More praise for *"Moby-Dick" and the Mythology of Oil*—

This unique reading of Melville's *Moby-Dick* reveals the place of poetry as an expression of a revelation in which myth and history collide, collude, and cooperate to offer a vision of nature disrupted by the hubris of humanity. Bob Wagner's book should be read by all those who find value in confronting the shadow side of human progress.

—— Dennis Patrick Slattery, Pacifica Graduate Institute, author of *The Wounded Body: Remembering the Markings of Flesh*

"Moby-Dick" and the Mythology of Oil presents an eloquent and compelling interpretation of Melville's epic romance as a cautionary tale no less germane to our times than to Melville's. The insatiable hunt for oil to fuel our consumer culture and our vanities—whether the oil is rendered from whales or pumped from the earth—is a form of apocalyptic risk-taking and portends natural disaster.

—— Gary Scharnhorst, distinguished professor of English at the University of New Mexico, author of biographies of Horatio Alger Jr., Charlotte Perkins Gilman, Bret Harte, and, most recently, nineteenth-century American journalist Kate Field

Bob Wagner's *"Moby-Dick" and the Mythology of Oil* provides a unique view of our hydrocarbon society from the perspective of the mythological backdrop of one of the great American literary masterpieces. Those of us in the oil business who have concern about our energy future will find rich ideas to ponder in this thoughtful and thought-provoking work.

—— Philip Cannon, independent oil producer, former headmaster of St. John's School, Houston

Moby-Dick and the Mythology of Oil

Moby-Dick and the Mythology of Oil

AN ADMONITION FOR THE PETROLEUM AGE

ROBERT D. WAGNER, JR.

ISBN-10: 1-453-68413-1
ISBN-13: 978-1-453684-13-9

Printed in the United States of America.

Artwork credits—Figures 1.1 and 1.2 used with permission of Taylor and Francis Books UK; figures 4.1 and 5.3 adapted and used with permission of Groppe, Long & Littell; figures 5.1 and 5.2 adapted from and used courtesy of the American Petroleum Institute.

Interior and cover design—Formandsubstance.com

This book is printed on acid-free paper.

CONTENTS

ILLUSTRATIONS

Figures

Tables

FOREWORD

Our relationship with the earth is in desperate shape. The rush to industrialize societies, now spreading around the world at breakneck speed, is fast diminishing the earth's resources—energy fuels, metals, minerals, clean air, and water—and this depletion may soon be irreparable. The situation with oil (the most pervasive energy fuel) and water (the most vital ingredient for the biological functioning of all species on the earth) is perhaps the most frightening.

The world can adjust, albeit painfully, to a shrinking supply of oil, but society cannot survive a fresh water scarcity. Sadly, the two resources are intimately intertwined—power generation and refining crude oil into finished petroleum products and transportation fuel both use massive amounts of water.

This apocalyptic view is not a religious myth but rather a serious crisis, which has now arrived. In *"Moby-Dick" and the Mythology of Oil*, Bob Wagner lays out a stunning story of this crisis through his thoughtful analysis of Melville's *Moby-Dick*.

I have known Bob Wagner since early 1974. We both came to Houston around the same time, just a few months after the Yom Kippur War, which changed the face of the oil business for decades. The control of oil flows and prices had moved from Standard Oil and its descendants to a loosely defined group of sovereign producers known as OPEC, becoming, in the process, a much more potent instrument of worldwide geopolitics than in previous decades. The result was that the price and availability of oil and natural gas became susceptible to swings in volatility that consistently disrupted simple market dynamics. It also made it quite difficult for most businesses dependent on energy flows to accurately manage their affairs over multiyear time horizons. Of these years, the 1980s were perhaps the most difficult, both for the oil and natural gas businesses of Texas and for their financial service providers, particularly banks and advisory firms. It was in dealing with the problems of these times that Bob and I developed a close relationship.

For much of our time together in Houston, Bob was a senior energy banker with major institutions in Houston and I was developing Simmons & Company International into a primary player in acquisition, divestiture and capital markets advisory in energy. Bob and I often worked together on deals and in forums as co-participant speakers. In the 1980s, when the aftermath of the volatility of the 1970s caused a massive collapse in energy prices and economics and in the broad commercial businesses of Texas, we saw ourselves working on many situations with which few of us had any experience or personal orientation.

The expertise needed to build businesses and asset bases and the skills needed to dismantle them to fit the realities of shrinking markets are radically different. So are the skills needed by the bankers and advisors to restructure the financial obligations for which many energy firms could not even pay interest. It was within such a dire environment that Bob and I realized our greatest talents as we helped save a shrinking oil service industry. And through these difficult years, Bob and I wound up forming lasting relationships with people in the markets of Houston and throughout Texas and the extended oil patch.

Over the past ten years, Bob and I have independently come to a conclusion that only a few knowledgeable people were even vaguely aware of the pending crisis the world would soon face, in what will be not only a fossil fuel scarcity but, even more alarming and dangerous, a water scarcity. This led me to develop and expand my speaking and dialogue engagements around the world. It took Bob to Pacifica

Graduate Institute in Santa Barbara to pursue an advanced degree in mythological studies, a pursuit that has resulted in the fascinating analysis that constitutes *"Moby-Dick" and the Mythology of Oil*.

In this book, Bob has developed a unique way to look at the condition of the human psyche and the planet today. Finding deep strains of discomfort with the evolving commercial markets of the nascent American economic society in Melville's treatment of whaling and the journey of the men of the *Pequod*, Bob has used the story of *Moby-Dick* as a deeply integrated allegory for our modern hydrocarbon society. The inclination to exploit such majestic creatures as whales to produce fuel for lighting or products for basic as well as trivial use arises from a deeply held set of beliefs in the western, Judeo-Christian psyche. These beliefs center on the view that humanity, particularly Judeo-Christian humanity, has a God-given right to exploit the earth's resources and its inhabitants, ad infinitum.

Melville's wonderfully colorful prose and his development of characters such as Ahab, Ishmael, Starbuck, and Queequeg, as richly diverse archetypal personalities, provide a spectacular story for all ages. Bob's analysis covers the tale Melville tells, and more. In his discussion of the commercial aspects of whaling, from the actual hunt over thousands of miles of ocean to the monstrous scenes of the harvesting of body parts, we see a reflection of similar conditions in the factories and railroad gangs of the nascent American Industrial Revolution. The emerging belief in humankind's invincibility over nature is captured in Ahab's speeches, behaviors, and actions. Although Ahab's views toward the natural world may seem outrageous to some of today's readers, Bob demonstrates that, in Ahab, Melville has given voice to the collective view of our current societal psyche that we humans really do have dominion over nature.

In *"Moby-Dick" and the Mythology of Oil*, Bob gives readers the insights to understand the underlying nature of this collective internal drive to exploit and consume. For it is in understanding the nature of our behavior, in understanding its origins and the deep-rooted patterns through which it is manifest, that we can begin to dismantle these proclivities and turn them around.

As Bob sees it then, the final voyage of the *Pequod*, as portrayed by Melville, has the characteristics of an apocalyptic journey of humanity into an underworld of its own creation, a hellish place of commercialism run amok. In this context, the White Whale, in all its power and majesty, is seen as an archetype of the natural systems of the earth; and the *Pequod*, led by Ahab, is a collective of men focused on proving their dominion over such systems. The final end to the conflict between Ahab, the men of the *Pequod*, and the White Whale is a prism through which we might divine a possible future for the human species . . . and to avoid such a calamitous end—for ourselves, for humanity, and for the planet—we need to heed warnings such as these and work to keep the sustaining ecosystems of the earth intact.

—Matthew R. Simmons
    Founder, The Ocean Energy Institute
    Retired chairman and founder, Simmons & Company International
    Author of *Twilight in the Desert: The Coming Saudi Oil Shock and the World Economy*

PREFACE

Oceans of oil . . . the bedrock on which we have built this complex economic society we call the modern world.

Oceans of oil . . . the rumblings beneath their feet that propelled the oilmen of Texas to struggle against overwhelming odds to produce the oil to win wars and build a peace.

Oceans of oil . . . the prize that drove the whalers of Nantucket to pursue leviathans of unequaled power over the watery surfaces of the world.

Oceans of oil . . . the image of catastrophes in the Santa Barbara Channel, the Bay of Campeche, Prince William Sound, and the Gulf of Mexico; oceans of oil that flow in and out of our consciousness.

Oceans of oil . . .

Consider a scene in the 2007 movie *There Will Be Blood*: independent California oilman Daniel Plainview is confronted by H. M. Tilford of Standard Oil, who is seeking to buy out Plainview's interest in an enormous oil discovery. Tilford's Standard Oil controls the bulk of the means to transport and refine oil in California (and nearly everywhere else in the United States). Tilford says to Plainview, "Where you going to put all that oil? Where? Build a pipeline? Make a deal with Union Oil? Be my guest. But if you can't pull it off, you got an ocean of oil under your feet, with nowhere to go."

Plainview stands firm, outsmarts Standard Oil, and builds a pipeline to get the oil to market by himself. Plainview demonstrates a resolve to combat all the odds, a resolve that is a big part of the story of oil in our consciousness and a primary reason that oil is such a dominant part of our society today.

Oceans of oil . . . It is what we are really all about.

I have been a banker for forty-four years; the focus of my engagement for much of that time has been oil, financing the oil and gas businesses of Texas. The years of my involvement in the business have been full of exciting events and characters, characters not unlike Daniel Plainview in his struggle against Standard Oil. It was the stuff of legends in American commerce.

Given my career in the practicalities of the oil business, that I enrolled at Pacifica Graduate Institute in Santa Barbara in 2003 came as a surprise to some of my colleagues. Perhaps even more so when, in time, I earned advanced degrees in mythological studies. To many, these two parts of my life seemed an unlikely combination. But I was driven by a lifelong interest in history and the historical backdrop of events and trends. To me, mythology—the study of the belief systems that form the bases for societal structures and for the philosophical, sociological, and spiritual worldviews of all cultures and communities—represented a connection and held a key.

The most fascinating element of my studies in mythology has been in discerning the mythos of so many historical periods through which I had lived, both in how such mythos were spawned and in how they seemed to be carried across disparate periods in time. In ancient, prehistory times, such belief systems were grounded in story, stories told over and over throughout extended communities. In later times, these systems were codified in treatises and canons emanating from universities, governments, and religions. However, even in these later times, the core energies of those systems were still very much grounded in story, in the literature, theatre, and art produced at the time.

With this as background, when I rediscovered *Moby-Dick* during my studies at Pacifica, I read it this time as having a mythological context that also reflected many of the events and trends that I had experienced over my life in the oil business. The synchronistic timing of Melville's writing the book in 1851, at the peak of the whaling era in American commerce, and the beginnings of the petroleum business in the discovery of the first commercial quantities of oil underground in

Pennsylvania in 1859 was startling. Recognizing the nature of *Moby-Dick* as an exploration into the dark side of the human psyche at the peak of the whale oil business began my process of exploring the underlying mythic systems that permeated Melville's tale. Comparing the elements of mythos that Melville developed in *Moby-Dick* against the issues that the human species faces today at the peak of the petroleum business seemed a timely and worthwhile venture. This book developed from that exploration; it was originally my doctoral dissertation for Pacifica.

Herman Melville's classic *Moby-Dick* is one of the great American epic stories, if not the greatest. Its preeminence has been chronicled by scholars and academicians continuously over the past ninety years. Many such scholars see Melville's story as a masterful exploration into the dark side of the human spirit. Surely the intensely lyrical nature of his prose and the intricate character and plot development he uses make it a masterful work, worthy of extensive study as demonstrative of exceptional American fiction. Beyond this, it is also a story of American commerce, about the early American system of whaling, which by Melville's time had become the first industry in which America ruled the world. It is a story of the hunting and plundering of whales for the primary purpose of providing an energy source for lighting the libraries, offices, and reading rooms of people all over the world. Melville provides as in-depth an analysis of the nature of whales and of the business of whaling as existed at the time. As such, it is also a dramatic story of the Industrial Revolution in its early development in the American experience.

Petroleum (crude oil and natural gas) is the defining commodity of today's economic society, which arose out of that time. In the hundreds of derivatives and thousands of products made from these substances, virtually everything we use or consume today uses petroleum in some fashion. Over the past century, the outcome of major wars has been determined by the access to petroleum supplies and national governments have used their access to these supplies as the driving force behind their development and implementation of critical geopolitical policies.

Petroleum has been a part of our economic activity for 150 years, a period we might call the Petroleum Age. Its development over that time has driven much of the structure of our societal systems, and the stories that abide in such development are an integral part of the history and folklore of this period. As we look into the facts of this history and the imbedded nature of oil and all its derivatives in every aspect of our lives today, we can see how this substance permeates our lives and how critical it has become to our very society.

Moby-Dick is primarily a mythic, epic story, conveying a complex structure of economic, sociological, and religious systems that had formed the nature of the American experience in its early history. However, the systems inculcated in *Moby-Dick* were so deeply grounded in the American experience in the broadest sense that they continued to develop over the ensuing generations. We are witness to those same systems operating in our modern society, in our Petroleum Age. In a sense, the compulsions that drove Captain Ahab and the crew of the whaleship *Pequod* to dominate the powers of nature that confronted them in their efforts to pursue a commercial trade are very much visible in the structure of our economic society today.

Another facet of this phenomenon is that the whaling business of Melville's time had grown to an extent that whale populations were diminishing and operating costs were rising dramatically. Within a decade of the writing of *Moby-Dick*, oil was discovered in Pennsylvania. In the years that immediately followed this event, subsequent discoveries made oil supplies seem limitless, and kerosene, a derivative of petroleum and an excellent fuel for lighting, became abundantly available at a fraction of the cost of whale oil.

The Petroleum Age had begun, inaugurating a titanic shift in energy sources, from whale oil to petroleum, to accelerate the development of the Industrial Revolution in the evolving American experience. But the underlying mythos remained the same. Although the shift in energy transformed how business was conducted, the mythological backdrop was the same as existed in Melville's time as a whaler. That is the core of the analysis here: the mythos of the whaling era of Melville's time was carried into and developed within the Petroleum Age, so much so that the story of Captain Ahab, Ishmael, and Moby Dick can be seen as our collective story as well.

In *"Moby-Dick" and the Mythology of Oil,* readers with an orientation to classic American literature will find a roadmap for an interpretation of Melville's tale that connects directly with today's world. Readers with a fascination for the mythos that permeates the major periods of the American economic experience, and with a deep concern for the future of the relationship of the human species with the earth will find much to ponder in the parallels between Melville's time and ours in the Petroleum Age.

After a brief prologue, "Loomings," to set the tone, this book is organized into six chapters, designed to provide a thorough understanding of my interpretation of Melville's classic as a representation of the shadow side of the human psyche at this pinnacle of the Petroleum Age. Although the flow of this analysis is critical in developing the thesis about *Moby-Dick* as a mythological representation of the emerging economic society of Melville's time and as a precursor to the position in which we find ourselves today, some readers may choose to approach the reading differently. Students new to the novel *Moby-Dick* will find that these chapters can also be read independently as standalone focused analyses. Those interested in more in-depth coverage of the topics will find an extensive bibliography at the end of the book.

Chapter 1, "Whales and Whaling," explores the nature of the whale species from a scientific and a mythical point of view, as well as the characteristics and history of the whaling industry from its earliest conception to its fall into decline. The condition of the whale population and the place of whaling in the mid-nineteenth century within the emerging economic and sociological culture of the United States at the time are important to establish. This chapter demonstrates how powerful the species of whale is as a centerpiece of the mythos of Melville's tale, how the whale was the only animal that could have carried the power of what Melville was trying to capture and that could speak to the presence of that mythos in our society today.

In chapter 2, "Melville: His Times, Life, and Works," Herman Melville's life and works are presented together with an analysis of the times in which he lived. The cultural environment that permeated the American Literary Renaissance of the first half of the nineteenth century and the emerging political and economic nation that was the United States created a fecund condition for the emerging author Melville. The developing Industrial Revolution fostered a sensation of grimness and fear among literary circles concerning the effect that this increasing activity was having on humankind and the earth. Grasping the impact that all of this had on Melville, the novelist, and on his view of whaling as a human activity and as an industry within the developing national economy, is a critical part of the analysis here.

Chapter 3, "*Moby-Dick*: The Tale as Myth and Epic," focuses on the story of *Moby-Dick*, emphasizing the key elements of the tale that correlate to the imagery and mythic nature of this analysis. Looking at whaling as a business, particularly a business of sourcing energy supplies, dissecting the journey of the *Pequod* as symbolic of the larger enterprise that was the emergent economic society of the United States, and exploring the rich religious and mythological imagery and references that Melville used, is the key focus. The epic struggle between the White Whale as a gloriously mythic animal and Ahab as a supremely confident whaling captain who has spent his life killing and harvesting whales, with Ishmael, as an everyday seaman caught in the middle of this conflict, becomes the centerpiece. This enables a series of analogous conclusions about the efficacy of rampant economic exploitation.

With the themes of *Moby-Dick* and their relationship to the analysis here established, the next three chapters focus on the Petroleum Age and the future ahead of us. Chapter 4, "The Petroleum Age: A Titanic Story," explores certain key elements of the history of the petroleum business over the last 150 years, with a particular emphasis on those aspects of the industry that have significant mythic parallels with the business of whaling.

Chapter 5, "Challenges of the Petroleum Age," focuses on the life cycle of petroleum and the position we are in today within that cycle. From that perspective, the concentration is on the impact that the hydrocarbon age, of which petroleum is the primary fuel, is having on the hierarchy of ecosystems that form the earth, and on the earth as a whole living organism. This discussion is a critical element of the analysis, designed to show the overall impact of our hydrocarbon society, the mythic parallels to the main themes of *Moby-Dick*, and the pressing need to find a more sustainable means for our species to source and consume energy in order for us to exist in harmony with the earth.

Chapter 6, "Industrialism and the Economic Society: Origins of the Mythos," synthesizes the foregoing analyses in such a manner as to allow the story of *Moby-Dick* to provide imagery and mythic insights into the questions of our energy and ecological present and future. It explores the roots of the belief systems that drive our economic society, from the concepts of the creation stories of the Bible, to the journey of the hero that is a fixture in our history and current psyche, to the obsession over wealth and consumption that is so much a part of our culture of life.

The epilogue, "From Dominion to Stewardship," projects into the future, searching for advice we might take from Melville's tale, set in the decline of the whaling industry, to our time at the pinnacle of the Petroleum Age, as petroleum resources become ever more scarce— and as our pursuit of those resources puts the critical human ecosystems of the planet itself in danger.

Finally, the journey of the *Pequod*, the confrontation of Ahab and the White Whale, is a classic journey of the hero. But the hero of this story is Ishmael. It is he who begins from a position of being distressed and lost in the world. He must travel into the "belly of the whale," into and through a titanic struggle with a leviathan of biblical proportions to achieve some understanding of the mythos of this experience. It is then, and only then, that he can be the survivor and return to "tell the tale." The final insight to be gained from this analysis, therefore, is to recognize that Ishmael, the ordinary seaman, is really all of us, Every-man. It is to recognize that his tale is our tale. It is the tale that all of us, all the peoples of the earth, desperately need to absorb at this time in human history.

—Houston, Texas
 July 2010

ACKNOWLEDGMENTS

Upwards of one hundred seventy-five thousand books are published in the United States in any given year. The sheer numbers might lead one to conclude that the process of writing a book should not be a particularly strenuous task. Would that my experience of producing *"Moby-Dick" and the Mythology of Oil* had mirrored such a judgment. This book, developed from my PhD dissertation of the same name, has been an endearing joy in my life (in spite of the gut-wrenching, ever-present anxieties that came with it), and has been accomplished only with the support of a host of people.

The dissertation committee that shepherded me through this process, Dennis Patrick Slattery, Debra Knowles, and Henry Groppe, were the first line in my army of confederates. Dennis provided the solid foundation in myth and epic that became the bedrock of the work. Debra added a strong grounding in depth psychology as well as a career background in finance on Wall Street. And Henry brought his fifty-five years of experience in the broadly defined energy and petroleum businesses to keep the focus on petroleum as fact-based and as well-reasoned as possible.

Many faculty, administrators, fellow students, and friends of Pacifica Graduate Institute were always willing to listen and comment with articulate and scholarly feedback. These include faculty members Hendrika de Vries, Christine Downing, Dawn George, Mel Gottleib, Laura Grillo, Aaron Kipnis, Patrick Mahaffey, Ginette Paris, Glen Slater, Lans Smith, Zaman Stanazai, and Elizabeth Terzian. Administrators and staff members include Edie Barrett, Elise Collins-Shields, Druscilla French, Diane Huerta, Mark Kelly, and Lori Pye. Those classmates who proved of enormous help in many respects were Amy Gardner, S. Ann Gramson-Hill, Nancy Parker, Terry Pearce, and Safron Rossi; others who provided feedback were Mara Applebaum, Joe Bogorad, Marla Carter, Suzanne Cloutier, Laurie de Nuccio, Stacy Erickson, Mark Hasencamp, Joe Leone, John Mahoney, Neora

Myrow, Candice Phillips, Jeff Reznikoff, Bob Roan, Phillip Roggow, Nan Savage, and Norland Tellez.

Authors and academicians with whom I was able to converse and who provided invaluable insight include Michael Dyer of the Kendall Institute and Melville Society in New Bedford, Massachusetts; Dennis Haugh of the University of Denver; John Irwin of Johns Hopkins University in Baltimore; Hershel Parker of Morro Bay, California; Gary Scharnhorst of the University of New Mexico in Albuquerque; and Richard Tarnas of the California Institute of Integral Studies in San Francisco. Special thanks to my esteemed colleague, Matthew R. Simmons, who graciously contributed conversations along the way and this book's foreword.

In the process of doing the work to convert the dissertation into the book presented here, a number of the people mentioned above provided useful suggestions; Pacifica classmate Terry Pearce was exceedingly helpful with ideas and introductions to editors and designers. In that category, Janet M. Hunter of Madison, Connecticut, and Helen Glenn Court of Silver Spring, Maryland, provided invaluable guidance and insights negotiating a more popular style of composition and navigating the labyrinthine world of publishing. I cannot say enough about their assistance.

Lastly, my family members were always there despite the vagaries of self-induced distraction and disruption which, at times, made my work space in the household an alchemical chamber of horrors for anyone present. My sister-in-law, Eleanor Arbeene, provided tireless and invaluable proofreading, and my children, Lisa McCulloch, Christopher Wagner, and Kimberly Heidt, were forever the cheering section. Behind it all, throughout the four years that encompassed the development of the concept through the writing of these words, my wife, Patty, was my enduring confidante and guide, my forever Virgil. This work is dedicated to her.

Loomings

The concept of dominion is firmly rooted in the Judeo-Christian psyche. Genesis 1:28, the first chapter in one of the earliest and most mythic texts of our Western culture, provides insight: "God said to them, 'Be fruitful and multiply, and fill the earth and *subdue* it; and have *dominion* over the fish of the sea and over the birds of the air and over every living thing that moves upon the earth'" (*New Oxford Annotated Bible*, 3rd edition, emphasis added). The idea that we are a higher order of being who has the right, a God-given right, to exploit the resources of the earth to suit our need for a sense of dominion seems a fixed part of our collective ethos.

However, we are clearly facing consequences resulting from the development of our economic society over the past five hundred years that could, in time, be catastrophic, yet we choose not to see. Why? Has the process of development, the evolution of this economic society of the West, left us with such a deeply ingrained disconnection with the earth that we cannot see? Today, in the early years of the twenty-first century, we seem to live entirely on synthetic surfaces, breathing synthetic, conditioned air, both of which we obsessively keep clean of dirt so that we never touch or feel the earth.

How have we come to feel so disconnected? Do we really believe that, with regard to our relationship with the earth, we have dominion as described in Genesis? Surely we are not in control. Our vulnerability to natural upheavals in the ecosystem is constantly before us. Hurricanes, tornados, earthquakes, tsunamis, volcanic eruptions, and firestorms consistently disrupt our carefully laid-out communities. Yet we struggle to accept such events as natural occurrences of nature to be embraced. We seek only to find some blame in our own inability to predict, to provide for, or even to prevent such "catastrophes." Even in today's world, other societies and cultures, those with more earth-centric views, are able to accept such events with resignation and deference; yet we seek only to lash out at the idea of some invisible hand at work or at some impotent character or force in our own psyches. Whence does this curious quality of our Western society emanate? How might it have been manifested in the collective consciousness over the period of its development? And what are the consequences of our continuing to believe in the fantasy of dominion?

In many ways, the scientific and commercial worlds that have been spawned within the exploitation of the resources of the earth over the last 150 years, a period we call the Petroleum Age, has been spectacular. It has given us a knowledge of the planet that has been extremely useful; it is truly laudatory how much we have learned, how much valuable information we have gained about the cosmos to help us understand its power and majesty. But, even with such knowledge, we seem to struggle with the idea of limits and with the need to consider change when such limits become manifest.

In all my years in working with oil businesses, there has always been one irrefutable fact: the ultimate supplies of petroleum, a non-renewable resource of the earth, are limited. However, as a society, we gave this fact no mind because the magnitude of the original resource base was so large that the reality of ultimately limited supplies seemed irrelevant. And, of more serious note, the prospects of a deterioration in the quality of our societal lives spawned by a diminution in such resource supplies, has not been considered a serious issue . . . until now.

In recent years, worldwide consumption of petroleum resources has grown to staggering proportions. Today all the human societies of the world burn in excess of forty thousand gallons of oil per second; and the speed with which we are depleting the resource base of petroleum is still growing. It would seem, today, that this could all soon begin to decline, perhaps rapidly. There is mounting evidence, notably in the rapid rise in the price for oil and in the heightened geopolitical tensions surrounding primary oil-producing regions, that we are reaching the pinnacle of worldwide petroleum supplies. To be sure, it is increasingly clear that the zenith of this economic age that we fuel with petroleum is upon us.

Herman Melville wrote his historic epic novel *Moby-Dick* in 1851. The central action of the novel is whaling, whaling when the New England whaling industry had grown to become America's first dominant commercial activity. Whale oil was a popular fuel used for lighting and products harvested from whales were shipped from New England ports to every economically developed society around the globe. And yet the activity of whaling, and the demand for whale oil, had grown so much that the whale population was being seriously depleted. Whaling expeditions had to range over much larger waters, and for longer periods, to find an adequate supply of whales. The effort needed to find and kill these creatures and to process the products derived from their bodily components increased sharply. The all-in cost to produce and deliver the commodity of whale oil, and the price to be paid by its consumers, continued to rise.

As is apparent from the long view of history, the life cycle of whale oil was then—in Melville's time—at the same point that we are today in the life cycle of petroleum. Adding to the unlikely symmetry of this timing is that whale oil virtually disappeared as an energy fuel within thirty years following Melville's completing *Moby-Dick*; it was replaced mainly by kerosene, a derivative product of petroleum.

Despite this symmetry, there is one major difference between the economic society of the mid-nineteenth century fueled by whale oil and today's society fueled by petroleum. Petroleum, like all other fuels derived from plant and animal matter (including whale oil), is a hydrocarbon. To create the energy to drive engines and to produce heat and electricity, we burn these hydrocarbons. To make products

3

for everyday use, we manufacture derivatives of these hydrocarbons, notably petrochemicals. In sourcing and burning hydrocarbons and in making and consuming products derived from petroleum, we release gases and particulate matter into the atmosphere and runoff and refuse contaminate the ecosystems that nurture and contain the species of the physical earth, including humanity.

Today, 150 years into the Petroleum Age, the accumulation of gases and particulates in the atmosphere and of refuse in the land and the oceans is beginning to alter, inexorably, the ability of the ecosystems of the earth to support life as we know it. The magnitude of the consumption of hydrocarbons in the accumulated levels of today is now such that the possibility of an apocalyptic outcome for humanity grows more real by the decade. In this context, a valid observation of Melville's epic is that it embodies some sort of stark warning to us.

Moby-Dick has a calamitous conclusion for the men of the whaleship *Pequod*. In their blind pursuit of the White Whale, driven by a mythically wounded Ahab, who irrationally seeks "vengeance on a dumb brute," they fail to heed the warnings about the dangers of their pursuit and are destroyed. The reality of the growing exploitation of whales by the economic societies of the time seems to impart a prophetic quality to Melville's characterizations. In mythic terms, then, the rampant, obsessive exploration, production and consumption of hydrocarbons that saturates our society today can be read much like the situation for the men on the *Pequod*. In symbolic terms, we, the developed societies of the earth, are the men of the *Pequod* pursuing myriad goals of incremental consumption in an accelerating pace that can result only in our own destruction.

"Moby-Dick" and the Mythology of Oil explores such a parallel, by discerning the mythic, archetypal power that the story of *Moby-Dick*, derived from the American economic society of the time, has for the economic society of today and for a similarly destructive, symbolic voyage in which we, the developed societies of the earth, seem to be currently engaged. In this book, I analyze the business of

whaling and whale oil in the context of the literary, political, and economic society of Melville's time, exploring the events and ideas that drove him to construct his wondrous and prophetic story. I compare this to the development of the business of exploration and production of petroleum over the last 150 years, which has resulted in the highly engineered, highly consumptive society in which we live today. Putting all of this into the context of the epic storyline Melville follows in *Moby-Dick* leads to the very plausible conclusion that the prospects for humanity in the not-too-distant future are, in mythic terms, very much like the outcome for the men of the *Pequod* in Melville's tale. Or might be if we hold to a view of our place in the world similar to Ahab's, as communicated to Starbuck that "I'd strike the sun if it insulted me" (140).

In all its mythic implications, Melville's American epic has been called the greatest American novel and one of the great American visionary fictions. The story as told by Melville has many mythemes (myths that are central to a society's core) that resonate in our American culture, and on many levels of our society. Joseph Campbell and others point out that the mythemes of epic stories like *Moby-Dick* portray significant archetypal energies that operate in many forms in the societies from which they emanate. The ultimate core of the analysis here will be that, in all the characterizations and all the forces engaged in Melville's tale, there is a journey that unfolds in the hunt for Moby Dick that is much more fundamental, much more sinister for our society today than is apparent on the tale's surface. It is, perhaps, one of which Melville himself may not have been entirely conscious.

In "Psychology and Literature," an essay first published in 1930, C. G. Jung calls *Moby-Dick* "the greatest American novel." Further, in "The Spirit in Man, Art and Literature," he discusses literature as having "the richest opportunities for psychological elucidation" and writes that stories like *Moby-Dick* are "constructed against a background of unspoken psychological assumptions, and the more unconscious the author is of them, the more this background reveals itself in unalloyed purity to the discerning eye" (*Collected Works* 15:137). There is, I believe, reasonable evidence that an all-encompassing objective psyche, and certain archetypal forces in the collective unconscious, were at work on Melville as he wrote *Moby-Dick*.

At its core, the novel portrays a journey into the depths, into the underworld of the Judeo-Christian, Enlightenment psyche that has formed the American economic society of today. If this society is really on a collision course with economic and ecological disaster, then the fundamental question for all of us is this: what is it in the depths of the collective psyche that drives this all-consuming quest, a quest that can only result in our own destruction? How can we be so consumed in a rush to our own ultimate annihilation, a rush akin to that of Ahab and his men in the final days of the *Pequod*?

In pursuing these questions, an important part of this analysis, therefore, is to explore those forces, to delineate with some precision how this epic sea voyage, this titanic pursuit of the great White Whale, presents much more than just a parallel to the oil and gas business as it has evolved. It delineates how Melville's tale, the journey of the men of the *Pequod*, foretells, in mythic terms, a potentially apocalyptic outcome for the planetary life support systems that nurture us all. We are led to the inevitable conclusion that the story of *Moby-Dick*, the activities of Ahab and the men of the *Pequod*, contains a powerful representation of our modern American economic society. And the journey of the lowly seaman, Ishmael, the real hero in this Campbellian story, is really the journey of all of us who are living in witness to this conflict.

1 Whales and Whaling

There Go Flukes

The coast of California winds a thousand miles from Mexico to Oregon, its western edge fronting the Pacific Ocean. This coastline and the relationship of the land to the ocean does much to define California and the lifestyle that it represents in the minds and hearts of its people. Highway 101 winds along and above the coastline, fronting the ocean for relatively brief stretches, including the fourteen miles from Ventura to Carpinteria. In this stretch, the road skirts along a bluff and the proximity of the Santa Ynez mountains to the shoreline limits the amount of commercial and residential development. As one drives this stretch in the early morning, with the sun behind, the water is a beautiful azure blue. Along the same stretch in the afternoon, the sun is over the water and its reflection creates the image of a gleaming orb. At either time, the water seems tranquil, and, when the air is clear, the horizon is a vivid line for 180 degrees. The vastness of this body of water stirs the imagination. As one looks to the horizon, past the Channel Islands of Anacapa and Santa Cruz, the endless stretch of water is mesmerizing, tens of thousands of miles to the next land mass of size and six miles deep at its deepest point. The average depth is more than a mile and, in the sheer volume of water, the entire mass is larger than all the other bodies of water on the earth combined.

Ferdinand Magellan called this ocean the Pacific, back in 1520, because he found its appearance to be peaceful. The soft rolling waves and the placid surface present the vision of serenity, belying the havoc that cyclones and tsunamis have brought to the Pacific's borders in various parts of the world. But, for all the imagery conjured up on its surface, it is in the depths of the Pacific that a deeper, more mystical world prevails. For in these thousands upon thousands of cubic miles of water, the whale, the great leviathan of the earth, seems eternally present in all regions and at virtually all depths, traveling thousands of miles in pilgrimatic migrations and reigning supreme in a kingdom of wondrous majesty and grandeur.

This mystical animal has stirred the imagination of humankind in many of its mythic systems, especially those cultures bordering on the sea. Herman Melville has made it the central figure in his glorious epic *Moby-Dick*. Melville's personal experience at whaling may have been the reason for his focus, but it is most likely more than that. It is, perhaps, that the whale, in all its forms and in all its symbolic ethos, particularly in its relationship to humankind in the practice of whaling, is a vital element of the story. The purpose of this discussion is to attempt to understand why, on a purely factual basis, independent of all the rich aspects of Melville's tale, the whale and the business of whaling are such powerful elements in this epic. It is to attempt to understand why the whale, as a species, in and of itself, and connected to humankind in the business of whaling, is the only creature on earth that could capture the force of the mythos attending Melville's story.

ORIGIN AND NATURE OF THE SPECIES OF WHALE

The whale, and all the categories of species assigned to it, is one of the oldest creatures on the earth. The formal name of the species is Cetecea, from the Latin, *cetus*, or whale. It is mammal, the only one that lives entirely in the sea. Researchers believe that a simple four-legged creature migrated from the land to the sea approximately fifty million years ago, by various estimates; we have no way of determining why it did so. The book *Whales*, written in 1958 by E. J. Slijper, late professor of zoology at the University of Amsterdam, provides perhaps the most comprehensive study of the species of whales. Reviewing the history of the species, Slijper notes that the original ancestor was probably the same creature that was the progenitor of most of the four-legged mammals that walk the earth today. In the long evolutionary process of adapting to the sea, each of the varieties of the species Cetacea, to include the dolphin and porpoise, fashioned singularly efficient bodily systems for living in that world.

The largest of the species is the blue whale, the largest animal ever to have existed on the earth, on land or sea, larger even than the largest of the dinosaurs. Whales roam in their undersea kingdom over thousands of miles following patterns that we still struggle to understand. Their annual life processes are largely shrouded in mystery. The watery kingdom in which they reign, with its depth and breadth and invisible underworld-like characteristics, is just not one that we humans can yet observe in any rigorous way, as we might observe life processes on land. Because of their size, whales also cannot be observed in captivity in any conclusive manner.

We do know that whales are traditional mammals. They are warm blooded; they must ingest air to breathe and facilitate bodily functions; they conceive their young internally and give birth, and they must nurture these young with sustenance and protection for some period of their lives after birth. They are significantly more advanced in the evolutionary chain than reptilian animals, which lay eggs and leave them to hatch and develop by themselves; most of the other creatures of the sea are reptilian.

Over the span of recorded history relatively little study was done on the whale before the development of the commercial whaling industry in the seventeenth to nineteenth centuries. Aristotle incorporated some analysis of dolphins in *Historia Animalium*. He was the first to examine their mammalian traits and their fundamental differences from other species of fish, but there was not much further research until the nineteenth century. As the commercial activity of whaling reached its climax, three independent works, by William Scoresby (1820), Thomas Beale (1835), and Charles Scammon (1874), provided the first development of extensive knowledge and understanding of whales and dolphins. These three men were active participants in the industry and observed the prominent cetacean species firsthand over many years.

Their pioneering work was not expanded upon, however, until the last half of the twentieth century, when another spate of analyses was completed, to bring the study of cetaceans to its position today. The primary works of this later period are E. J. Slijper's book *Whales*, mentioned earlier; Richard Ellis's *The Book of Whales* (1980) and *Men and Whales* (1991), and Hal Whitehead's *Sperm Whale* (2003). Because the latest group presents a more informed and in-depth source of knowledge of whales, with a generally higher level of scientific foundation, these are the primary sources used here.

The cetacean species includes all of the varieties of species of whales, dolphins, and porpoises. Richard Ellis, in *The Book of Whales*, notes forty-seven species of cetaceans, broken down into two groups: toothed whales and baleen whales. The toothed whales (which include porpoises, dolphins, killer whales, sperm whales, and pygmy sperm whales) have teeth to masticate their food. The baleen whales, by contrast, have a porous membrane of light flexible whalebone across their mouths that allows them to capture food in bulk in their mouths and expel the water through the membrane, retaining the food and beginning to digest it in the process. There are five genera of baleen whales: rorquals, gray whales, humpbacks, right whales, and pygmy right whales. The primary species of the rorquals, in the baleen whale group, is the blue whale. The primary species of whale that are the center of myth and story are the blue, the gray, the humpback, the right, and the sperm. Of these five, only the sperm whale is toothed, giving it a unique characteristic in myth and story.

All five of these species of whale have significant differences in body shape and bodily functions; yet all are believed to be descended from the same ancestral species. However, the sperm whale is the one people tend to picture when they envision the whale and, in the history of American whaling, it occupies center stage. The sperm whale is therefore the focus of this analysis.

The connection of the cetaceans to their earlier land-based ancestor is evident in the skeletal structure and cardiovascular systems, both in embryonic as well as fully mature form, when compared to current-day land mammals. Figure 1.1, from Slijper's *Whales*, shows the comparison of skeletal structures of a horse and a blue whale; the similarities are relatively clear and the differences easily understood in the context of fifty million years of adapting to the sea (see following page). Key considerations are the similarities in the rib cage, spinal chain to the tail, and elements of front legs in the whale's fins.

Figure 1.1 Skeleton of a Blue Whale and a Horse

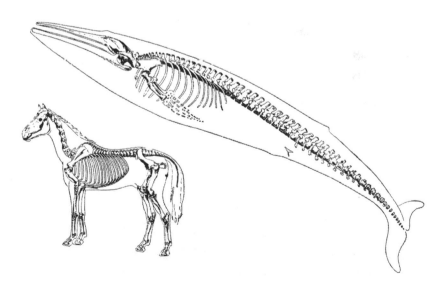

Source: Reproduced with permission from Slijper 1958, fig. 21, p. 59.

From its four-legged ancestor, the whale's front legs turned into paddle-shaped flippers, but the bone structure of those flippers still resembles the digits of the forelimbs of land mammals. The similarities are even more apparent in the shape of the limbs in the early embryonic stages of the modern-day whale. As the whale evolved, the back legs disappeared entirely, although "the buds of hind limbs are visible in the embryos of cetaceans" (Ellis, *Book of Whales*, 8). The tail grew considerably larger and widened horizontally into two fin-like extensions, called flukes. The creature turned whale lost most all body hair, "a uniquely mammalian trait" (8), as well any bodily protuberances, such as ears. It developed a thick layer of fat, called blubber, to keep warm at depth and in the polar regions of the oceans. The skull elongated and the nostrils shifted to the back of the head, becoming the blowhole, to aid in breathing at the ocean's surface; the blowhole is the primary breathing organ.

Thomas Beale, in *The Natural History of the Sperm Whale*, provides some detailed evidence of the operation of the blowhole as a breathing apparatus in the process of diving and surfacing, demonstrating the whale's capacity to stay submerged for periods of an hour or more. It is apparent that the Cetacean creatures developed an entire series of adaptations related to diving, allowing whales to stay submerged for extended periods and to dive to depths of three thousand to five thousand feet. These include the ability to store more oxygen in the blood and muscles, and more blood volume relative to body size than land mammals.

Additional evidence of the similarities between the cetacean species and its distant land-based relatives is apparent in figure 1.2, also from Slijper (158). It shows the arterial systems of a bottlenose dolphin and of a horse.

As noted, the tail of the earlier ancestor changed considerably in adapting to the sea, widening horizontally to become flukes. Flukes are dense, powerful tissue with strong, highly developed muscles. They are extremely powerful, and are the primary means of propulsion. Being horizontal, they are unlike the tails of most fish, which are vertical. The fins or flippers on the side of the body of the whale are used primarily for steering, not for propulsion. Today's science seems to suggest that the evolutionary process of development of the modern species of whale, occurring over a period of fifty million years, resulted in an extremely efficient body and organ structure, a machine designed for rapid and easy movement in the water. Estimates of size and speed of whales have been difficult because of the nature of their activities and habitats; the available data are less than precise. However, according to the sources used here, estimates for the lengths, mass, and sustainable speeds for five primary species of whale are shown on the following page in table 1.1.

Figure 1.2 Arterial System of a Bottlenose Dolphin and a Horse

Source: Reproduced with permission from Slijper 1958, fig. 89, p. 158.

The conclusions that can be drawn about the awesome nature of the power of the whale are clear, even more so when one takes into account Jim Murphy's estimate in *Gone a Whaling* that the maximum "fleeing" speeds of the blue, humpback, right, and sperm whales is 20 to 25 knots, and that of the gray is 10 knots. Beyond these extraordinary speeds, some evidence indicates that these animals possess a sensory capability, level of intelligence, and empathetic view of the world that is equally remarkable.

Table 1.1 Size, Mass, and Speed of Five Types of Whales

Type	Feet	S/Tons	Sustainable Knots
Blue	90	100	14
Gray	40	35	5
Humpback	50	30	5
Right	60	60	5
Sperm	70	80	12

Source: Author's compilation based on Ellis 1985; Murphy 1998; Scammon 1968; Slijper 1958.

Sensory Characteristics

Slijper provides a lengthy analysis of the brain size, senses, and central nervous system of the primary species of whale. Of the sensory functions, the sense of smell is almost nonexistent and the capacity of sight is somewhat limited because of the medium of water in which they live and the absence of light at deeper water depths. The positioning of the eyes on some whales, particularly the sperm whale, in which the eyes are on the flat side of the head, also limits vision significantly. That being said, however, hearing and vocalization are extremely well developed in many of the species and give them an unusually high level of sensory perception.

There are two aspects of this function. The first is the capacity to receive and process sound. According to Slijper, "the hearing of Cetaceans is second only to bats" (204). The auditory system is entirely mammalian, but, because of the enormous pressures of the water depth to which whales have been known to descend (more than three thousand feet), the evolutionary process has provided the whale with a much more intricate auditory network than many land-based creatures possess. The second aspect is a capacity, in some species, to send out sound waves and receive back and process the reverberations of the sounds. This second function, called echolocation, is, for certain species of whale (particularly the sperm whale) the primary manner of sensing the exterior world. This feature is similar to that of bats; it gives the animal a very strong sense of what is before it, working in much the same way as sonar (in the sea) and radar (on land). High-pitched sounds and clicking noises, some of which have individual signature qualities, are emitted in a pattern with their echoes being received back and processed. Studies, particularly of dolphins, show that these sounds are clearly a sonar-type signal that allows the cetacean to navigate around obstacles with great accuracy.

Sperm whales' complicated combination of knocks, bangs, and clicks has been recorded. Researchers believe that these echolocation patterns are generated from different points in the head and nose, most probably from the case that is the spermaceti organ. Ellis notes in *Book of Whales* that spermaceti oil has been found to have a high level of "sound-transmitting qualities" (113). The echolocation function and capacity of the spermaceti organ is further explained in Hal Whitehead's *Sperm Whales*, where he notes that the "vast nose of the sperm whale is . . . a massive click producer." Whitehead goes on to say that "Sperm whales arrange their clicks in various patterns . . . and use them in a variety of circumstances. The two broad classes . . . are echolocation and communication" (134). His analysis focuses on the nature and qualities of all the sounds and the possible uses thereof. The broad conclusion relevant to this analysis is that the echolocation and communication capabilities of the sperm whale, centered in the spermaceti organ, suggest a highly developed, quite advanced species with unusual social characteristics. This is particularly apparent in various elements of their behavior.

Intelligence and Social Behavior

With regard to intelligence, much work has also been done to estimate the brain capacity of whales in comparison to that of other mammalian species. The earliest method used was to measure the size of the brain both in absolute terms and in relation to various body measurements and processes. As Slijper summarized, cetaceans have the brain capacity, including a certain deductive capacity, equivalent to that of the species of great apes. In this regard, their intelligence is at the high end of the mammalian chain, approaching that of man. In an October 2006 article in the *Journal of Applied Animal Behaviour Science* titled "Into the Brains of Whales," Mark Simmonds, international science director of the Whale and Dolphin Conservation Society, puts forward a compelling case for a high level of intelligence among cetaceans. Simmonds sees the methods of measuring absolute and relative brain weights and sizes as inadequate because, although whales score very high in absolute brain size (the sperm whale has the largest brain on earth), they are low in relative terms, given their enormous body size and the size and weight of the various body systems needed to deal with the harsh environments in which they live.

Instead, Simmonds compares the behavior and social interaction of the various cetacean species and of other mammals. He notes four basic indications of a more advanced cognitive capacity in cetaceans: an ability to learn, a complex social system, a capacity for self-awareness, and advanced cultural development. In summary, Simmonds's work supports Slijper's analysis. Much of the research has been done on dolphins, especially those in captivity; by contrast, whales have been more difficult to study because of their size, life patterns, and the inability to observe them in captivity. However, from the analysis that has been done, Simmonds and other sources, notably Slijper and Whitehead, conclude that there is reasonable evidence of an intense level of social interaction among whales, a deep empathy for each other, and a capacity to relate to others, including humans, in a manner beyond that of most other mammals.

Cetaceans, sperm whales in particular, live in complex social environments. Whitehead notes that their communities, or schools, can be sizable, with populations of hundreds. The schools are highly nomadic, traveling up to thousands of miles in a year. The young remain with their mother for extended periods. The young males split off in their teens and tend to aggregate in bachelor groups until they reach sexual potency, when they move on to larger communities. Whales live for widely varying periods, some as many as eighty to ninety years. The societal structures are in place for most of their lives and the communal bonds that develop seem quite strong. In a number of observed situations, distressed whales have been accompanied closely by other whales, and, when attempts were made by human groups to provide aid to the distressed whale, its protectors would not relinquish their protective positions. There are also the curious instances of a distressed whale beaching itself in a process of dying, not responding to attempts to refloat it, even when it can still swim. There are no known biological explanations for this behavior.

A November 2006 article by Andy Coghlan, "Whales Boast the Brain Cells that 'Make Us Human'" in *New Scientist*, a peer-reviewed journal based in London reporting on new scientific discoveries, reports that spindle cells have been discovered in a number of species of whales, including sperm whales. These spindle cells are "specialized brain cells that are involved in processing emotions and helping us interact socially. . . . the cells that are credited with allowing us to feel love and to suffer emotionally" (6–7). The co-discoverers are Patrick Hof of New York's Mount Sinai School of Medicine and Estel van der Gucht of the New York Consortium in Evolutionary Primatology. Hof is quoted in the article:

> It's absolutely clear to me that these are extremely intelligent animals. We must be careful about anthropomorphic interpretation of intelligence in whales, but their potential for high-level brain function, clearly demonstrated already at

the behavioural level, is confirmed by the existence of neu-
ronal types once thought unique to humans and our closest
relatives. They [whales] communicate through huge song
repertoires, recognize their own songs and make up new
ones. They also form coalitions to plan hunting strategies,
teach these to younger individuals, and have evolved social
networks similar to those of apes and humans.

The article also reports, from Hof and Gucht's work, that the
cellular evolution in whales was entirely independent from that of
humankind and primates, despite the shared land-based ancestry,
and that it is different among other cetacean species. The cetaceans'
evolutionary process, however, seems to have taken place over a much
longer period than that of the human species and its predecessors.

We can conclude that the whale's evolutionary history, its bodily
features and capabilities today within the harshness of its environment, its capacity to move in this environment, and its level of intelligence and empathy for the world around it are quite amazing. The
whale, more than most other mammals, appears to have a level of
consciousness and a capacity to perceive its broader environments
that parallels those of humankind. It is also possible that, over the
much more extensive period of its evolution, the whale has reached
a level of consciousness and environmental symmetry—a connection
to the broader ecosystems—that is superior to humankind. Several
interesting indications of this in the interaction between whales and
humankind over the history of whaling are explored in the following
section.

PRACTICE AND BUSINESS OF WHALING

Humankind has been connected to whales, particularly in coastal
societies, for much of human history. For purposes of this analysis, it
is important to understand the evolution of this relationship, from its

earliest days to the rampant excesses of the mid-nineteenth century, as chronicled in *Moby-Dick*. The significance of whales as a center-piece of Melville's epic has particular meaning in the context of the relationship of whales to humankind that developed up to, and during, Melville's time.

The practice of hunting and killing whales to harvest their parts for food, clothing, fuel, and implements of everyday life appears to have begun in prehistoric times, initially with whales that had washed up on the beach. Slijper provides a good summary of the early activity, noting the evidence of the hunting of whales in the coastal waters of the northern North American and European continents in the second millennia BCE. The people inhabiting what is now Iceland and the Norwegian coast were actively engaged in hunting whales in the sea as early as the ninth century CE and are generally regarded as the first community of active whalers.

The ensuing seven centuries saw increasing activity in the northern Atlantic and Arctic Oceans by the peoples inhabiting the lands bordering those waters. From harvesting whales that had washed up on the beach, the practice of trapping whales in coves and inland waterways and driving them to the beach for slaughter allowed for a much more sustained source of food and other needs for people living on or near the coasts of traditional whale provinces. Much as the buffalo was the staple for the Native Americans on the Great Plains, the whale provided many products to support indigenous livelihoods in the coastal communities. A richly deep symbiotic relationship existed between whale and these coastal communities much as it did for the buffalo and Native Americans. Commercial whaling, the hunting and killing of whales and the harvesting of their body parts for sale in a commercial setting, however, did not begin in earnest until the fifteenth and sixteenth centuries, then primarily by the Spanish and British.

The Basque whaling industry, which began in the Bay of Biscay, was the first to develop many of the methods for killing and harvesting whales beyond the practices of indigenous peoples. Whaling expeditions extended away from coastal regions and eventually ranged all over the eastern North Atlantic. Whales were killed in open seas and floated to nearby ports for harvesting, or the harvestable body parts were cut up and stored on board to be processed at port. The British followed suit, as did the Dutch a bit later, and the activity levels of all three were great enough that the whales inhabiting these regions, primarily the various species of right whale, experienced a serious decline in their populations by the late seventeenth century.

The British settlements of the northeastern coast of North America in the seventeenth century were driven by a number of cultural forces, not the least of which was the excellent fishing potential of the inland and coastal waters of these virgin, rugged coastlines. The European whaling activities had concentrated in the eastern and far northern areas of the Atlantic; Basque, English, and Dutch fleets had not ventured much below Newfoundland on the Atlantic's western edge. American whaling, in the seventeenth century, however, concentrated on bay whaling, hunting and killing whales in close-in coastal waters and then rendering them in nearby ports. Most of the whales so hunted were various species of right whales. However, as Ellis recounts in *Men and Whales*, a sperm whale washed ashore in Nantucket in 1700 and was harvested by the population of the small whaling community developing there. Its high-quality products surprised the residents. In 1712, an early Nantucket whaleship was blown out to sea by a storm and, happening upon a group of sperm whales, its crew was able to kill one and drag it back to port, demonstrating that this species could be hunted successfully in the open sea. Thus began the storied relationship of American whaling and the sperm whale, centered initially in Nantucket.

The abundance and high quality of the products rendered from this species sparked the imagination of the small Nantucket whaling community of the time. Sperm whales were bigger and thought to be more aggressive than the right whales; they were also not seen in the coastal waters. But the discovery of their presence in waters farther south, off the mid-Atlantic coast of the American colonies, and the realization that they were not so aggressive as to preclude capture, was enough to spark a new whaling focus. Nantucket had also become a Quaker haven by the early eighteenth century, and the rigorous work ethic of Quakerism as it developed in the New England colonies made the Nantucket community well poised for the development of a robust whaling trade, despite the risks.

The success of the Nantucket whalers quickly spread to other parts of the American colonies. Over the eighteenth and early nineteenth centuries, led by the whalers of Nantucket, the American sperm whale fishery flourished, basing its operations in various ports of New England, Long Island, and the northern Atlantic coast.

From its roots as a bay whaling trade, the industry also developed a series of efficient processes for hunting, killing, and rendering sperm whales. These included larger ships capable of larger crews and more extensive voyages; faster, sleeker whaleboats; careful mapping of whale migrations leading to enhanced strategies to find whales; more aggressive tactics used in hunting and killing; and refinements of the tools and processes for landing whales and dismembering their bodies. According to Ellis in *Men and Whales*, one of the most significant breakthroughs was the development of onboard tryworks for processing blubber. These consisted of large cauldrons set in stone or brick furnaces and mounted on the deck of the whaleship amidships so that the whale blubber and other parts could be cooked down into oil at sea, right after the kill, with the resultant fresh oil stored in barrels. The tryworks mechanism replaced the older systems of dragging slain whales to port for processing, or storing unprocessed whale body parts on board for processing later, in port. Slain whales and unprocessed body parts tended to decay rather quickly, whereas processed oil, particularly oil from sperm whales, remained unspoiled for extended periods. This innovation allowed for much longer whaling voyages over much wider areas; it also opened all the oceans of the entire world to the whalers from a single port.

By the early to mid-nineteenth century, the American whaling industry, particularly with its focus on the sperm whale fisheries, now dominated the world. In terms of the aggregate value of sperm oil, whale oil, and whalebone sold, the peak years of the American whale fishery were the 1840s and 1850s when the aggregate value approximated $10 million in 1840 dollars (Starbuck, 98–148). The gross domestic product (GDP) of the United States at the time was in the nominal range of $3 billion (147). Although the position of whaling in the American economy was therefore quite small, it was the first experience of American economic dominance in comparison to whaling elsewhere in the world. As such, whaling became one of the earliest indications of the American capacity to pursue commercial advantage, a capacity that seemed ingrained in the diverse, and politically liberal, human communities that were the American British colonies.

The products derived from whales varied significantly. In the early years, the primary use was food. By the time of the height of the American whale fishery, uses were extensive. Oil rendered from blubber or extracted from other body parts was used primarily for lighting (including candle making). It was also used as a lubricant, a raw material used in the production and manufacturing of other products (as such, it is referred to as feedstock), and as an additive in the manufacture of a number of products including soaps, cosmetics, paints, and varnishes. Bones were put to a variety of uses, from building materials and tools to decorative pottery. The membrane that constituted the baleen from the various mysticeti (or baleen) whales had equally diverse uses, including "corset stays, umbrella rods, fishing rods, buggy whips, and carriage springs" (Ellis, *Men and Whales*, 55). Before the acceleration of the Industrial Revolution, which took hold in the mid- to late nineteenth century, when petroleum became the primary source for a variety of fuels and manufactured products, the whale was a primary source for many products used in everyday life.

The whale fisheries also became a source of employment for diverse populations. The crew of a whaleship could include people from all over the colonial landscape as well as a number of indigenous people from remote corners of the world. Runaway slaves, Polynesian and African tribesmen, barely pubescent farm boys from the American hinterland, and immigrants and refugees from oppressed European societies might all be part of a whaleship crew. Some of the more difficult and strenuous tasks fell to indigenous people from more tribal cultures, those whose lifestyle and cultural backgrounds gave them superior strength and durability and made them capable of performing certain grueling tasks, like manning the harpoon, with grace and skill. Although a ship's masters, its captain and mates, tended to be exclusively white, Anglo-Saxon, and Protestant, the ship's community could be a truly universal society.

But life aboard ship was always harsh and fraught with risk. The conditions on a whaleship under voyage were much akin to the extremes of life in the factories of the rapidly growing industrial cities, so much so that the whaleship under sail was, in effect, a floating factory of the early Industrial Revolution. Although entirely different in the particular circumstances, these conditions were equal in perversity to those of the factories and tenements of lower Manhattan in the early years of the nineteenth century. Voyages were long (up to four years), accommodations were cramped and crowded, there were no bathing facilities, food was generally intolerable, fresh water was scarce, and the risks of serious injury and death were ever present.

Rendering a whale was an atrociously foul and hazardous business. The dead whale was pulled alongside the ship and, through a series of strenuous maneuvers, its skin and blubber were peeled off in long strips, hoisted on board, and dropped into a *blubber room* in the hold. There it was cut into smaller strips, hoisted back on deck and placed in the cauldrons where the blubber was reduced to oil. The discarded whaleskin was used as fuel for the furnace; its burning produced a dense, black, foul-smelling smoke. The hot oil was scooped out of the cauldrons with enormous ladles and poured into barrels. Risks of injury throughout the process were high (Ellis, *Men and Whales*, 168–202).

Compensation for all hands on a whaling voyage was contingent on the success of the voyage. Seamen were equipped beforehand with basic equipment such as overalls, boots, and gloves, the cost of which became their personal liability. Each was paid for his work on the voyage only in a share of the profits of the venture. Such share was designated in terms of a *lay*, a percentage of the total profits of the voyage. The size of each lay depended on the seaman's relative status within the hierarchy of men on the vessel. At the conclusion of a voyage, and after the final accounting of the overall revenue and expenses of the venture had been completed, each seaman was awarded his lay, his share in the profits. The final determination of each seaman's net proceeds was made only after deduction for the original cost of his equipment. If the venture was successful, there might be a reasonable net payment to each man. If it was not particularly successful, then seamen could end up owing money to the owners of the ship or the backers of the voyage, the capitalists who bankrolled the venture. Because the lays were the smallest for the lowest level seaman, any net burden from a less than successful voyage would fall the hardest on the most junior of men (McNally, 95–98).

The oil from sperm whales was superior in many respects to that from other cetacean species, a fact that, given their focus on sperm whales, significantly enhanced the fortunes of the major participants in the American whaling industry. Three kinds of oil derived from sperm whales: sperm oil, spermaceti, and ambergris. Compared to oil of the other whales that were hunted actively, sperm oil (whale oil rendered from the blubber of sperm whales) was superior as a clean-burning lamp oil and a highly effective lubricant. Spermaceti (a waxy substance from the spermaceti organ in the sperm whale's head) was used to make a very high quality candle, one that was very clean burning, odorless, and smokeless; no other substance existed at the time delivering such a high quality candle. Ambergris was a waxy substance that occurred in the intestines of whales, purportedly as a result of some sort of impaction in the intestines. It was extremely valuable, with an intoxicating scent, and was used in the manufacture of cosmetics and perfumes.

The fortunes of the men of capital who developed and financed these endeavors rose significantly in the progression of the American whale fishery in the eighteenth and nineteenth centuries. The primary whaling communities of New England saw the development of one of the first group of American families whose substantial wealth was derived from an American industrial experience. One of those families was Starbuck and one of its members was Alexander Starbuck, who published *History of the American Whale Fishery* in 1876. His is an exhaustive, intensely data-based survey of the American whaling industry from its earliest days. Despite the enormous risks—a voyage could be a complete loss with one mishap, and there was no guarantee of success—the returns could be significant. Starbuck chronicles the results of virtually all vessels working the fishery from all the ports of New England and New York from 1715 to 1876, when the book was written, though he was able to develop hard data only for the period 1804 to 1876. The data is recorded as of the year that a ship returns to port, no matter how long the voyage lasted, so the data for any given year is not a true reflection of the activity of that year. In the peak year of 1845, 257 ships returned to thirty-two ports from Portsmouth, New Hampshire, to Wilmington, Delaware. Their aggregate rendering was 158 thousand barrels of sperm oil, 273 thousand barrels of whale oil, and 3.2 million pounds of bone for a total value of approximately $9.2 million. In all, in the extended period from 1715 through 1876, approximately twenty-seven hundred ships sailed, executing almost twelve thousand voyages. From 1804 through 1876, according to Starbuck's record, the total harvest was 5.1 million barrels of sperm oil, 8.5 million barrels of whale oil, and 75.3 million pounds of bone, with a total dollar value of $331.9 million. (It should be noted that Starbuck uses both barrels and gallons in different tables and analyses. For this discussion, gallons have been converted to barrels based on 31.5 gallons per barrel, which was the measurement of the time.

The modern measurement of 42 gallons per barrel was adopted by the petroleum industry in 1866 in Titusville, Pennsylvania.) Starbuck reports that one ship, the *Envoy*, returning to New Bedford in 1848 after a voyage of less than a year, brought in an aggregate of fifty-three hundred barrels of oil and seventy-five thousand pounds of bone for a gross value of $138, 450; the cost to fit the voyage was $8,000 (147).

The aggregate of all this activity staggers the imagination; activities like this enabled the Industrial Revolution and the urbanization of western society in the nineteenth century. Starbuck reports that, based on the aggregate statistics for the activity between 1804 and 1876, a total of 419,043 whales (225,521 sperm whales and 193,522 right whales) were killed in the American whale fishery. Naturally, the effect of such abundant activity was to deplete the resource base of whales and drive up the cost; in effect, the plundering of the resource base of whales, escalating without restraint, sowed the seeds of the industry's own demise. From the decade of the 1820s to that of the 1860s, the average price of sperm oil went from $.65/gallon to $1.80; whale oil, from $.32 to $.88; and bone, from $.15/pound to $1.08 (Starbuck, 660). This was at a time when inflation was not as much a part of the economic landscape as it is today; all other things being equal, the cost of an item did not change in price for decades. For the whaling industry, facing a decline in available whales and a higher cost to acquire its primary commodity, whale oil, the only result was an escalation in price and the potential for a more competitive product to emerge and replace it.

The decline of whaling in America, then, followed that of the European industry. From its peak in 1845 of 257, the average annual number of voyages returning to port for the decade of the 1870s was less than one hundred. Whale as a fuel was replaced by kerosene, a derivative of petroleum. Whale oil (including sperm oil, spermaceti, and ambergris) as a lubricant and raw material for manufacturing continued to be in demand; however, without the fuel market, the higher levels of activity could not be sustained and the industry experienced a long and protracted decline. Although whaling on a very limited basis continues in certain parts of the world today, the last American whaling vessel sailed in 1926.

THE WHALE IN LITERATURE AND MYTH

Few animals have occupied as powerful an image in the human psyche as whales, fewer still of those that are as inaccessible to close human contact as the whale. In Genesis 1:21, God creates the "great sea monsters and every living creature that moves, of every kind, with which the waters swarm." The words *whale, great sea monster,* and *leviathan* were used interchangeably in most early literature. It is reasonable to assume that, when the words *sea monster* were used, the factual basis for the image was the whale. Indeed, whales and dolphins were known to frequent most all the major oceans and seas, including the Mediterranean and Red Seas and the Persian Gulf, so that an image of these animals swam in the collective consciousness. The words *sea monster* and *leviathan* appear many places in the Bible, notably, in the Book of Jonah, where a "large fish" is used by God as a vehicle to renew and redeem Jonah and his faith in, and dedication to, God. *Leviathan* is also used in Isaiah 27:1), Psalms (74:14, 104:25, 26), and Job (3:8, 41:1–34). In many of these references, Leviathan is seen as a serpent and a symbol of evil, which God crushes to protect the faithful. In Job 41, God characterizes Leviathan as an all-powerful creature against which man is entirely impotent, to demonstrate to Job the vulnerable and inconsequential nature of his existence.

Robert McNally, in *So Remorseless a Havoc*, provides an excellent review of the presence of the cetacean species in myth and literature. Dolphins are present in a number of Greek myths, McNally tells us, notably in the Homeric hymn of Dionysus and in the story of the musician of Apollo, Arion. In the mythologies of a number of far northern cultures bordering the sea, notably those of Iceland and Norway, and in the mythic systems of the Inuit of

Greenland, northern Canada and Alaska, the whale is a frequent presence. The whale is also prominent in a number of Polynesian and Japanese myths. In virtually all these, the dolphin or the whale is either a savior of some protagonist in danger of drowning in the sea, a vehicle for transportation, or a vessel for transformation of a god or human into another form, either physical or mythical. In the early Christian traditions up through the Middle Ages, there is very little reference to whales or dolphins, but many maps of the world feature a myriad of sea monsters, many resembling whales, adorning the waters at the edge of the known world, effectively appearing as threshold guardians at the edge of the unknown.

McNally's recounting of the presence of whales in Western consciousness notes that it was not until the late eighteenth and nineteenth centuries that a number of books appeared, both documentary and fiction, occasioned by the emergence of whaling. In 1752, Voltaire wrote a fascinating fictional short story, "Micromegas," in which the whale plays a small part. The primary character, named Micromegas, is an individual of prodigious size and intelligence, an inhabitant of a remote planet in the system of the star Sirius. Micromegas travels around the universe, experiencing a number of unusual situations, until he finally comes to earth. He is so large that he cannot find any inhabitants of this planet until he encounters the whale, which, though still incredibly small from his perspective, he assumes to be the primary form of life. Soon, however, he discovers a group of earthly philosophers. After developing an elaborate means of communicating with such a small species, he proceeds to find them somewhat ridiculous in their beliefs. The story is an early version of science fiction, but it is primarily an elaborate spoof on much of the conflict between religion and science of the time. The significance of whales in the story is limited, except, perhaps, to indicate that their size validated their being a species worthy of recognition as an inhabitant of the earth, especially in contrast to the puniness and absurdity of humankind.

McNally devotes a number of pages to Melville and *Moby-Dick*, which he calls "one of the best of all books ever" (173). Clearly, in the context of whales and whaling in myth and literature, *Moby-Dick* is center stage, from virtually every aspect anyone might look at this subject; the mythological constructs that can be developed therefrom are numerous and are covered, in detail, in chapter 3.

In virtually all societies, myth is the fundamental ethos that gives form to the central belief systems and, as such, myth exists in many forms. The stories only give them life in the consciousness. As a vibrant example, the relationships of the cetacean species to humankind in the coastal communities of indigenous people around the world are deeply mythic; they are very similar to that of the buffalo in the Native American systems. Both are steeped in a very powerful mythos. The bond between the Native Americans on the Great Plains and the buffalo was deeply spiritual; the tribes that hunted the buffalo cherished its spirit and drew strength from their relationship to it. The tribal communities used virtually every part of the animal. They celebrated the hunt, both before and after, and they paid homage to the buffalo for giving its life to them. It seems to have been the same with whales and the indigenous coastal people who relied on whales for their livelihood. Dick Russell, in *Eye of the Whale*, an extensive study of the gray whale and its migratory patterns, outlines the relationship of the gray whale to the Inuit in the same fashion. Although actual mythical stories of the whale in societies like the Inuit have not been recorded to the extent of the buffalo in Native American societies, the parallels are very strong.

In more modern times, there is the occasional treatment of the whale in fairy tales and film. The story of Pinocchio includes an episode in which the living puppet is swallowed by a whale and discovers his creator, Geppetto, trapped inside. He devises a plan for both of them to escape and, in doing so, realizes his dream of being transformed from a wooden puppet into a real boy. Three recent films— *Free Willy* (1993), *Whalerider* (2002), and the animated film *Finding*

Nemo (2003)—all highlight the whale as a means of transformation and, as such, are similar to the myths of earlier cultures. Of these films, *Whalerider* is the most relevant here. It is the story of a young girl, Pai, of the Maori people of Whangara, on the northeastern coast of New Zealand. Pai believes she is the rightful heir to the role of chief, but is rebuffed by the elders who believe that only a male can ascend to this role. Despite showing unusual skill in a number of trials and outperforming all the male pretenders to the role, she finally wins out by a heroic act of saving a group of right whales who have beached themselves. Her achievement includes riding on one of the whales as she leads the group back to the sea. She almost drowns in the process, a symbolic death and rebirth of mythic proportions. Her experience is so much like that of an ancestor, a renowned chief once saved by a whale, that she is accepted as the rightful heir to the chief. Much can be concluded about the choice of a young girl in a patriarchic tribal culture, about the behavior of the whales here in beaching themselves, and about their responding only to Pai in the process of being returned to the sea. Throughout, the power of the whale to influence the culture and behavior of the Maori people is a strong motif.

The dominant theme in the stories in so many diverse cultures is the presence of the whale as a spirit of transference and redemption. Even in the early Judeo-Christian systems, where the whale is seen as some sort of instrument of fear or evil, the result of its presence is a process of transference or redemption for humankind. All of this and more, much more, is present in the mythic experiences chronicled in *Moby-Dick*.

WHALES, WHALING, AND *MOBY-DICK*

The answer to the question asked at the beginning of this chapter about the significance of the whale as a central presence in Melville's tale can be addressed in four parts. The first of these involves the startling physical characteristics of the animal itself. Clearly, the whale is enormously large, powerful, and massively dominant in its environment. It evolved over millions of years in its ocean environment, resulting in an ease, grace, and power of movement that is majestic. It also has sensory and communication systems, and lives in a social environment that seems quite advanced as compared to the social environments of other life forms on both land and sea.

Within the context of the nineteenth-century whaling industry, the whale's strength and ease of movement also gave it the capability to destroy virtually any human or craft that endeavored to kill it. That whales did not generally do so is curious. The various stories of the rogue whale, although infrequent, are very demonstrative of its power. The one that is most documented is the story of the plight of the whaleship *Essex*, on which the story of *Moby-Dick* was loosely fashioned. In 1820, the *Essex*, out of Nantucket, was attacked by a sperm whale, subsequently named Mocha Dick, in the eastern Pacific Ocean, west of the Galapagos Islands. The ship was in the process of pursuing a number of sperm whales when Mocha Dick appeared and swam directly at the ship, ramming it just off the bow. He swam under the ship and appeared again on the other side, stationary, but seemingly taking aim for another collision with the ship.

The first mate of the *Essex* was a Nantucketer named Owen Chase who wrote an account of the incident titled *Shipwreck of the Whaleship* Essex. The captain of the ship was in one of the whaleboats, so Chase was in command. Chase wrote that, as the whale sat there, "he was enveloped in the foam of the sea, that his continual and violent thrashing about in the water had created around him, and I could distinctly see him smite his jaws together, as if distracted with rage and fury" (20). The whale then swam across the ship's bow and disappeared. After a few moments, he appeared again swimming toward the *Essex*, this time "coming down apparently with twice his ordinary speed, and to me at that moment, it appeared with tenfold fury and vengeance in his aspect" (21). The whale struck the ship much as he had done the first time and swam off. The *Essex* sank within ten minutes of the second ramming. The crew managed to get into two whaleboats with some provisions and sail away. They commenced an equally hazardous journey over the eastern Pacific until, after much hardship (including eating the flesh of dead fellow seamen to survive), they were chanced upon by another whaleship and rescued. The story, as told by Chase, became well known throughout the whaling community and became familiar to Herman Melville, who met and befriended Chase's nephew during a whaling voyage.

It is useful to put some further perspective on the destructive capacity of the sperm whale. Numerous stories in the literature, including *Moby-Dick*, discuss the sperm whale's ability to demolish a whaleboat with one flick of its flukes. Its ramming capacity, however, is the most fascinating. The frontal aspect of the sperm whale seems almost as if it developed as a natural battering ram. It presents a five to seven foot, mostly flat vertical plane, slightly tapered laterally, to give it the prospect of a flat edge, rounded at the sides. The exterior of this facade is a tough layer of skin and membrane covering the interior skull and spermaceti organ. Whitehead, in *Sperm Whales*, discusses how the males engage in ramming and battering opponents in mating rituals, so that there is plentiful evidence that the male of the species uses its strength in this way. To give this power and strength some perspective, consider the physics of an 80-ton whale, swimming at a rate of 20 knots and striking a nineteenth-century whaling ship (which typically weighed approximately 300 tons) stationary in the water. In comparison, the force can be likened to a moderately sized diesel train engine of today striking a stationary object weighing 300 tons. If this engine were traveling at 20 miles per hour and struck a comparable 300-ton object (say, six large tractor-trailer trucks assembled, bound together, and sitting stationary on a crossing), the impact would be enormously destructive. The experience of the *Essex* seems quite understandable in the light of such facts.

Yet, to a large measure, the whale did not use this strength. Its reluctance to do so reflects the nature of the whale as a species that is highly evolved and highly gifted, yet fully integrated in its environment. This brings us to the second point on the efficacy of the whale as a central focus of Melville's tale. Within the environment in which it lives and within the times in which Melville's story is set, it was as if, as a species, the whale sensed being a part of a larger ecosystem, that it felt some need to be sacrificed to sustain the larger system. In this sense, its similarities to the buffalo and the environment on the North American plains surface again. The development of the whale fisheries was significantly aided by this general lack of aggressiveness of whales, especially the various species of right whales, which had been hunted almost to extinction by the European and Scandinavian whalers. The whale's tendency to beach itself in times of deep stress or when it is approaching death may have some of the same import, the whale making itself available to the ecosystem. It is also as if, in doing so, it senses a longing to return to land whence it originally came, as if this were part of a final passage.

McNally discusses some similar themes. He explores the view that the cetacean species really has developed a higher level of consciousness. He notes that the nature of their environments and their inaccessibility to humans make it difficult for us to comprehend their world, but the curiously advanced nature of their sensory systems and their capacity for a relatively wide range of communication suggest a high level of intelligence. He posits that it all speaks to a species that has transcended the world experienced by humans, the world we have come to call "the human condition." He sees the cetacean as a species that has "slipped the bonds that hold us fast in our predicament" (229).

The third and fourth points of the central question here are the contrasts of the whaling industry as an economic enterprise within the American consciousness at the time of *Moby-Dick* and the incredible devastation that this economic enterprise was having on a species as mystical as the whale. Whaling had emerged as the first standard-bearer of the new American economic society, the emerging ability of our "free" society to out-produce the world and create significant financial wealth in the process. This industry was roundly praised in the emerging nation; it was seen as indisputable testament to the capacity of this new and incredibly diverse amalgamation of the world's outcasts to build economic power. Yet it achieved such distinction through the merciless, remorseless slaughter of hundreds of thousands of one of the earth's most glorious creatures. Within Melville's era, the species of whale and the experience of whaling seem the perfect backdrop to his exploration of the American ethos.

The legacy of whaling in the human consciousness is very much the legacy of the age of industrialization. Whaling is a much-reduced activity today, limited by a number of international bans on its practice over the last fifty years. But in the carnage of the eighteenth and nineteenth centuries, when the harvesting of whales left hundreds of thousands of carcasses stripped of skin and bones to float in the open sea, the scene was a parallel to the piles of carcasses of skinned buffalo in the same era, left on the Great Plains by white hunters looking for buffalo skins. Perhaps the image of the daily piles of trash and waste on our streets and in our landfills today is another parallel, the refuse of a similar exploitation of the earth toward questionable ends. How could so many hundreds of thousands of majestic creatures have been so slaughtered, solely to provide lighting for further industrialization and a profusion of products, many of which had no more value than to satisfy a passing fancy? And, although most of the species of whale survive today and whaling is nowhere near the level of the mid-nineteenth century, haven't we, the people of the developed societies, just turned our attention to a plunder of other resources of the earth, the image of which has many mythic parallels? The plunder of the future, the staging of an apocalypse for our children's children, the rape of Gaia: can we see the parallel between whaling and buffalo hunting?

McNally's book, *So Remorseless a Havoc*, is an attempt to put the relationship of humankind and whales into a framework for understanding the total experience that whaling is within the history of human consciousness. He starts with a wonderful quote, from chapter 105 of *Moby-Dick*, in which Melville discusses the position of the species of the whale in the environment of the earth over geologic time. (The concept of geologic time is a part of the analysis of petroleum in chapter 4.) Whereas Melville questions the validity of the parallel of the whale as facing the risks of extinction of other species like the eastern buffalo herds of Illinois and Indiana, his rich and mythic wording provides an excellent perspective and, perhaps, a prophetic conclusion to this analysis of whales and whaling:

> But still another inquiry remains; one often agitated by the more recondite Nantucketers. Whether owing to the almost omniscient lookouts at the mastheads of the whaleships, now penetrating even through Behring's straits, and into the remotest secret drawers and lockers of the world; and the thousand harpoons and lances darted along all the continental coasts; the moot point is, whether Leviathan can long endure so wide a chase, so remorseless a havoc; whether he must not at last be exterminated from the waters, and the last whale, like the last man, smoke his last pipe, and then evaporate in the final puff. (352)

Melville's tale vacillates between the poles of many mythemes in the society of his time. In his discussions of the whale, he is as enamored of the glory of the New England whaling industry as he is dismayed by the activities of slaughtering and rendering each of the species of whale. But it is in the inherent contradictions of this treatment that the true majesty of the epic derives its greatest power. For what Melville seems to be saying is that, in the unrelenting pursuit of this economic activity, the only outcome of "so remorseless a havoc" is the extinction of both whale and man. The parallels to the economic activities of our twenty-first century hydrocarbon society and the potential results of our "so remorseless a havoc" may be larger still.

2 Melville: His Times, Life, and Works

Fast-Fish and Loose-Fish

Herman Melville was born on August 1, 1819, of Dutch and Scottish lineage, a line that had significant involvement in the history of colonial America. Both his grandfathers were heroes of the American Revolution. His birthplace, 6 Pearl Street, lay at the foot of the island of Manhattan, less than a half mile from the corner of Broad and Wall streets, where George Washington took the oath of office in 1789. In the sixty-two years between this event, which marked the beginning of the U.S. governmental system, and Melville's writing *Moby-Dick* in 1851, the new American society, spawned from the European process of world colonization, experienced phenomenal growth and change in virtually every aspect.

The man, Herman Melville, lived and breathed this environment of growth and change, and participated in it in a unique and fascinating way. The mythic systems that permeated this new nation, the mythological constructs that formed the bases for the emerging worldview of America of the early nineteenth century, were a major influence on the literary genius who created the story of the White Whale. This chapter sets forth a review of the conditions of the evolving American society of the early nineteenth century and of the circumstances of Melville's family, personal, and literary life as a background to his telling the story of *Moby-Dick*.

THE DEVELOPING NATION

The United States of 1789, the former thirteen colonies, extended primarily along the Atlantic Coast, from Portsmouth, New Hampshire, to Savannah, Georgia, a distance of eleven hundred miles. The western boundary of the territory was the Allegheny and Blue Ridge Mountains. Most of the settlements were within 150 miles of the Atlantic coast. It was originally a series of colonies founded over the prior 182 years, colonies that were either religious havens for Protestant or Catholic outcast sects escaping oppression in the continuing religious conflicts in Europe or commercial outposts of European business interests designed to exploit the resources of the vast new continent. The new societies that developed within these colonies faced enormous struggles and established ways of life that were unique and diverse. Their aggregating to form the bond that successfully opposed Britain was equally unique; it set the stage for the development of a new nation that was unparalleled in the history of humankind to that point. It was a new nation of enormous resources and advantages; its growth and development from the start were electric.

According to the first census, taken in 1790 as prescribed by the new constitution to determine the representation in the House of Representatives, the aggregate population of the new nation at inception was 3.9 million and its GDP, a measure of economic output, was $190 million (U.S. Census Bureau). In the ensuing sixty years, to the time that Melville wrote *Moby-Dick*, the number of states increased from thirteen to thirty-one. The land mass expanded westward, first to the Mississippi, and then to the California coast. The land west of the Appalachians, from the Great Lakes to Florida, was acquired from Britain in the Revolutionary War and its aftermath; much of that was designated the Northwest Territories and had only been lightly explored. The Louisiana Purchase in 1803 added the great swath of land from the tip of Louisiana up the Mississippi and Missouri rivers to the Pacific Northwest; and the Texas revolution, its subsequent annexation, and the Mexican War of 1846 added the Southwest from Texas to California. By 1851, the new nation included all the lands to the Pacific. The tremendous growth in landmass, and the excitement of a new nation organized wholly differently from the traditional, more oppressive societies of Europe, attracted enormous flows of immigration from Europe and Asia and fueled the rapid growth of commerce and industry. By the 1850 census, the population had grown to 23.2 million and the GDP, to $2.6 billion.

It is hard to imagine today the excitement and energy that this new nation, within the world of the early nineteenth century, was generating around the globe, not to mention the enormous change taking place within its evolving borders. The spirit of revolution was sweeping through Europe, but the long-entrenched repressive regimes of those societies were thwarting its progress. In America, by contrast, the spirit of revolution was alive and in place. Enormous expanses of land were available to all who had the energy and sense of adventure to explore and homestead them. The exploding industrialization of the major cities also provided myriad economic opportunities for the adventurous.

This new nation also had deep, dark shadows, specters that were as frightening as its new sense of liberty and expansiveness were electrifying. The entrenched institution of slavery in the South, the creeping dehumanization of the industrialization of the North, and the exploitation of the Native American societies of the West belied the legitimacy of the expansionist zeal. But these deplorable systems and conditions did little to stem the progress of the development of the new nation as the land of opportunity. The time held a sense of opportunity whose limits seemed without any sense of boundaries.

EMERGING POLITICAL AND ECONOMIC SOCIETY

The United States populace of the Revolutionary War generation had grown up as British subjects. Despite the intellectual discourse about human and societal freedoms, the nation's early leaders retained a sense of the need for a ruling class, a patrician nobility or landed gentry. The idea of a nation ruled entirely "by the people" was still more of a concept than a practical reality. However, as the new governmental system took root and the last of the Revolutionary War generation died off in the 1820s, the tone of government turned more to concepts of a truly democratic society, the rights of all people to aspire to government. This tone was particularly strong in the ascendancy of the administration of Andrew Jackson, beginning in 1829. Jackson was the first president who was neither of the Revolutionary War generation nor a direct descendant of one of the Founding Fathers. Perhaps more important, Jackson was born in Tennessee and therefore a true son of the frontier. He was seen much more as a man of the people of this new expanding nation, and his ascendency fueled the expansionist zeal.

The doctrine of Manifest Destiny developed within the administration of the Jacksonian Democrats; it conveyed the belief that it was the right of the American nation to dominate the North American continent, from the Atlantic to the Pacific. Furthermore, the spirit of the frontier, of individual freedoms and the rights of the individual to seek land and fortune, spawned an independence of mind and spirit that infected the entire social body.

The Industrial Revolution, which was by this point a century old in Britain and Northern Europe, took on a unique flavor in the new nation and resulted in the explosion of the urban complexes of Boston, New York, and Philadelphia, as well as in a host of smaller cities from Maine to Virginia. The invention and development of a number of new mechanical processes, and the infusion of immigrant labor from Europe and Asia promoted explosive growth and facilitated the emergence of a truly American industrial economy, one whose capacities could grow beyond the expectations of the societies of the time.

As with the innovations developed by Yankee ingenuity that made the New Bedford whalers the dominant players in the worldwide whaling industry, inventions like the cotton gin, sewing machine, automatic reaper, the adaption of steam power to engines aboard ship, and the rapid expansion of the railroads and telegraph systems created a uniquely American industrialization. In short, "the thousands of inventions, major and minor, made between 1790 and 1850, utterly transformed methods that had been employed almost unchanged for hundreds of years in manufacture, transportation, mining, communications and agriculture" (Beard and Beard, 195). A land initially envisioned as a source of raw materials to support European industrial and commercial production began to emerge as a manufacturing power in its own right.

The shadow elements of the expanding nation had much to do with the explosive industrial development. The rapid rise of the industrial complexes of the major cities was, in no small way, aided by the institution of slavery in the South, allowing for raw cotton fiber to be produced and shipped to northern mills as cheaply as possible. The settlement of lands to the west, facilitated by the continual displacement of the Native American tribes, provided sources of food for the growing populace and raw materials for the industrial processes. And the influx of immigrants from Europe and Asia allowed for an incredibly cheap and exploitable labor base to provide the workers for the factories and railroads.

The deplorable conditions in the cities were exacerbated by the emergence of economic cycles of boom and bust that began to plague the national economy during this period. The first of these economic crises occurred in 1819 and was followed by another in 1829; 1837 marked the beginning of the third and most severe crash in the history of the United States up to that date, it lasted for about five years. Then, a "brief recovery was only a prelude to a fourth collapse in 1847" (Beard and Beard, 203). The overcrowding in the cities and the difficult living conditions that it spawned, combined with the economic hardship of the business cycles, resulted in the development of the first of labor movements and the emerging philosophical and social

41

conflicts between owners, capitalists, and management on one hand, and labor on the other.

AMERICAN LITERARY RENAISSANCE

In parallel with the developing political, sociological, and economic forces at work in the new American society, came a striking emergence of literary accomplishment. F. O. Matthiessen, professor of history and literature at Harvard, first developed the idea of this period as an American literary renaissance. In his landmark classic, *American Renaissance*, published in 1941, Matthiessen explored the profusion of literary genius that emerged in the third, fourth, and fifth decades of the nineteenth century. He saw this as a major breakthrough for America within the world's intellectual societies. Indeed, the confluence of American-born literary genius that appeared on the scene in the first half of that century is particularly notable. Consider that in the period between 1803 and 1819, the following individuals were born:

1803	Ralph Waldo Emerson
1804	Nathaniel Hawthorne
1807	Henry Wadsworth Longfellow
	John Greenleaf Whittier
1809	Oliver Wendell Holmes
	Edgar Allan Poe
1811	Harriett Beecher Stowe
1815	Elizabeth Cady Stanton
1817	Frederick Douglass
	Henry David Thoreau
1819	Julia Ward Howe
	James Russell Lowell
	Robert Lowell
	Herman Melville
	Walt Whitman

For the three decades leading up to the Civil War in 1861, these individuals provided an unusual outpouring of literary achievement virtually unmatched in the American experience to today. In the five years from 1850 to 1855, *The Scarlet Letter*, *The House of Seven Gables*, *Moby-Dick*, *Walden*, and *Leaves of Grass* were written. Commenting on these and a number of other less well-known works produced within this five-year span, Matthiessen observes that it was "one extraordinarily concentrated moment of expression. . . . You might search all the rest of American literature without being able to collect a group of books equal to these in imaginative vitality" (vii).

What was it about this period in our history, the three decades leading up to the Civil War, that allowed for such a productive outpouring of literary achievement? Looking at parallels in other times in known history provides some clues. Periclean Athens in the fifth century BCE, which saw the rise of the philosophical schools of Socrates, Plato, and Aristotle, was also the age of Aeschylus, Sophocles, and Aristophanes, and of the genesis of the theatrical arts. Elizabethan England in the late sixteenth and early seventeenth centuries saw the unusual confluence of Shakespeare, Jonson, and Marlowe, and the development of the modern literary stage. Interestingly, these periods were also times of momentous political and social change, ones in which new, relatively stable societies, based on new principles of individual freedoms were established in the aftermath of periods of momentous disruption. The conditions in the new American society, while not without significant shadow qualities, have strong parallels with these earlier historical periods.

The new American society was the first founded on the principles of equality of all men and the rights of all men to live a free and independent life. Despite the fact that *men* meant only white males and, in its early decades, primarily white men of property, these principles were still a major breakthrough in the history of the species. The unique republican form of government, the vast areas of land opening up, the opportunities for economic gain in the exploding industrial-

43

ization and commercialization of daily life—together, these created a sense of excitement that spawned a creative energy across all elements of society.

Literary Themes of the Period

As in Periclean Athens and Elizabethan England, the new American society of the early nineteenth century saw significant expansion of the scope and breadth of literary expression. It forged new ground and explored diverse themes that transcended the contributions of the periods immediately prior to this time.

In *Beneath the American Renaissance* (1989), David Reynolds, of Baruch College at New York's City University explores three elements present in the themes and writings of many of these authors, elements he characterizes as Conventional, Romantic/Adventure, and Subversive. Conventional authors dealt with traditional, mythic themes of society, themes often inherited from the traditional British genres. Romantic authors employed conventional elements but were more adventurous. James Fenimore Cooper, for example, wrote many stories whose style and subject matter were in this vein. These authors dealt with events and experiences in the American scene that were of mythic proportions, ones that were, according to Reynolds, "action-packed and sometimes dark but usually stylistically restrained" (8). In contrast, the Subversive authors were much more focused on the shadow elements of American and European society and of the human experience in general. This group included the major writers listed earlier, as well as Emily Dickinson (born in 1830) and Louisa May Alcott (born in 1832).

Subversive: Focus on the Shadow

The Subversive group can be broken down into the essayists and poets (including Emerson, Thoreau, Whitman, and the others listed) and the novelists and fiction writers (including Hawthorne, Melville, and Poe). In writing of these novelists, Reynolds asserts, "While the Subversive had roots in eighteenth-century British criminal and Gothic fiction, it took on distinctly American characteristics when reinterpreted by authors who wished to find literary correlatives for the horrific and turbulent aspects of perceived reality in the new republic" (8). Reynolds also saw the works of all of these authors as "often highly irrational and rebellious" and, with regard to the final achievements of the icons of this age (Emerson, Thoreau, Hawthorne, Melville, and Whitman), he saw "an enormous compression of varied cultural voices in an explosive center" (9).

The works of the Subversive writers, particularly the essays of Emerson and Thoreau, the poetry of Whitman, and the novels of Hawthorne and Melville, seemed to have three main currents behind the surface elements of their writings:

1. the repressiveness of the traditional Calvinistic view of Christian doctrine and everyday Christian life that was prevalent in the primary societies of seventeenth- and eighteenth-century New England, New York, and Pennsylvania;
2. the profound human degradation of the entrenched institution of slavery in the South and the plunder of the lands of the Native American in the West; and
3. the pillaging of the earth inherent in the rapidly growing activities of commerce and industry, and the exploitation of those, mostly immigrant, populations whose livelihoods were inexorably bound to the urban industrial activity.

Emerson, Thoreau, and Hawthorne lived in the fascinating cultural community of Concord, one of the first inland settlements in Massachusetts. It was here that the American Revolution began in April 1775, with the historic ride of Paul Revere to warn the colonial militia positioned outside the town of the approach of the British regulars. In the early part of the nineteenth century, Concord emerged as a cultural magnet, beginning with Emerson and Hawthorne and continuing through Thoreau, Dickinson, and Alcott. This was also Puritan New England, with a sense of the oppressiveness of the more strict and devout Protestant sects, which were steeped in a staunchly dualistic view of the world. Unitarianism, which emerged in the American colonies in the late seventeenth and early eighteenth centuries in opposition to these traditional beliefs, was accepted by large followings. It was a core belief system for the literary and intellectual community that eventually found its home in Concord.

Unitarianism rejected the idea of a multipersonality godhead, with a hierarchy of lesser deities, and espoused instead a single entity in God and a deep connection between God and nature, to include humanity. It saw a fundamental connectedness between God, nature, and humanity that resulted in the development of a much simpler, more humanistic view of the world.

Unitarianism was a part of the development of a less repressive religious orientation that accompanied the advent of the philosophy of Romanticism in Europe; it was, indeed, a break from the Enlightenment thinking of Francis Bacon and John Locke. The central idea of the Enlightenment was that reason, based on empirical studies of the physical world, was the primary basis of knowledge. Although this idea had a profound influence on the political thinking of Thomas Jefferson and other Founding Fathers, by the early 1800s, Romanticism emerged as a counterbalance to the Enlightenment, focusing on a much more humanistic view of the world, a view that had its genesis in the thinking of philosophers such as Immanuel Kant. Beyond the purely rationalistic focus of the Enlightenment, Romanticism saw the world as inherently sublime, in and of itself, independent of reason, and every human spirit as unique and mirrored in nature.

Contemporary author Susan Cheever, in *American Bloomsbury*, reviews the cultural and intellectual makeup of the literary community in and around Concord, particularly the development of Transcendentalism, which has been called American Romanticism. This movement focused on a much stronger link between man and nature, and a belief that God, man, and nature were inexorably intertwined. Emerson was Transcendentalism's primary spokesman and, beginning in the 1830s, this movement counted Emerson, Hawthorne, Thoreau, Margaret Fuller, and Bronson Alcott (father of the Alcott sisters) among its core. Emerson's essay "Nature," first published in 1836, was a primary text. It systematically explored the relationship of man to nature and to a concept of God as intertwined in nature. Emerson challenged each man and woman to unite with the nature of his or her own connection, to pursue a "philosophy of insight and not of tradition, and a religion by revelation to us" (7). Beyond its break with the Enlightenment, the result for Transcendentalism was a radical movement away from the traditional views of the world as inculcated in the primary Protestant religions of the northeastern United States.

Hawthorne, a native of Salem, the scene of the seventeenth-century witch trials, focused some of his best fiction on the repressiveness of the traditional Puritan view of the world, dramatizing it in deeply allegorical terms. Both *The Scarlet Letter* and *The House of Seven Gables* spotlight deeply held beliefs about the nature of sin. In both of these novels, however, the protagonists, although sinners in a biblical sense, are portrayed as the victims of misplaced societal judgments. In their steadfast commitment to a sense of the psychic honor and purity of self, they rise to the level of hero or heroine.

From misplaced societal judgments, it is not a far leap to the second underlying theme of the evolving American literary society of the time: the question of slavery and the exploitation of the Native American populations in the nation's march to the Pacific. The unspoken rule among the Founding Fathers, specifically the framers of the Constitution and the early members of Congress, was that the enigma of slavery was to be avoided in debate, at all costs. Even in the early days of the Republic, this required some effort. (Slavery was far from isolated: there were more than six hundred fifty thousand slaves in the original 1790 census.) Joseph Ellis relates in *Founding Brothers*, a wonderful study of the icons of America's earliest leadership, how this pact of silence developed after an intense debate in the first session of Congress in 1790. The belief at the time was that, for the Union to remain intact, the business of government would have to be conducted without the subject of emancipation ever being on the agenda. The solution, promulgated by Washington and Madison, was that the legitimacy and legality of slavery was a problem for each state to decide for itself, not the federal government.

For most of the next quarter century, this pact remained. But as the tone of government shifted toward a more democratic view and as the intellectual society developed, the voices silenced in 1790 began to be audible again. The existence of slavery and its tolerance by the very fabric of government was a most damning fact of life of the new American scene; it was the fact that belied the major tenets of the nation's founding. Beginning in the 1830s, slavery's existence was increasingly debated in society, sometimes violently, and the specter of this horrendous shadow began to roil in the nation's consciousness. As new states were organized and sought entry into the Union, slavery became a central factor in the debates over admission. Both sides wanted the balance of control in Congress to remain equal, with the number of states permitting slavery being equal to those opposing it. Thoreau's famous essay, *Civil Disobedience*, developed a position that has found use in a variety of protest movements well into the twenty-first. century; it was occasioned by his decision to refuse to pay a poll tax in 1846, in opposition to the Mexican War and the likelihood that it would extend slavery in the Union. Thoreau opined that the individual had an obligation to obey a higher law, and to disobey a civil law, if the higher law found the lesser, the civil law, to be wrong. He found that prison was "the only house in a slave state in which a free man can abide with honor" (9).

In 1850, the debate over slavery reached a fever pitch, with the proposed admission of California to the Union. The resulting Compromise of 1850 allowed California admission to the Union as a free state, prohibited slavery in certain territories, and passed a strict and harsh Fugitive Slave Law. This piece of legislation made it illegal for anyone, anywhere in the Union, in a slave or a free state, to aid and abet the escape of any slave from his or her master. One of the first tests of this law, in Boston, was decided by the Massachusetts Supreme Court, whose presiding judge was Lemuel Shaw, Herman Melville's father-in-law.

In 1852, in her revulsion toward the Fugitive Slave Law, Harriet Beecher Stowe, a Connecticut teacher and abolitionist, wrote *Uncle Tom's Cabin*, which was based on the lives of a family of slaves brutally treated within the system of slavery. An involved story that contains many of the stereotyped portrayals of black men and women in the South before Emancipation, it was one of the most popular books of the nineteenth century and did much to educate the public on the conditions of the lives of the slaves in the South.

The third aspect of literary focus, and perhaps the most important for Melville, was the exploitation of the resources of the earth, including the human spirit, inherent in the Industrial Revolution and the rampant commercialism of the new American nation. The abuse of immigrant populations from Europe, who provided the bulk of the labor to support the development of factories and the building of the railroads was one example. The Transcendentalists, who disdained the dehumanizing aspects of the materialism of the emerging economic society, also focused on opposition to this abuse.

Thoreau's *Walden* has a number of references to the effect of commerce on the landscape and the lives of men. In an explanation for choosing to live alone on Walden Pond and seek the simplicities of life in nature, he comments, in his traditional metaphorical terms, about the complexities of the national life inherent in the commercial and industrial development. "The nation itself . . . is just such a wieldy and overgrown establishment, cluttered with furniture and tripped up by its own traps, ruined by luxury and heedless expense" (89). In the same vein, he discusses the oppressive growth of the railroads, probably the most central element in the development of industrial capacity.

He writes about how the ties underlying the rails are really Irish men, workers, each a tie, "The rails are laid on them, and they are covered with sand, and the cars run smoothly over them" (90).

The Economic Undercurrent

These three underlying currents of the emerging literary society were inexorably bound, all integral elements in the new nation's drive to build the economic societies of the new industrialism. At the first, the institution of slavery was fundamental to the economic core. Almost as important, the displacement of the Native American tribes was necessary to access and develop the necessary resources of the land; and the surging immigrant populations were needed to staff the factories and the railroad gangs. But most significantly, the traditional religious systems, both Protestant and Catholic, provided an element of philosophical legitimacy to support these dark and sinister systems. All the traditional Christian religions were attendants to the establishment of the colonial networks that promoted slavery and exploited native populations. In addition, the concept of a Protestant ethic, as a philosophical system to promote hard work, frugality, and investment, regardless of any underlying abuse of the human spirit, was a core of the Puritan, Quaker, and other Protestant systems. It provided a theoretical, theocratic basis for the drive to build and aggregate industrial capacity.

In 1905, the early sociologist Max Weber wrote *The Protestant Ethic and the "Spirit" of Capitalism*. The thesis of this work concentrated on the evolving view of the world within the Protestant societies of northern Europe of the seventeenth and eighteenth centuries; it focused on the idea that the accumulation of wealth in such societies—wealth beyond what was needed for the sustenance and security of one's immediate and extended family—was being pursued as a measure of one's favor in the eyes of God. This view developed in the context of the emerging industrialism to become a theoretical and philosophical basis for the growth of the economic societies of Europe and America. Wealth was to be accumulated through constant, self-less, hard work, and reinvested within the commercial enterprises of the time to promote the accumulation of more wealth. This system also eschewed frivolous spending and the ostentatious demonstration or use of wealth, "the conscious enjoyment [or] outward signs of social esteem" (24). Interestingly, Weber uses many of the proverbs ascribed to Ben Franklin (for example, "time is money," "money begets money," "a penny saved is a penny earned," and "the good paymaster is lord of another man's purse") to describe the development of these systems (10–12).

The development of the economic society of the new American nation was built on entrenched systems of planetary exploitation and supported by both the traditional religious systems and the new freedoms of the emerging society. This development resulted in a rush to consume the resources and the people of the earth as a means to acquire wealth. The literary commentators of the time, the icons of the American literary society, focused on these sinister elements of the American psyche that either profited from or blindly tolerated such exploitation. Their focus provides excellent testimony to how a mythology, the mythic system that supports a worldview, is seeded, germinates, and grows in the collective psyche of a nation. Herman Melville, as a man of these times, clearly developed a view of the world and of the human condition from his experiences in this expanding American nation, so much so that these mythemes became the center-piece of many of his works.

THE AMERICAN MAN, HERMAN MELVILLE

The serious study of Herman Melville as a member of the American literary experience began in the 1920s when, thirty years after his death, his books were recognized for a level of literary accomplishment that was not acknowledged during his lifetime. This "revival" of Melville has continued to this day, especially with new discoveries of documents and archival material. Over this time, beginning in the 1940s, a number of excellent biographies have appeared, including those by Newton Arvin of Smith College (1950); Eleanor Melville Metcalf, granddaughter of Herman Melville (1953); Edwin Haviland Miller of New York University (1975); Hershel Parker of the University of Delaware, in two volumes (1996 and 2002); and Andrew Delbanco of Columbia University (2005). Hershel Parker's is by far the most exhaustive; he is also an editor of the Norton edition of *Moby-Dick* as well as of editions of Melville's other works.

As with many of his peers in the emerging literary society, Herman Melville was born into a family of privilege; his was particularly situated in the privileged classes of the American revolutionary society. (The original spelling of the family name was without the final *e*, which Herman's mother, Maria Gansevoort Melville, added in 1832.) His paternal grandfather, Thomas Melvill, was a Boston merchant, a member of the Sons of Liberty, who, disguised as Mohawk Indians, dumped ninety thousand pounds of tea into Boston harbor in 1773 to protest unfair tax regimes. His maternal grandfather, Peter Gansevoort, was a Dutch patroon, a wealthy landowner, and a general in the Continental Army. General Gansevoort's valiant defense of Fort Stanwix against the British General Burgoyne in the Mohawk Valley north of Albany in 1777 made him a Revolutionary War hero. The Melvills were Scots of some position and wealth in Scotland. Thomas Melvill's father immigrated to Boston in the early eighteenth century. The Gansevoorts immigrated in the early seventeenth century and were active as major brewers of beer in the upper Hudson and Mohawk valleys. Over the years, they had intermarried with many of the prominent Dutch families of New York, including the Rensselaers.

Herman Melville's father, Allan Melvill, was a merchant like his father. He was active in New England and New York in the merchandising of goods from Europe, particularly France. Trafficking up and down the Hudson, he met Maria Gansevoort in Albany and settled there in 1814. His success enamored him of New York and, after the birth of their first son, Gansevoort, in 1815, they moved to New York, where Herman (the third child and second son) was born. The first eleven years of Herman's life were years of significant privilege:

> The Manhattan household of the boy's first decade consisted of loving (almost doting) and apparently wealthy parents, supported by attentive if transient nurses, tutors (at times a live-in teacher), and other servants (three or more at a time, sometimes including, besides the female cook and house-maids, an almost supererogatory male waiter). (Parker 1:22)

Allan Melvill's business acumen, however, lacked a certain financial practicality. As the family grew to a total of eight children, they moved a number of times, to successively larger homes, and they became active in the emerging Manhattan social scene. However, in the recurring financial cycles of the emerging economic society, his fortunes deteriorated to the point where in October 1830, the Melvill family was forced to abandon their New York home and lifestyle and flee to live with the Gansevoorts in Albany. Their move from New York was more of a late night flight from creditors than a normal relocation. The eldest, Gansevoort, and his mother left a few days early with most of the siblings. Allan and young Herman, then eleven, packed the last of their belongings and left in the late evening of Saturday, October 9. With a suddenness and a sense of drama and intrigue, the family's life of privilege ended in a furtive boat ride up the Hudson River.

His father continued to struggle and was successively bailed out by family and friends, until a growing despondency resulted in rapidly deteriorating health. Allan eventually died in January 1832, at the age of fifty. Both Herman and his older brother Gansevoort were enamored of their father; he had traveled extensively and regaled them with stories of European society. Until his declining financial condition and health took their toll, he had a lively and open outlook on life. Melville biographer Newton Arvin suggests that, given the family history and the life of wealth and privilege of their early years, the experience of their father's business collapse (though readily apparent to the world from the weakness he had shown in financial dealings) must have been traumatic for both the boys. Arvin explains it this way: "Deprived of an idolized father on the very verge of adolescence, the boy Melville underwent an emotional crisis from whose effects he was never to be wholly free" (23).

In the aftermath of their father's death, Gansevoort and Herman could no longer continue their schooling at the level they had. Herman began work as a bank clerk; he was not yet thirteen. Over the next six years, he worked first in an Albany bank, and then for his older brother who, at the age of seventeen, had taken over his father's merchant business. Gansevoort was modestly successful and, amidst some brief periods of prosperity, Herman was able to attend school. In 1837, in the economic collapse and financial panic that was the most severe of the nation's economic cycles to that time, the family merchant business under Gansevoort failed, and Herman went to work as a teacher in a small town in western Massachusetts, near Pittsfield.

After a full semester of teaching, he went on to odd jobs, to include a failed effort as a surveyor. Finally, in early 1839, with his family's fortunes continuingly grim and burdened with the anxieties of virtually all his teenage years, Herman signed on to a merchant ship bound for Liverpool. He returned later that year on the same ship, having spent two months, between the respective voyages, in the dreary backwaters of industrial Liverpool and its environs, including the "pestilent lanes and alleys" of this grim industrial city (Parker, 1:150). His return voyage also gave him exposure to the experience of poor Irish and German immigrants in steerage quarters aboard the merchant ship.

Returning home to Albany, Melville found work as a schoolmaster in Greenbush, across the Hudson from Albany. The family fortunes deteriorated further, such that his mother and sisters had become almost entirely impoverished. After less than a year of teaching, in early 1840, Herman, then twenty, journeyed to Galena, Illinois, to see an uncle, Thomas Melvill Jr., and to seek employment in the new West. He traveled around the upper Mississippi Valley for a time, but found no prospects for employment. Returning home, he found nothing there either, so, in late 1840 he traveled to New Bedford and signed on to the whaleship *Acushnett*. Two of Melville's cousins, Thomas Melvill and Leonard Gansevoort, had been on whaling voyages a few years earlier, so the idea of such an adventure was already in the family lore.

The *Acushnett* set sail in early January 1841, with H. Melville on the roster as a seaman, but there is no record of Melville's experiences aboard ship over the ensuing eighteen months. It is assumed that he found the voyage grueling, so much so that, in July of the next year, he "jumped ship" as the *Acushnett* lay at anchor off the island of Nuku Hiva, in the Marquesas group of islands, part of the vast island grouping of French Polynesia. He escaped inland and lived for a period of three to four weeks among the islanders of the Taipi tribe in an immense volcanic valley in the midst of the island. Fearing that he was being groomed to be part of a cannibalistic ritual, he finally fled the valley, found his way back to the shore, and signed onto another whaling ship, the *Lucy Ann*.

At Tahiti, in September 1842, a revolt aboard the *Lucy Ann* ended up with Melville and a number of others in chains for mutiny. Charges were eventually dismissed and, after wandering the island for some time, Melville signed onto a third whaler, the *Charles and Henry*, which got him to the town of Lahaina, on Maui. Here he was released from service, and spent about three months touring the Sandwich Islands, as the Hawaiian Islands were then called. His odd jobs during this time included setting pins in a bowling alley (Parker, 1:253). In August 1843, he signed on as a seaman aboard the U.S. Navy frigate *United States*. The various voyages of the *United States* brought him to Boston in October 1844. He had, by then, been at sea or amongst the islanders of the Pacific for three and a half years.

Melville's experiences on both the Marquesas and the Sandwich Islands coincided with significant European colonial activity. As Melville alludes to in *Typee* (293–98) and Parker notes in his essay in the Norton edition of *Moby-Dick* titled "Before *Moby-Dick*: International Controversy over Melville" (465–66), the French were establishing their dominion over the Marquesas in the colonization effort that would eventually establish the very extensive French Polynesian group of islands. The British briefly held claim to the Sandwich Islands in the early 1840s before the islanders established their independence, with some help from the United States whose frigate the *United States* was present to support the islanders.

Upon his return to the United States, Melville found his way to Albany and then to Lansingburgh, where his mother and younger siblings (ranging from two to eleven years younger than Melville) now lived. They were in somewhat meager circumstances but not quite as destitute as earlier, thanks to Gansevoort's efforts and the support of family and friends. In the ensuing weeks after his return, Melville regaled them all with stories of his adventures. These stories proved so captivating that all suggested he write a book. It turned out that the target audience for popular literature of the time fit the profile of the women of the Melville household perfectly, according to Andrew Delbanco (64).

After a few months, he moved to New York to stay with his brothers, the elder Gansevoort and the younger Allan. He began writing of his adventures and, by late 1845, he had completed his first book, *Typee*, whose name was a stylized version of the name Taipi or Taipai, the tribe with whom he spent those few weeks in 1842 in the interior of Nuku Hiva. The story was cast as an account of his personal experiences, but with various exaggerated and fictionalized elements. In his attempts to get it published, he was rebuffed by the largest and most influential of the New York publishers, Harper Brothers, who saw the accounts of Melville's experiences as improbable.

His brother, Gansevoort, had become active in political affairs in the intervening years since Herman left and had successfully worked on the presidential campaign of James Polk. This activity gained him an appointment in the American legation in London. From this position, he was able to submit Herman's manuscript to a London publisher and to promote the book with friends and acquaintances in London. As the process of publishing it in London was developing, a visit by Washington Irving to the American legation gave Gansevoort the opportunity to show the manuscript to him. Irving liked it and recommended it to his New York publisher, G. P. Putnam, of the firm of Putnam and Wiley in New York, who was also visiting in London. Putnam agreed to publish *Typee* and it first appeared in print in New York, as well as London, in February 1846.

Melville's story line and descriptions in *Typee* represented the first time that an account of actual life among the Polynesian people had appeared in print, as contrasted to mere records and observations of "scientists, sea captains and missionaries" (Parker, 1: 400). The book was vivid and lively, almost erotic, and the writing style was quite captivating. It appealed to the interests of the English as well as the growing American readership of the time. Both Hawthorne and Whitman gave it enthusiastic reviews. Melville immediately began work on the sequel, titled *Omoo*, a name taken from the sound, to Melville, of the Tahitian word for "a rover, or rather, a person wandering from one island to another" (326). Its story line began at the point that Melville left the Marquesas and continued until he got to Maui. Its style is very much like that of *Typee*, continuing with the author's enchantment with the natural life of the Tahitian islanders. In addition, as Tahiti was well into the process of colonization by the French, it also expressed a rather dim view of the oppressive treatment of these natives by the Europeans, particularly the missionaries who strenuously imposed their Christian views of God, nature, and sin on the Polynesian culture. *Omoo* was published in 1847 to an equally warm reception by the literary world, although there was some criticism of his treatment of the missionaries.

Omoo was followed, in relatively quick succession, by three additional texts: *Mardi* in 1849, which is an entirely fictional account of a young American seaman who tours various islands in the Pacific; *Redburn*, also in 1849, which tracks Melville's experiences on the merchant ship to Liverpool in 1839; and *White Jacket* in 1850, which recounts his experiences on the military frigate *United States*, these last two being fictionalized accounts of his adventures much in the manner of *Typee* and *Omoo*. *Redburn*, *White Jacket*, and *Mardi* also have increasingly dark and critical themes about the life experiences of the protagonist. *Redburn* attempts to capture the grimness of life in the lanes of Liverpool and in the steerage quarters of the mostly Irish and German immigrants traveling by ship to New York. There are also comparisons of New York's Lower East Side, to which these immigrants were headed, to the inner city of Liverpool. *White Jacket* portrays the harsh and cruel conditions of life aboard a military ship, to include random, brutal, and many times undeserved floggings. *Mardi*, however, besides being entirely fictionalized, was a significant departure for Melville, in that he attempts to use much more mystical, metaphorical imagery to describe the experiences of the protagonist. In the process, he also creates a number of places, people, and events that are not-so-veiled allegories of his times. For a literary public that had enjoyed his vivid imagery of real-life experiences, this work's themes met with very mixed reviews.

However, during this period, Melville achieved considerable overall fame, which had the effect of improving the family's fortunes dramatically. Gansevoort had died in mid-1846 at age thirty-two, the victim of continuing decline in his health, driven by financial mishaps. He left the family in relative poverty. As the success of *Typee* and *Omoo* began to improve their lot, Melville moved everyone to New York and settled them there in late 1847. In August of that year, he married Elizabeth Shaw of Boston, the daughter of Chief Justice Lemuel Shaw of Massachusetts, who had been a close friend of his father and who had provided some early assistance to the struggling Melville family.

The literary scene in New York during this time had become quite active, surpassing that of all other U.S. cities and rivaling those of Europe. Herman Melville, with his new and exciting approach to writing, which many saw as an extension of the new American Romanticism, was very much in the midst of this ascendancy. In mid-1850, however, partly because his wife and mother were enamored of the country around the Berkshire Mountains in western Massachusetts and partly because he was tiring of the New York literary scene and its incessant squabbling, Melville moved to Pittsfield with his immediate and extended family. In September of that year, he bought a farm, which he called Arrowhead. At this time, he was well into writing his sixth and greatest book, *Moby-Dick*. His efforts on this project, and indeed, his larger worldview, encountered their greatest stimulant at this time when, in early August 1850, he met Nathaniel Hawthorne.

Hawthorne was born in 1804 in Salem, Massachusetts, and grew up there, a fourth-generation member of the Puritan community that settled in the region in the early seventeenth century. A great uncle had been one of the judges in the witch trials in Salem in 1692. Hawthorne was educated at Bowdoin in Maine, where he was a classmate of a future president of the United States, Franklin Pierce. He began his writing career in the mid-1820s, writing mostly short stories and articles, and was first published in 1828. He moved to Concord in 1842 to become a member of the literary community there. In 1849 he moved to Lenox, only a few miles from the farm that Melville would buy a year later. On August 5, 1850, at a picnic hosted by a New York lawyer friend of Melville's, a party that also included Oliver Wendell Holmes, Hawthorne and Melville met for the first time. The events of the day evolved in a fashion such that Melville and Hawthorne ended up spending a couple of hours by themselves; it is apparent that, during this short time, a deep and abiding friendship was formed. Melville had known of Hawthorne, and in the immediate aftermath of their meeting, he wrote a review of Hawthorne's anthology of stories titled *Mosses from an Old Manse.*

In this review, "Hawthorne and His Mosses," which appears in the Norton edition of *Moby-Dick* (517–32), Melville describes Hawthorne's influence upon him, saying that he had "dropped germanous seeds in my soul" (529). Hawthorne's collection of stories was originally published in 1846, a few years before *The Scarlet Letter,* his first full-length novel. The Mosses stories seem to have taken Hawthorne's study of the human condition to a much deeper, darker level. In his review, which he did anonymously, Melville explores "that blackness in Hawthorne . . . that so fixes and fascinates me" (522). It is a blackness that Melville likened to Shakespeare, finding parallels in those "deep far away things in him; those occasional flashing-forth of the intuitive Truth in him; those short, quick probings at the axis of reality" (522).

Hawthorne and Melville were fifteen years apart in age, and, in appearance, demeanor, and life experiences, they were starkly different. Susan Cheever, in *American Bloomsbury,* describing the profoundly human experiences of the men and women central to the American literary renaissance, devotes a chapter to the relationship of Hawthorne and Melville. She calls it "intense, erotic and platonic" (97). Contrasting them, she sees Melville as rough hewn, rugged, and unpredictable and Hawthorne as reserved, frail, and rigid in his daily routine. Hawthorne had hardly left New England, whereas Melville had traveled halfway around the world, living "the kind of life Hawthorne could only dream about" (97). "Melville was Pan to Hawthorne's Apollo" (99).

They were neighbors for a little more than a year, during which time they met with and wrote to each other with some regularity. Given their eventual literary stature and the impact they seem to have had on each other, it may have been one of the most significant years in American literary history. Cheever believes that "Hawthorne's intensity, his refusal to treat life as anything less than a controlling metaphor for man's moral nature, seemed to be contagious" (98). Melville labored over *Moby-Dick* during this time; there is evidence that much of this work went through significant revision as a result of the discourse with Hawthorne. The impact of the relationship seemed to be mutual, as Hawthorne wrote *The House of Seven Gables* during this time as well.

There is reasonable evidence that Melville's revisions of *Moby-Dick* during this time profoundly deepened the story. John Bryant, in "Moby-Dick as Revolution," explores the theory that there are two *Moby-Dicks*. According to this theory, the first was a book Melville originally intended, which would have been a pseudo-fictionalized story of whaling much in the form of earlier works such as *White Jacket*. The second, occasioned by the relationship with Hawthorne, was one that developed "a Shakespeareanized story of Ahab" (67), which took the book to the levels it eventually achieved. Melville's character development of Ahab is thought to have been significantly deeper and more involved than it had been in early drafts. In addition, it is believed that some of the structural anomalies of the book and the curious early characters that are developed and then disappear, such as Bildad and Bulkington, also point to the possibility of Melville's extensive revisions.

Hawthorne moved back to Concord in the late fall of 1851. This was about the time that *Moby-Dick* was originally published, first in London and then in New York. The New York edition was dedicated to Hawthorne, but despite Hawthorne's enthusiasm for the work, Parker believes that Melville refused to let him review it, either out of respect for their friendship or fear of possible rejection (2:15). In the literary community, the book received a wide range of responses. Jay Leyda's *The Melville Log*, a detailed accounting of the daily events in Melville's life, provides a smattering of excerpts from various reviews, some positive—"a singular medley of naval observation, magazine article writing, satiric reflection upon the conventionalisms of civilized life," "far beyond the level of an ordinary work of fiction, not a mere tale of adventures, but a whole philosophy of life," "characters and subjects set off with artistic effect, and with irresistible attraction"—and a bit more of them, negative—"an ill-compounded mixture of romance and matter-of-fact," "falls short of being a great work," "the chief feature of the volume [is] a perfect failure, and the work itself inartistic" (1:430–39). *Moby-Dick* did very poorly in sales, particularly in America; Melville's total earnings from the American edition were $556.37 (Delbanco, 178).

Melville brooded over the book's poor showing for some time, but by early 1852 he was on to his next book, *Pierre or The Ambiguities*, which was published in July of that year. It is a curious story about a boy, raised by a very domineering mother, who marries a delicate society type and is then torn by his need to feel and experience a deeper, passionate relationship. The book was destroyed by the critics, who found little redeeming value in Melville's explorations of the deeper human emotions inherent in the crossover of familial and conjugal love. One critic, echoing the tone of many, called it "A bad book! Affected in dialect, unnatural in conception, repulsive in plot, and inartistic in construction. Such is Mr. Melville's worst . . . book" (Leyda 1:463).

Coming so soon in the wake of *Moby-Dick's* tepid reception, this reception put Melville into a seriously depressed state. In the ensuing years, he wrote two more novels, *Israel Potter* in 1855 and *The Confidence-Man* in 1857, and one series of short stories, *The Piazza Tales*, in 1856. *Israel Potter* is a story of an actual Revolutionary War veteran who leaves his parents' farm as a boy to fight at Bunker Hill and is captured by the British and shipped off to England. He escapes in England and spends many years in an Odyssey-like series of escapades trying to return to Boston. The *Confidence-Man*, on the other hand, is a story of a fictionalized confidence man on a Mississippi River steamboat who, in a variety of disguises, systematically fleeces different passengers in a range of wild ruses. Of the *Piazza Tales*, one— "Benito Cereno"—is a masterful work about a slaveship in distress on which the slaves are able to take over the ship and wreak unspeakable horror on their captors. It was seen by some, particularly among the abolitionist community, as one of the best stories about the complexities and absolute horrors of slavery in the New World.

The declining popularity of Melville's books, however, limited his income significantly. His various attempts to obtain a political appointment of some kind, with the support of influential family members, were to no avail. With funds from his father-in-law, he made an extensive tour of Europe and the Near East in late 1857 and early 1858, following which he conducted a number of lecture tours throughout the United States, relating his experiences.

In 1863, he moved with his family from Pittsfield back to New York, and took up residence again in lower Manhattan. In 1866, he secured a position as inspector of customs of the Port of New York, a post he held until 1885. He wrote considerably more poetry than fiction during these years, the greatest of which—an eighteen-thousand-line poem titled *Clarel*—was published in 1876. It is the story of a young man who tours the Middle East, particularly the Levant and the Holy Land, in search of some sort of higher meaning to his life. Much of it harkens back to Melville's own tour in 1857 and 1858. It is an exhaustive work with much imagery and symbolism covering a wide range of ideas and vistas, but it was seen as too fragmented and received no support within the literary world. However, the intensity of the imagery and the literary composition provides some valuable insights into Melville's complex and anxious view of conditions in the world. The following lines from an exchange while the protagonist is in Bethlehem sets the tone of how his view of Western industrialism had developed:

> The Anglo-Saxons—lacking grace
> To win the love of any race;
> Hated by myriads dispossessed
> Of rights—the Indians East and West.
> These pirates of the sphere! Grave looters—
> Grave, canting, Mammonite freebooters,

> Who in the name of Christ and Trade . . .
> Deflower the world's last sylvan glade. (4.9:117–25)

Melville spent his final years in the late 1880s writing what came to be his second greatest work, *Billy Budd*, about a very likeable young sailor of that name who is pressed into service on a British man-of-war during the Napoleonic era. Billy is a pure soul, of remarkable beauty and innocence, who is nonetheless harshly treated by Claggart, the ship's cruel master-at-arms. Because of his disdain for Billy, Claggart fabricates a set of charges that Billy has been inciting some of the crew to mutiny. Speechless at the charge, Billy strikes Claggart in a rage. Despite the apparent perversity of the master-at-arms' actions, the captain is forced to find Billy guilty under the British Navy's articles of war and have him hanged. It was an excellent story, once again showing Melville's capacity to deal with the darkest of elements in the human psyche. By the time Melville wrote it, however, he was so much forgotten that *Billy Budd* was not published. Melville died in relative obscurity in 1891, at the age of seventy-two.

In 1920, the Oxford World Classics series republished *Moby-Dick*, which had been out of print since 1886. In the emerging revival, Melville came to be seen as "a writer who had anticipated James Joyce's literary innovations, and who . . . sinned blackly against the orthodoxy of his time," according to Delbanco (11). *Billy Budd* was finally published in 1924 and favorably received. The revival received one of its greatest early boosts in the personage of D. H. Lawrence who, in 1923, published his *Studies in Classic American Literature*, a review of a number of the early nineteenth-century American authors. With regard to Melville, Lawrence became the first of noted authors to capture his brilliance. Toward the end of his commentary, in his review of the conclusion of *Moby-Dick*, Lawrence observes,

> So ends one of the strangest and most wonderful books in
> the world, closing up its mystery and its tortured symbol-

ism. It is an epic of the sea such as no man has equaled; and it is a book of esoteric symbolism of profound significance, and of considerable tiresomeness. But it is a great book, a very great book, the greatest book of the sea ever written. It moves awe in the soul. (168)

Perspectives

In the context of his times, and of the life and practices of his contemporaries, the story of the life and work of Herman Melville seems a unique phenomenon. After eleven years of a pampered child's life, to be the sole companion to his father in a midnight flight from creditors in New York; to watch his father, an admired fatherly figure, decline into a state of depression and death over his inability to negotiate the vagaries of the commercial marketplace; to watch his older brother, only seventeen when his father died, struggle with the same system and come to the same end at age thirty-two; to escape to the sea, first on a merchant ship to Liverpool at the beginning of the diaspora of Europe's poor and disadvantaged, then on a series of whaling expeditions and, finally, as a seaman on a man-of-war frigate, all such voyages taking him halfway around the world; and, then, to return to New York, the economic heart of America, and become a celebrated writer with virtually no training, all before the age of thirty, illustrates that Melville was an amazing individual. In the first eleven years of his writing career, from 1846 to 1857, he wrote nine full-length novels and one anthology of short stories, all of which were published. In all, during these eleven years, his published works came to a total of thirty-six hundred pages (based on the Library of America's complete works in three volumes).

The question arises: whence developed this seemingly magical literary talent, this profound capacity for creation of deep human story, told with vivid description and poetic expression? His life to this time cut across much of what was happening in and around America, and he experienced it in a unique way. His writing came largely from his experiences, but what was the source of his unique skill at composition?

Melville's formal education was limited, as was his involvement in the literary communities of the time. There is some evidence that he was an active reader from an early age, and he seems to have gained some academic awards for scholarship and composition during his brief time in various schools in Albany in his middle to late teens. Merton Sealts, professor of English at the University of Wisconsin and an acknowledged Melville scholar, compiled *Melville's Reading: A Check-List of Books Owned and Borrowed*, which was published in series in the Harvard Library Bulletin from 1948 to 1950. Sealts notes in exhaustive detail all the evidence of Melville's reading, from these early days at school through his involvement in literary activities in Albany, to the possibility of his access to shipboard libraries during his sea voyages, and through the literary period beginning in 1846. Some of the evidence is anecdotal, and much of it is from interpretations of commentaries by some of the main characters in his novels. From 1846 on, however, upon his return from sea and embarking on his literary career, it is clear that Melville read everything of value that he could access. Sealts compiled lists from various sources, which included virtually all the classic authors back to antiquity. Melville seemed to develop a particular love of Shakespeare; it is believed that he read most of Shakespeare's major works in the immediate years up to and during his writing of *Moby-Dick*.

Melville's capacity to create his own unique view of the world in literary form developed in a way equally as fascinating as his composition. He clearly took to the activity of writing with enormous energy and a consummate, innate skill, even though there was little indication of this being a primary interest for him much before he started in the mid-1840s. He wrote entirely of his experiences, and, from the first, with an almost unique flair and language. He quickly moved from the popular memoir style of *Typee* and *Omoo*, to delve into a more metaphorical and psychological orientation in *Mardi*, and, subsequently, to seek the lowest strata, the more grim elements of the contemporary human experience in *Redburn* and *White Jacket*. With the stimulation of Hawthorne, he then plunged headlong into the depths of the human psyche, both from the point of view of his contemporary era as well as a more timeless vein, in *Moby-Dick*. Although he was very much attuned to the current events of the day in the American scene at the time, he seemed to have had much less of an orientation to the deeply philosophical elements of the American experience before he met Hawthorne in 1850, as he was writing, and then re-writing, *Moby-Dick*. His connection with Hawthorne therefore looms large in understanding the outcome of his creative efforts from 1850 on.

Chasing the Shadow

The works after *Moby-Dick* continued the trend developed in that epic. *Pierre*, as a psychological analysis of the human psyche, was wholly unlike anything seen to that time. The *Confidence-Man* dealt with the darkness of certain financial and economic elements of the American society; this one focused on the Mississippi River Valley scene, one that Mark Twain similarly exploited later in the nineteenth century. Melville's despair over the weak showing of *Moby-Dick* and *Pierre* within the literary community, however, seriously diminished the productivity he had shown in the early years of writing. But the deep, human themes continued in all his works. At the end, *Billy Budd*, like *Moby-Dick*, was a masterpiece of exploration into the dark side of the human spirit.

If we put this progression of Melville's works into the context of the times in which he lived and his experiences therein, it is clear that he was increasingly dealing with a blackness in the human soul and, particularly, the American soul. The shadow elements of the emerging American society, as elaborated in the three literary themes discussed, were coming into sharper and sharper focus in the progression of his works. The most critical element was that, as opposed to all of his peers, Melville experienced them firsthand in a unique and focused way. His commentary in his review of Hawthorne's *Mosses from an Old Manse*, described earlier, provides some further indication of the evolving themes in his mind. He seems to be talking of his own mind when he says that Hawthorne

> is shrouded in blackness, ten times black. But this darkness gives more effect to the ever moving dawn, that forever advances through it, and circumnavigates his world. Whether Hawthorne has simply availed himself of this mystical blackness as a means to the wondrous effects he makes it to produce in his lights and shades; or whether there really lurks in him, perhaps unknown to himself, a touch of Puritanical gloom,—this I cannot altogether tell. Certain it is, however, that this great power of blackness in him derives its force from its appeals to that Calvinistic sense of Innate Depravity and Original Sin, from whose visitations, in some shape or other, no deeply thinking mind is always wholly free. (521)

His references to Puritanism and Calvinism seem to be something much more than religious; rather, the idea of a sense of "Innate Depravity" stemming from "Original Sin" (the capitalizations are his), and a blackness that is never illuminated by an "ever advancing dawn" are a condition of the human psyche that haunts the "deeply thinking mind."

Melville wrote no essays or philosophical treatises or commentaries. He knew few of his major contemporaries. Aside from Hawthorne, there is some probability that he knew Whitman in New York. But he never met Poe (Parker, 1:370) nor did he know any other members of the Concord crowd. "Hawthorne and His Mosses," which Melville wrote before he spent much time with Hawthorne, conveys some interesting views of the religious traditions of the early American experience. Whence might these have emanated?

Religion and the Early American Worldview

Melville's religious upbringing was staunchly Protestant, in the Dutch Reformed and Scottish tradition. He was rooted in the American Dutch settlement of New Amsterdam, which became New York in 1664 when the British seized that colony, and in the Puritan and Quaker systems of Massachusetts. In 1943, William Braswell of Duke University and the University of Chicago completed a summary of Melville's religious background and life views in *Melville's Religious Thought*. He shows Melville to be a man reared in a "God fearing tradition" who seemed to attend church on an occasional basis, to include missionary churches in the Pacific, but who, as a result of his experiences, comes to struggle with the nature of God.

Similarly, Lawrence Thompson of Princeton provides an analysis of the conflicts in Melville's worldview in *Melville's Quarrel with God*, published in 1952. In both books we see a man tortured with a vision of God that he cannot reconcile with his experience in the world. Both these books also deal with Melville's treatment of God in *Moby-Dick*. Braswell understands Ahab as believing that "if good is to be attributed to the omnipotent deity, then so must evil" (58). Thompson sees one of the goals of Melville's writing of *Moby-Dick* to be "to tell a story which would illuminate, obliquely, his personal declaration of independence not only from the tyranny of Christian dogma but also from the sovereign tyranny of God Almighty" (147).

In 1856, during his trip to the Middle East, Melville visited in Liverpool with Hawthorne who had been appointed consul there by his old school friend, and now president, Franklin Pierce. This was after Melville had been devastated by the poor reception of the works he had considered vastly superior to his more popular first novels. Hawthorne was struck with the changes in Melville and wrote in his journal:

> I think he will never rest until he gets hold of a definite be-
> lief. It is strange how he persists—and has persisted ever

since I knew him, and probably long before—in wandering to-and-fro over these deserts, as dismal and monotonous as the sand hills amid which we are sitting. He can neither believe, nor be comfortable in his unbelief; and he is too honest and courageous not to try to do one or the other. If he were a religious man, he would be one of the most truly religious and reverential; he has a very high and noble nature, and better worth immortality than most of us. (Braswell, 3)

Equally significant in his emerging view of the world is Melville's exposure to many elements of the Industrial Revolution during his life. The recurring economic depressions and collapses of the emerging industrial and commercial system, in the 1820s and 1830s, particularly in New York, the financial heart of the new economic society, had—as mentioned earlier—a devastating effect on Melville and his whole family. Further, in his travels, Melville witnessed various scenes of the more grim and destitute experiences of the American economic society.

In all of this, and in the work that refined his skill and his view of the world, Melville developed an unusual capacity to weave theme and story, to deal with the interlocking nature of all the dark currents of his society. It is, perhaps, one of the greatest elements of his work. For in all the disparate events of his times, and in all his experiences of the shadow side of the new American psyche, he developed a strain of themes woven into story that few could grasp. No wonder that the books of the second half of his eleven-year run, that period from 1851 to 1857, were so poorly received. Despite all that was happening in America, how many readers would choose to deal with all that Melville saw and portrayed so grimly in many of his works, and so notably in *Moby-Dick*?

These interwoven themes for Melville—the influence of the Protestant ethic in the Calvinistic and Puritan systems, the economic underpinnings of slavery and the degradation of the Native American, and the exploitation of the earth and of humanity in the emerging industrialism—these were much of the backbone of the new American nation, the soft underbelly of the emerging economic society. These are elements that still hold a very dark power in the psyche of America of the twenty-first century. Indeed, it is Melville's treatment of these themes in *Moby-Dick* that provides the power that this mythic epic conveys for us today.

As but one example, consider chapter 89 of *Moby-Dick,* which is titled "Fast-Fish and Loose-Fish." This chapter presents another of Melville's famously lengthy descriptions about the particulars of whales and whaling. Here he describes the rules of the sea, as developed by the American whalemen, regarding the rights of any whaler to land any particular whale. The rules were meant to address the problem of a dispute arising where one ship landed a whale but suffered its escape, or, if already dead, its unharvested carcass somehow broke away, and it was later captured by another ship. The simple rule followed by all, according to Melville, was: "I. A Fast-Fish belongs to the party fast to it. II. A Loose-Fish is fair game for anybody who can soonest catch it." He goes on to say that "alive or dead a fish is technically fast, when it is connected with an occupied ship or boat, by any medium at all controllable by the occupant or occupants" (308). After a discussion of a particular dispute, Melville suggests that "these two laws touching Fast-Fish and Loose-Fish will, on reflection, be found the fundamentals of all human jurisprudence. . . . Is it not a saying in everyone's mouth, Possession is half the law, regardless of how the thing came into possession? But often possession is the whole of the law" (309).

At this point, Melville enumerates a litany of analogies of Fast-Fish and Loose-Fish, writing: "What are the sinews and souls of Russian serfs and Republican slaves but Fast-Fish" in comparing Russian serfdom and American slavery. His list includes many items that fit the currents of social, political, and literary focus of the times. And, in Melville's imagination, it also provides an excellent small picture of his view of the world as he was writing this masterpiece of American fiction:

What to the rapacious landlord is the widow's last mite but a Fast-Fish? What is yonder undetected villain's marble mansion with a door-plate for a waif; what is that but a Fast-Fish? . . . What is the Archbishop of Savesoul's income of £100,000 seized from the scant bread and cheese of hundreds of thousands of broken-backed laborers (all sure of heaven without any of Savesoul's help) what is that globular 100,000 but a Fast-Fish? . . . What to that redoubted harpooneer, John Bull, is poor Ireland, but a Fast-Fish? What to that apostolic lancer, Brother Jonathan, is Texas but a Fast-Fish? . . .

What was America in 1492 but a Loose-Fish, in which Columbus struck the Spanish standard by way of waifing it for his royal master and mistress? What was Poland to the Czar? What Greece to the Turk? What India to England? What at last will Mexico be to the United States? All Loose-Fish.

What are the Rights of Man and the Liberties of the World but Loose-Fish? What all men's minds and opinions but Loose-Fish? What to the ostentatious smuggling verbalists are the thoughts of thinkers but Loose-Fish? What is the great globe itself but a Loose-Fish? And what are you, reader, but a Loose-Fish and a Fast-Fish, too? (309–10).

Were there any doubt, Herman Melville makes clear in this litany that he has told the tale of *Moby-Dick* to a much larger end.

THE AMERICAN WRITER, MELVILLE AS ISHMAEL

Finally, in preparation for a more detailed exploration of *Moby-Dick* in the next chapter, it is useful to talk about how that epic begins, to wit: "Call me Ishmael" (18). Melville does not say, "My name is Ishmael," nor "I am Ishmael." He tells us to call him Ishmael. Melville's style in much of his work, his penchant for using a first-person narrator, was very much tinged with strong autobiographical elements. There is an almost universal belief within the Melvillean community that, in *Moby-Dick*, much of the character of Ishmael is infused with psychic elements of Melville himself. The conditions that Ishmael recounts as prompting him to go to sea—"the damp, drizzly November in my soul" (18)—recall the conditions that may have affected the young Melville who shipped on a merchant ship in 1839 and on a whaler in 1841. In the beginning of *Moby-Dick*, he seems to be saying that this story, a story of whaling and of the journey of a particular whaleship, mostly fictionalized characters and events with some basis in fact, that this story must be told by him. But why Ishmael? Why this name?

In Genesis 12:1–5, God chooses Abraham to found a new nation in the land of Canaan; this is the beginning of the Hebrew people, and the beginning of the Hebraic tradition. In Genesis 16:1–16, Sarah, wife of Abraham, has failed to become pregnant and is concerned about succession as Abraham and she are aging. She gives her slave-girl Hagar to Abraham as a mate. With Hagar, Abraham sires a son and potential heir whom he calls Ishmael, which name means "God gives." Subsequently, in Genesis 17:15–19, God makes Sarah fertile and in Genesis 21:1–7, she gives birth to Isaac. Finally, in Genesis 21:9–14, Sarah expresses resentment toward Ishmael and Hagar and declares to Abraham, "Cast out this slave woman with her son; for the son of this slave woman shall not inherit along with my son Isaac." Abraham is concerned and seeks God's counsel, but he is told to follow Sarah's wishes. God pledges to watch over Hagar and Ishmael and give them a separate nation.

In the Hebraic tradition, then, the covenant between God and the Hebrew people is passed to Isaac, and not Ishmael, the elder son. In the Islamic tradition, Ishmael and Hagar travel to Mecca, where Ishmael establishes the nation there promised by God. He is visited by Abraham, and together they build the Kaaba, the shrine in the middle of Mecca. Mohammed, the prophet and founder of Islam, is a descendent of Ishmael, and the nation of Islam is based in Mecca.

Melville's choice of this name for the narrator of the story of *Moby-Dick*, then, seems to have powerful historical significance. Melville has chosen a name, his name, Ishmael, from an individual who was the chosen one, by God, to be Abraham's descendant, the leader of the new Hebrew nation, the progenitor of the entire Judeo-Christian civilization. However, because of the circumstances of his birth, he is cast aside and denied his birthright. Instead, he founds a separate society, one whose evolving tradition led to the founding of the second largest religious system on earth, Islam, second only in size to Judeo-Christianity. Abraham is the father of both, and the genesis of each has arisen from a sibling conflict.

Looking at the status of the two systems today—Judeo-Christianity and Islam—at the nature of the conflicts that have developed between the two, at the position of oil as the underlying currency defining the root of value for each in the world of the twenty-first century, it seems that Melville could not have chosen a more prophetic or a more profoundly mythic name than Ishmael. For, as we confront our world today, at the beginning of the twenty-first century, at the pinnacle of the Petroleum Age, in all its inherent political, social, and economic conflicts, the mythological relevance of the idea of Ishmael as narrator of this story seems striking indeed.

3 Moby-Dick: Myth and Epic

There! She Breeches

Moby-Dick, as a mythic, epic, poetic tale, can be read on many levels. The story of one man's titanic obsession with a monstrous animal, a Leviathan of biblical proportions, and of the scribe, Ishmael, who recreates it for us, encompasses a number of themes that reflect the core elements of American and human society during the nineteenth century. Melville's original intent seems to have been to tell a story of whales and whaling, much as *Typee* and *Omoo* chronicled Polynesian life and *Redburn* and *White Jacket* scrutinized merchant seafaring and naval military life, respectively. Whales are animals of epic proportions, and, up to that time, their story had not been told, nor had the story of the American whaling industry, in the popular style that Melville had perfected in his earlier works.

And, yet, *Moby-Dick* is much more than a story of whales and the whaling industry. Melville's interaction with Nathaniel Hawthorne (as observed in chapter 2), seems to have provoked a much more intense exploration into the human experience in *Moby-Dick* than originally intended. It is in this exploration, in Melville's attempt to plumb the depths of the human experience in the dramatic enactment of the men of the *Pequod*, and to do so within the epic activity of whaling, that the true mythic power of this tale is found. Christopher Sten, in *The Weaver God, He Weaves*, explains that "*Moby-Dick* is an incredibly rich and complex work with as intricate a set of symbols, image patterns, and motifs as is to be found in a work of literature anywhere in the world" (139). To understand the richness of this story, and its epic design, particularly how they apply to our focus here, it will be useful to deconstruct the tale, the critical elements of its mythic meaning, as it appears Melville intended to portray them, and as they inform the American economic experience both of Melville's time and today.

MYTH AND EPIC

Joseph Campbell's four-volume work *The Masks of God* is his definitive expression of the place of myth in the human experience. It is meant to explore all the mythic themes that have been inculcated in human society since the emergence of the species into consciousness. The first two volumes, *Primitive Mythology* and *Oriental Mythology*, reviewed the multitude of mythic systems and focused on the roots of myths in pre-history and on the development of mythic systems in the emergence of the major religions of Egypt, the Levant, India, China, Southeast Asia, and Japan, respectively. The third volume, *Occidental Mythology*, gathered the underlying themes in the early development of Western systems. The fourth volume, *Creative Mythology*, traces the development of myth in the West over the past eight hundred years, beginning in the High Middle Ages of the twelfth century. In the first chapter of this fourth volume, Campbell notes that the themes inherent in the human experience up to that point were generally quite consistent, writing that "Millenniums . . . rolled by with only minor variations played on themes derived from God-knows-when" (3).

At the transition from the High Middle Ages to the Renaissance, however, there arose significant changes in fundamental human systems of thought. In setting the stage for his exploration of the Western experience that began at this time in history, Campbell asserts that

In our recent West, since the middle of the twelfth century, an accelerating disintegration has been undoing the formidable orthodox tradition that came to flower in that century, and with its fall, the released creative powers of a great company of towering individuals have broken forth: so that not one, or even two or three, but a galaxy of mythologies— as many, one might say, as the multitude of its geniuses— must be taken into account in any study of the spectacle of our own titanic age. (3)

In his introduction to the fourth volume, Campbell provides his four functions of myth, which are repeated in many forms in his later works. These are: first, "to reconcile waking consciousness to the *mysterium tremendum et fascinans* of this universe as it is;" second, "to render an interpretive total image of the same, as known to contemporary consciousness;" third, to enforce "a moral order; the shaping of the individual to the requirements of his geographical and historical social group;" and, fourth, "to foster the centering and unfolding of the individual in integrity, in accord with himself (the microcosm), his culture (the mesocosm), the universe (the macrocosm) and that awesome ultimate mystery which is beyond and within himself and all things" (4–6). In discussing the third of these functions, Campbell says that, in the enforcement of a moral order, in the shaping of the individual to the group, an actual break with nature may occur, which would include ritualized acts that sever the body or elements of the earth from their natural condition. In short, nature can become subservient to society as rituals and practices are pursued that actually denigrate the natural system (5). The fourth of the functions Campbell calls the "most vital, most critical function of a mythology" (6).

The last two of these provide the sense of creative mythology, where the human society has adopted the capacity to shape its mythologies independent of nature or any sense of a higher order. It is in these latter two that the capacity of the human species to foster a mythic system that breaks with an earth-centric view of the world can appear, as did those that began to appear in the West over the last five hundred years.

Finally, he defines myth in the context of these four functions as follows: "A mythological canon is an organization of symbols, ineffable in import, by which the energies of aspiration are evoked and gathered toward a focus" (5). The effort in chapter 2 was to describe the fundamental belief systems that pervaded the society of early nineteenth-century America, those from within which Herman Melville wove story. In its mythic form, the tale that is *Moby-Dick* fulfills the elements of Campbell's analysis in the manner in which it weaves the themes we have outlined. The underlying activity of the novel, whaling, has, as its fundamental underpinnings, the pursuit of economic gain. The product of the economic activity, whale oil, was a core consumable within the economic landscapes of America and the world. It was harvested and processed in an activity that involved enormous risks and in which the probability of serious injury was great, mirroring many of the economic activities of the Industrial Revolution. The economic enterprises that conducted the processes were highly structured and financially integrated into the societies of the time. The exploitation of nonwhite, non-Anglo-Saxon workers and the exploitation of nature were as much a part of these activities as they were in the other industrial activities of the time.

The mythic systems that permeated these times—the new political system of the United States and the expansion that it promoted; the repressive religious systems of the underlying culture; the rampant exploitation of African, native, and immigrant American peoples masked by the broader ethos; and the pursuit of economic opportunity enabled by these systems, at whatever costs to the underlying society and the natural world—comprised the integral elements of the consciousness of the time. The belief systems that informed the underlying patterns of behavior very much served to shape the individual to the requirements of the social group that was America. To paraphrase

Campbell's principle of myth, they served to center the individual integrally, in accord with the culture. And, finally, in *Moby-Dick*, it is the multitude of the myths of the time, interwoven in story and echoing Campbell's "galaxy of mythologies [that inhabit] our titanic age" (3), that stir the imagination and allow the stark parallels to be drawn with our modern age. It is the multitude and the power of the myths in which a diverse people, an American nation, are engaged that make *Moby-Dick* so rich and enduring.

However, the epic element of this tale, the masterfully expansive adventure that it engages, may be even more powerful than the mythos in which the story is woven; it is its epic stature that seems to cause larger-than-life energies to stir in the psyche. Bainard Cowan calls it "the greatest example of epic in the modern Western world" (217). Cowan understands epic as encompassing majestic and idealized themes, of importance to the societies from which they emanate. He views *Moby-Dick*, however, as a significant departure from the epic tradition of the historical giants such as Homer, Virgil, and Milton. In the prose of a novel rather than in poetic form, *Moby-Dick* represents a different approach, a more plebian one, from the ancient masters. Nevertheless, in the manner in which Melville weaves the themes of his time, in the context of the events in the greater consciousness, the treatment of the ethos of the story is still majestic, reflecting the full tradition of epic.

The business of whaling loomed large in the psyche of early nineteenth-century America, even if the general public was not aware of its scope and breadth. The whale is a majestic animal, lionized as Leviathan in biblical texts and present in equally powerful forms in much of world myth and literature for millennia. The species of whale that was hunted by the American whaler, the sperm whale, was uniquely powerful and more dangerous and aggressive than its counterpart species. As it does today, it ruled the ocean that is the Pacific, a body of water so vast as to stir everyone's imagination. The process of the whale hunt, executed with incredible intensity over profound time lines and distances, was dangerous, exhaustive, and heroic. The story that is *Moby-Dick* contains many of the attributes of Campbell's hero's journey: the calling, the descent to the underworld, and—for Ishmael at least—the return. The ultimate outcome of the whaling voyage, the delivery of barrels of oil and pounds of bone to be made into such products as lighting fuel, candles, lubricants, tools, building materials, buggy whips, and corset stays seems incredibly pedestrian. However, in the context of the larger consciousness of Melville's time and in the context of what is happening today, with the importance of whale oil's successor, petroleum, to the world's societies, it retains its epic proportion.

Cowan sees the novel form as epitomized in *Moby-Dick* as a unique and different medium in American, and, ultimately, world consciousness; he sees it as epic because it takes the ordinary man, Ishmael, and propels him into extraordinary circumstances. He calls the novel "radically democratic," because it is a story of the journey of Ishmael, the quintessential nineteenth-century ordinary American, being drawn into a confrontation with the great whale himself (222). It becomes epic for our own time as well because it involves Ishmael, the ordinary American, in a struggle between the whale and an economic society infused with a sense of dominion, the sense of dominion that is epitomized by Ahab's monomania over the White Whale's seemingly invincible power to resist capture.

THE STRUCTURE AND STORY THAT IS *MOBY-DICK*

The 427-page Norton edition of *Moby-Dick* includes the title page, table of contents, and a series of eleven pages of etymology and "Extracts," which incorporate Melville's research notes about whales. The actual story as written by Melville is presented in 135 chapters, whose organization and flow provide a simple structure for analysis of the story. The tale is, in concept, a very simple one. It is primarily that of a journey of a typical, if not archetypal, whaleship. As used in this work, the terms *archetype* and *archetypal* are generally meant in their classic Jungian sense, that is, to refer to definite forms or universal images inherent in the collective unconsciousness (Jung, "The Shadow," *Collected Works* 9:88–90). The use in this instance is perhaps broader than Jung intended, to denote qualities of people or things that are the essence or core element infusing that person or thing with a certain universality. Thus, the *Pequod* is referred to as an archetypal whaleship because it retains all the universal qualities of the successful nineteenth-century American whaleship. The purpose of the voyage is to kill and harvest whales; it is that of a commercial enterprise of killing whales and harvesting barrels of whale oil and spermaceti for the commercial markets of the world. It is also a journey to pursue one man's revenge on one particular, larger than life, notorious whale.

Christopher Sten's book *The Weaver God, He Weaves*, mentioned earlier, provides one of the best breakdowns of the story. He segments it into five sections, as follows:

Chapters	Content
1–23	Staging and preparation for the journey of the Pequod and the hunting of whales.
24–47	Introduction of the purpose and characters of this journey and of the general lore of whaling.
48–76	The process of the pursuit, killing, and rendering of whales as a commercial enterprise.
77–105	The capture of the whale; the journey into the interior of the realm of the whale.
106–35	The confrontation and conflict with Moby Dick; "the trial in the whale's belly." (138)

Sten studies each of these sections in great depth, finding significant mythic parallels. The focus here is a relatively short recap of the story, to orient the reader in the flow of the tale and in the elements of the story that speak to the themes of this analysis.

The opening chapter is devoted entirely to Ishmael's decision to return to the sea, to go on a whaling adventure, from Nantucket Island via New Bedford, Massachusetts. It begins with Ishmael describing his being in a mood of dark melancholy, "a damp, drizzly November in my soul" (18), and elaborating, at some length, on the lure of the sea as a healing medium in the human consciousness. Very little is told of his background or origins, other than that he journeyed to New Bedford from Manhattan. He casts himself as a simple, somewhat ordinary man with a simple outlook on life. In his first night in New Bedford, he meets and immediately befriends a Polynesian harpooneer named Queequeg.

The interaction of Ishmael and Queequeg and their developing relationship consume the better part of twelve chapters. Sten and others draw significant parallels between Melville's opening and the beginnings of many other epics, notably Dante's *Inferno*, Milton's *Paradise Lost*, and T. S. Eliot's "The Wasteland," to include the relationship with Queequeg, who is seen very much akin to a guide like Virgil to Dante in the *Inferno*. Melville casts Queequeg as a superhuman being, of enormous strength, with a simple world view that Ishmael finds refreshing, particularly in contrast to Ishmael's Christian views of life. To the Christian of the time, Queequeg is the pure primitive savage, but he is of noble blood from an island "not on any map" (59). He is possessed of enormous strength and skill, his view of life is simple and straightforward, and his solutions to everyday problems epitomize common sense. He is also an idolater, worshiping a god he calls Yojo, in the form of a small wooden statue, with whom he seems to commune regularly. Despite their differences, Ishmael respects Queequeg's view of life and accepts his ways as equal to his own. He defers to his simple solutions and respects his spiritual sense, his "traces of a simple honest heart" (55). In one of their first interactions, when contemplating their having to share the same bed, Ishmael considers the man, Queequeg, and quips, "Better sleep with a sober cannibal than a drunken Christian" (18).

Together they sign on to the *Pequod*, a whaleship of unusual quality and adornments. Ishmael describes it as follows:

a rare old craft . . . a ship of the old school, rather small if anything; with an old fashioned claw-footed look about her. Long seasoned and weather-stained in the typhoons and calms of all four oceans, her old hull's complexion was darkened like a French grenadier's. . . . Her venerable bows look bearded. Her masts—cut somewhere on the coast of Japan, where her original ones were lost overboard in a gale—her masts stood stiffly up like the spines of the three old kings of Cologne. Her ancient decks were worn and wrinkled, like the pilgrim-worshipped flagstone in Canterbury Cathedral where Becket bled. But to all these . . . were added new and marvelous features pertaining to the wild business that for more than half a century she had followed. . . . Built upon her original grotesqueness, inlaid all over with a quaintness both of material and device. . . . She was a thing of trophies, a cannibal of a craft, tricking herself forth in the chased bones of her enemies (60–70).

In the days leading up to, and the events surrounding, the preparations for sailing, a number of episodes and characters appear in the tale, carrying significant mythic and allegorical power. In one such incident, Ishmael attends New Bedford's Bethel Chapel and encounters its pastor, Father Mapple, who is an ex-whaler turned venerable cleric. The church has numerous plaques and memorials adorning its walls, in remembrance of whalemen lost at sea, mostly in battles with whales. As he prepares to deliver his sermon, Father Mapple ascends a unique pulpit, shaped like a ship's prow with an elaborately adorned rope ladder; upon reaching the perch, he pulls up the ladder, isolating himself in the pulpit. The sermon is on the Book of Jonah and of the perils of rejecting the call of God. There is a significant parallel here to the experience of Ishmael in journeying to Nantucket, heeding the call to go whaling and ending up in the grip of Ahab's journey. Jonah is called to deliver the word of God to the people of Nineveh, but he rejects the call and tries to distance himself from God. He is eventually swallowed by a whale, which becomes the vehicle for his redemption. Ishmael, on the other hand, accepts the call, and, in a different sense, the whale in *Moby-Dick* becomes a source of healing for him as well.

In another incident, a tattered vagabond named Elijah mysteriously questions Ishmael and Queequeg about their knowledge of Ahab and provides them with veiled, sinister warnings about the impending voyage. Asking if they had signed on to serve on the *Pequod*, he adds, "Anything down there about your souls?" (87). His questions about their knowledge of Ahab have a further ominous ring; Elijah is the name of the biblical prophet who denounces Ahab, King of Israel, in I Kings, for his idolatrous leanings (17:1–21:27).

Last, the interaction of Ishmael with the primary owners of the *Pequod*, the former captains, Peleg and Bildad, who are charged with preparing the vessel for the journey, provide a contrasting view of the Quaker ethos so prevalent on Nantucket at the time. Bildad is staunchly rigid in his Puritan view of the world, using all the Quaker idiom in his speech, much as Ahab does. Peleg is entirely worldly in his actions and speech. But both are "fighting Quakers. . . . Quakers with a vengeance" (73). In discussing Bildad, whom he notes to be more rigid in his ways than Peleg, Melville reports that he has been educated "according to the strictest sect of Nantucket Quakerism" (74). Melville reveals his disdain for the duplicity of the American Protestant systems, as carried in men like Bildad, when he, Melville, referring to the Quaker refusal to take up arms in military battle, says of Bildad that, "for all this immutableness, there was some lack of common consistency [that, while] refusing, from conscientious scruples, to bear arms against land invaders . . . yet he had, in his straight bodied coat, spilled tuns and tuns of leviathan gore." As a note to the book explains, "A tun is an enormous barrel containing 252 gallons" (74).

In a similar inconsistency, Bildad tries to cheat Ishmael out of a rightful share of the results of the voyage, by proposing a pitifully small share, or "lay." In response, Peleg chastises Bildad mercilessly. As with

Father Mapple and Isaiah, Ishmael's experiences with these individuals are rich in mythological idiom, echoing the themes of the nineteenth-century American economic society that is the focus here; they also enhance the dark and sinister character of the unfolding story.

The chapters following the initial sailing, primarily the second section in Sten's breakdown, are devoted to the study of whales and whaling, to the introduction of the main personages and their roles in the hierarchy of the vessel's crew, to the particulars of daily life aboard a whaling ship, and to a myriad of stories about the characters and the ship. Of particular note are chapters 36, 41, and 42, which are key in the staging of the story line of the tale.

In chapter 36, "The Quarterdeck," Ahab reveals to the crew, including all the officers, the precise nature of the voyage: that it is a hunt not for whales in general but for one particular, notorious whale. Despite the nefarious nature of such a focus, Ahab's stature as a whaling captain and his passion for this quest engages everyone and enlists their support. Starbuck, the first mate, the most realistic and moralistic of the ship's company, objects. But the force of Ahab's presence prevails, and Starbuck acquiesces to his demands. Ahab then has everyone take a vow: "Death to Moby Dick! God hunt us all if we do not hunt Moby Dick to his death!" (142).

Chapter 41, "Moby Dick," provides the history of the whale, Moby Dick, of Ahab's encounter with him, and of the travails of Ahab in the aftermath of having had his leg severed. The intensity of Ahab's feelings toward the White Whale and of his obsession to exact revenge as expressed by Melville is particularly striking and is a focus of a discussion of Ahab later in this chapter.

Chapter 42, "The Whiteness of the Whale," describes the particular qualities of the color of the whale, especially as seen by Ishmael. This is significant as an indication of the duplicitous nature of evil in the mind of Melville, and of Ishmael's doubts about the true nature of the White Whale and of the likely outcome of Ahab's quest. Later in this chapter, a discussion of the character of Ishmael returns to this point.

The elements of the novel dealing with the whale as a species and with the business of whaling, both within and before the American experience, are of a depth and level of detail that seems almost out of place for a novel of this genre. At least twenty-five chapters, almost 20 percent of the novel, are devoted, in whole or in significant part, to elements about whales and whaling, the facts of which, on the surface, would appear to have only limited applicability to the evolving story. At the beginning of the novel, between the table of contents and chapter 1, Melville lists a number of quotes and references about whales and whaling under the general heading of Extracts (pages 8–17 in the Norton edition). These are, generally, the sources for his various treatments. It would appear that Melville, for whatever reason, was trying to provide as complete an analysis of the subjects as he could, intending a summary of all the known scientific, natural, and economic facts about whales and whaling, sourcing all the major texts of the time.

The extent of Melville's focus on whales is such that Howard Vincent, one of the early Melville scholars of the twentieth century, in his definitive analysis of the tale, *The Trying Out of "Moby-Dick,"* labels a vast portion of the middle of the tale, chapters 32 to 105, as "The Ceteological Center." This comprises the second, third, and fourth sections of Sten's breakdown. Vincent says, "The ceteological center of *Moby-Dick* is the keel to Melville's artistic craft" (121).

Speculation might lead one to conclude that, from his experience with whales, Melville believes that the general knowledge about whales in the world consciousness was so limited, and the animal and its life and environs so majestic, that a detailed schooling on the subject was necessary. In this work's chapter 2, a summary of the current knowledge about whales and whaling is provided. Much of that is the result of study done after Melville's time, and it significantly advances the knowledge of the whale as a species. All of this enhances the knowledge of whales as presented by Melville and leads to the conclusion that this creature is even more wondrous than the impression Melville was trying to convey.

However, the question remains as to why Melville seemed so intent on such an exhaustive treatment. Vincent concludes that it is all critical to what Melville was attempting:

In a strange and remarkable way, our quickly and easily acquired information about harpoons and lances, whaleboats and lines, blubber and bones, the pursuit of the whale and the flight from the whale, informs us so thoroughly and profoundly concerning whaling life that we identify ourselves with the *Pequod* crew as they abandon themselves to the delirious pursuit of the albino whale so soon to destroy them. (125–26)

It would also seem that, in his lengthy descriptions of the majesty of the whale and in the differentiation he ascribes to Moby Dick as a particularly powerful whale, Melville has assured an epic stature to the story. It also becomes clear that this treatment is one of the key reasons why *Moby-Dick* has achieved the stature it has within the literary history of America and the world. No other animal or any other human activity of the time could have conveyed such power.

The third section of Sten's breakdown, chapters 48 through 76, ranges over a myriad of subjects related to the hunting of whales, their capture and the process of rendering, and the interaction of the *Pequod* with a number of other whaling vessels in chance encounters on the open sea. The first chapter of this section, chapter 48, "The First Lowering," shows the high risks of whaling, as the skiffs in pursuit of the whale are caught in a storm and barely survive. This is particularly grueling for Ishmael, who was tossed into the sea with his boat's crew and who was the last to return to the *Pequod*. The epic nature of the story is echoed in Ishmael's description of the adrenaline rush of the confrontation with the mighty sperm whale, in the unmediated confrontation with such a majestic beast as well as in the high-risk business of whaling as a human activity.

At this point, moreover, five strangers appear from below, a special crew for a whaleboat to be captained by Ahab, apparently having been smuggled aboard prior to sailing. These are the "five dusky phantoms" (180), headed by an Indian Parsee named Fedallah, one of the incidents that Elijah forewarned. It is a secret crew clearly brought on board by Ahab as a special force to be used in his vengeful hunt for Moby Dick. Melville's wording here, the "dusky phantoms," who were hidden below deck to be brought forth for the hunt, appears a fascinating metaphor for the shadows inherent in the nineteenth-century American experience as developed in chapter 2.

These five men are quite mysterious and sinister in appearance; although they are seemingly dark complexioned, no mention is made of their origins and—with the exception of Fedallah—they are not given names. Some of the crew see Fedallah, whose history with, or connection to Ahab is never mentioned, to be the devil incarnate. Ishmael refers to him as "a creature that civilized, domestic people in the temperate zone only see in their dreams" (191). The implication to be drawn is that Ahab's quest is being cast by Melville as a mythical pact with the devil, with certain native people in the role as the devil's agents.

The encounters with other whaleships, called *gams*, each contain a story line seemingly separate and independent from the *Pequod*. However, in varying degrees they enrich the central story, particularly as it relates to Moby Dick. The particularly long story of the *Town-Ho* is most instructive here. The *Town-Ho* was a homeward bound Nantucket whaler that had had an encounter with Moby Dick on a previous voyage. The *Town-Ho* story concerns a conflict between a particularly wicked and cruel mate who insidiously provokes one of the crew into striking him, a situation that escalates into near-mutiny and is resolved only by the mate's unrelated death at the hands of Moby Dick. It is told by one of the *Pequod*'s crew, who had heard it secretly from a *Town-Ho* seaman during the gam. The story was said to have been generally unknown to the *Town-Ho*'s officers and other men.

Interestingly, the story is related in *Moby-Dick* by Ishmael, as he purports to have told it in a bar in Lima, Peru, some two years hence.

The significance of the *Town-Ho* story is a bit curious, especially as to its length and detail; some scholars believe that in the conflict of the wicked mate and the seaman, there is evidence of an original story line for the book, *Moby-Dick*, before Melville's interaction with Hawthorne resulted in its rewriting. Edgar Dryden, in *Melville's Thematics of Form*, notes this possibility and reports, additionally, that the twist of Ishmael's telling of this story at some time in the future fulfills his destined role at the end of *Moby-Dick* to be the lone survivor returning to tell the tale (111–12). In the particularly cruel treatment of a seaman by one of the mates in the *Town-Ho's* story there is significant resonance with the story of *Billy Budd*, written by Melville from 1889 to 1891, in the last years of his life. It seems to be indicative of Melville's obsession with the nature of evil in the human experience, a theme he is working to develop at a much more intricate level in *Moby-Dick*.

Chapter 61 presents the novel's most vivid portrayal of the actual hunt, capture, and death of a whale. In vivid imagery, the mythic power of the interaction of whale and whaler, and the actual process of killing explode into consciousness for the first time in the story. As the whale in this particular hunt tires of the chase and the whaleboat is finally brought even with the animal, the mate, Stubb, darts his lance into the whale repeatedly, trying to find and pierce its heart. When he finally does, "gush after gush of clotted red gore, as if it had been the purple lees [sediment] of red wine, shot into the frighted air; and falling back again, ran dripping down his motionless flanks into the sea. His heart had burst" (233). The vivid imagery here, of the underlying nature of whaling as a human activity in the emerging industrialization of the time and of its impact on the natural world, conveys a sense of horror and outrage that seems not too far under the surface for the young Ishmael.

Chapters 77 through 105 constitute the fourth section of Sten's schematic. The coverage deepens, exploring the interior of the whale and of the process of whaling. Melville's descriptions of whales and whale parts are more elaborate here than in the earlier sections and he presents detail concerning the ingenious processes developed by the American whalemen to render the sperm whale. A gam with the whaleship *Samuel Enterby*, out of London, provides a report of a ship whose officers and men have had extended encounters with Moby Dick, including a disastrous skirmish in a battle the previous year, wherein the English captain lost his arm, in much the same manner that Ahab had lost his leg. The captain, who has avoided pursuing Moby Dick in recent sightings, is shocked to see Ahab's passion to hunt Moby Dick. His ship's surgeon says, "Bless my soul, and curse the foul fiend's . . . this man's blood—bring the thermometer—it's at the boiling point!" (340). From this point, each successive gam provides more reports of Moby Dick's capacity to exact devastation on whalers who deign to pursue him. With each such encounter, with each successive gam, the likelihood of a catastrophic outcome for the *Pequod* is clarified, as the stories of the White Whale's strength, cunning, and viciousness become more pronounced.

In chapter 96, "The Try-Works," Melville describes the structure and use of the furnace placed amidships on the *Pequod*'s deck with its immense pots poised over the fire chamber. Called tryworks, this apparatus is used to heat the blubber and reduce it to oil. The furnace, fueled with crisp remnants of whaleskin from which blubber has been removed, burns very hot and creates a particularly acrid smoke and odor. In the story, as the process of rendering the blubber continued into the night, the redness of the fire, the foul blackness of the smoke, and the rolling of the ship on the waves in the darkness created a striking eeriness. Ishmael sums up the scene, saying, "the rushing *Pequod*, freighted with savages, and laden with fire, and burning a corpse, and plunging into the blackness of darkness, seemed the material counterpart of her monomaniac commander's soul" (327). In the presentation of scenes like this, the drama and intensity of Ahab's and the *Pequod*'s rush to judgment builds dramatically.

The concluding chapters, chapters 106 through 135, the fifth group in Sten's blueprint, encompass the build-up to and the intense drama of the conflict with Moby Dick. A series of incidents put the escalating narrative into focus. Ahab's whalebone leg cracks, so he has the carpenter fashion a new leg for him out of recently harvested whalebone; there is much attendant discussion about this process and about the efficacy of a leg made from a whale as part of the pursuit of the whale who took the original leg.

Ahab and Starbuck have a number of conversations about the substance of the journey in this section. Starbuck has been the voice of reason, a ship's officer driven by a certain deference to a code of whaling, to the business of whaling as a business, and to the natural order of that world. Increasingly he pleads with Ahab to relent from his murderous quest. At one point, Starbuck considers killing Ahab to save them all from a disastrous end; but he is compelled to desist out of a sense of duty and a deep affection for the man who is his captain, one who has served in his profession with distinction for so many decades.

In chapter 119, "The Candles," the *Pequod* is caught in a terrifying electrical storm in which the masts are lit up with electrical impulses. In front of the terrified crew, Ahab seems to defy the elements and quench the flames with his hands. The electrical storm disables the compass, and Ahab fashions a new one out of a few simple elements. In a number of successive speeches, some delivered as soliloquies, Ahab becomes more and more intense in his rhetoric. His comments become more and more blasphemous, evincing a deep-seated belief on his part that he has the power to defy God and nature.

All these experiences and the growing proximity of Moby Dick, as other whaleships report engagements, increasingly forebode the likelihood that the *Pequod* and all of its crew will meet a catastrophic end. As the *Pequod* makes its way into the preferred hunting ground of Moby Dick, Ahab and Starbuck have a particularly tender exchange in which Ahab seems suddenly hesitant, questioning the logic and efficacy of the hunt. He laments:

> What is it, what nameless, inscrutable, unearthly thing is it; what cozzening, hidden lord and master, and cruel, re-morseless emperor commands me; that against all natural lovings and longings, I so keep pushing, and crowding, and jamming myself on all the time; recklessly making me ready to do what in my own proper, natural heart, I durst not so much as dare? Is Ahab, Ahab? (406)

Throughout this exchange, Starbuck is pleading with him to cease in his fantasy, to turn the ship around and return to Nantucket. But, in the end, Ahab is too resolute; he reaffirms his commitment and rejects Starbuck's pleadings.

The last three chapters are of the hunt itself, with increasingly fierce and disastrous skirmishes with the White Whale. Each day Ahab's boat is smashed and men are killed, until, on the last day, Moby Dick's onslaughts result in Ahab's death, in the *Pequod* being rammed by the whale, and a vortex being created that sucks the ship and all its crew and paraphernalia into the sea.

The closing line of the last chapter, before the epilogue revealing Ishmael's survival, is "and the great shroud of the sea rolled on as it rolled five thousand years ago" (427). This seems a logical conclusion, the sea swallowing the great drama that was Ahab's and the *Pequod*'s quest. Five thousand years seems biblical in its orientation, a reference to the history of the world as believed in the religious systems so prevalent in Melville's day. A footnote in the Norton edition confirms this by noting that five thousand years is the biblical period from Noah's flood to the present day.

The epilogue begins with a quote from Job, "And I only am escaped alone to tell thee" and it ends with Ishmael reporting that the whaleship *Rachel*, the last ship with which the *Pequod* had gammed and which had been searching for missing seaman from an earlier skirmish with Moby Dick, has found and rescued him. He is floating on a sealed box that had been Queequeg's coffin; Queequeg had had it made by the ship's carpenter some months before when he was concerned about his own life. In the tale's final line, Ishmael reports that the Rachel, "in searching after her missing children, had only found another orphan" (427).

With Ishmael as the only survivor from the journey of the *Pequod*, the tale seems to end in classic Campbellian fashion, much as it began with Ishmael heeding the call. Ishmael's return can be seen as the natural outcome of the myth of the hero's journey, where Ishmael, the outcast, returns to tell the tale.

THE *PEQUOD* AS AN ECONOMIC ENTERPRISE

The *Pequod*, under sail and at sea from Nantucket, is as complete an organization of men and tasks as could be found in the nineteenth-century American sociological or economic experience. In structure, staffing, organization, and economic mission, it carries many parallels to the American economic society of Melville's time and to the archetypal commercial organization of the twentieth century as well. As an organization of men focused on a task that becomes increasingly more sinister and life threatening as the weeks and months roll on, the *Pequod* and its journey have also been likened to the American nation in the 1850s as it plunged toward the near catastrophic conflict of the Civil War (Delbanco, 158). For these reasons, it is useful to look at the basic structure and elements of the vessel as an enterprise.

First, the choice of the name *Pequod* deserves some attention. It is a misspelling of the name of a branch of the Mohecan Indian nation called the Pequot, a nation that had historical significance in the early American experience. As the early English settlers were expanding their footprint inland from the New England coast during the first half of the seventeenth century and the Dutch were doing the same northward from New York, significant conflicts developed with the Native American tribes which had occupied these lands in significant numbers for centuries. Many of these tribes had been in conflict with each other as well, fighting for control of the lush river valleys of what is now Connecticut, Massachusetts, and New York.

The Pequot nation, which occupied parts of central and western Connecticut and Massachusetts, were the most aggressive and resistant of these tribes. In 1636 and early 1637, a number of small skirmishes blamed on the Pequots resulted in the deaths of a few settlers and traders; these initiated what has been called the Pequot war. In May 1637, a militia of men from the Massachusetts Bay Colony, together with a contingent of members of the Niantic and Narragansett tribes, attacked a major Pequot village near the site of modern-day Mystic. By various estimates, up to seven hundred Pequot were killed, many of whom were women and children. Most were killed when the settlers set fire to the village from three sides. Only seven individuals were reported to have survived.

Alfred A. Cave, in *The Pequot War*, wrote that the final stages of the attack on the Pequot compound constituted the beginning of a well-orchestrated effort by the commander of the militia, Captain John Mason, to eradicate the Pequots as a nation, saying that, in Mason's view, "the incineration of the Pequots was an act mandated by God to punish savages guilty of arrogance and of treachery against God's Chosen" (151). Cave sees this as an act of genocide and one of the earliest examples thereof perpetrated by the Europeans against the Native American. It was this war, according to Cave, that defined the relationship of the American psyche with the Native American for the next two hundred years. As Cave wrote, "The images of brutal and untrustworthy savages plotting the extermination of those who would do the work of God in the wilderness, developed to explain and justify the killing of Pequots, became a vital part of the mythology of the American frontier" (168).

Melville knew the general story of the Pequot from having read Benjamin Trumbull's *A Complete History of Connecticut,* published in 1797 and revised in 1818. In the story, Melville refers only to the ship's name as "the name of a celebrated tribe of Massachusetts Indians, now extinct as the ancient Medes" (69, footnote 4). But what he has done in the choice of this name is to create a powerful link to the emerging political realities of the American economic and political scene of the nineteenth century, when the exploitation of the Native American became a vital element in the growth of the economic nation.

The hierarchy of the men of the *Pequod* is also a direct parallel to that of the economic enterprises of the growing Industrial Revolution. At the lowest ranks of the ship are men of every race and nationality. In chapter 40, Melville creates a scene in which the seamen of the *Pequod* engage in a lively exchange of simple worldviews. He lists sailors from Nantucket, Martha's Vineyard, and other parts of the American colonial world as well as men from Africa, China, Denmark, England, France, Iceland, India, Italy, Portugal, Scotland, and the islands of the Azores, Cape Verde, Malta, Tahiti, and Polynesia. It is a ship of men, only men, but men from all the corners of the globe; and this organization of men is ruled only by New Englanders, four white men, of Anglo-Saxon Protestant stock.

At the head of this organization is the supreme ruler, Ahab, a captain of extensive experience, forty years as a whaler. In his own words, he is the god of the *Pequod.* In chapter 109, when Starbuck questions his decision to ignore the accumulation of loose oil in the hold, indicating that some of the sperm oil casks may be leaking, Ahab rejects him and says, "There is one God that is Lord over the earth and one Captain that is lord over the *Pequod*" (362). But Ahab is also extremely competent, as warranted by Peleg in chapter 16, to lead and manage a ship of men in the business of hunting and rendering whales. Per Captain Peleg, "Ahab's above the common" (78). In his years as a whaling captain, he has demonstrated his superior skill in hunting whales; his experience has also led him to amass unusually detailed maps, charts, and data on the movement of whales through the oceans of the world (167–69). It is this information that he uses to find Moby Dick.

As described in the story, Ahab is tough, seemingly fair, and a leader who suffers no fools. In the whole of the story, Ahab portrays the intelligence, demeanor, and visage of authority, the command presence of the archetypal captain of a whaleship. In the mythology of captains and rulers, and of business managers in our industrial world, he is also the archetypal organizational leader, despite the manner in which he distorts some of his obligations and the responsibilities of command. Upon first seeing him on the quarterdeck, Ishmael describes him as standing "erect, looking straight out beyond the ship's ever pitching prow. There was an infinity of firmest fortitude, a determinate, unsurrenderable willfulness, in the fixed and fearless, forward dedication of that glance" (109).

The officers under Ahab were arranged in order of command, with Starbuck, Stubb, and Flask, as the first, second, and third mates, respectively. Each of these has respective duties and each is the commander of a boat crew in the actual whale hunts. Starbuck is a Nantucketer, a Quaker, fit, trim, described as "long, earnest . . . prepared to endure for long ages to come . . . uncommonly conscientious . . . and endured with a deep natural reverence" (102). He is steadfast, practical, and as courageous as is necessary to execute the duties of first mate with resolute precision.

Stubb and Flask are lesser men, but of no small stature in the scheme of things on a whaling mission. Stubb is from Cape Cod, a Cape Cod man in the vernacular of the industry. He is "calm and collected, . . . good humored, easy and careless" (104). He approaches the task of whale hunting with a relaxed, perhaps too nonchalant attitude. Flask is from Martha's Vineyard; he is described as a "short, stout, ruddy young fellow, very pugnacious concerning whales, who somehow seemed to think that the great Leviathans had personally and hereditarily affronted him; and therefore it was a sort of point of honor with him, to destroy them whenever encountered" (105). His attitude toward whales also gave him an "ignorant, unconscious fearlessness" (105).

Each of the whaleboats commanded by these three has a specific harpooneer and a total crew of seven—the mate, the harpooneer, and five oarsmen. The mate uses an oar as the rudder at the stern, and the harpooneer and the crew man the oars. The skill of the harpooneer is critical, for, at the command of the mate, as the boat approaches a whale with the oarsmen pulling with all their strength, the harpooneer must drop his oar, seize his harpoon, stand and turn in the boat, and hurl the harpoon into the whale.

Queequeg is assigned to Starbuck's crew and Ishmael is one of the five oarsmen in that crew. The harpooneer for Stubb's boat is Tashtego, a Native American from the western end of Martha's Vineyard, a tip of land called Gay Head. At the time there were a few remaining members of this Native American group; they were all called Gay Headers. Melville recounts that they were once celebrated trackers and describes Tashtego as "an inheritor of the unvitiated blood of those proud warrior hunters" (106). The harpooneer for Flask's boat is Daggoo, a six-foot, five-inch tall African, "a gigantic, coal-black negro savage, with a lion-like tread" (106).

All the harpooneers, then, are men of color, natives from the corners of the earth where the white Europeans have been planting their colonial flags for three hundred years, up to the time of Melville's writing his epic. To each of these three, Melville attributes unusual human strength and skill and simple, strikingly pure views of life.

Beyond the mates, harpooneers, and oarsmen of the whaleboats, there are also men who are never engaged in the boats; these are the shipkeepers, some of a particular skill, like a carpenter and blacksmith, others in more menial roles such as cooks and stewards. On the *Pequod*, two of these, Doughboy and Pip, are black, performing roles not unlike what they might have been doing ashore in the America of the time.

When Melville discusses the make-up of the officers and crew of the *Pequod*, he speaks of the diversity of the crew, saying that "as with the American army and military and merchant navies, and the engineering forces employed in the construction of the American Canals and Railroads . . . the native American [the colonial] liberally provides the brains, the rest of the world generously supplies the muscles" (107).

The primary activity, therefore, the pursuit and the killing of whales, is undertaken by a unit of seven men, in whaleboats of 30 feet in length and a beam of 6 feet in width, chasing whales of 60 to 80 feet, weighing 60 to 80 tons, cruising at 10 to 12 knots. As a commercial business of the mid-nineteenth century, the epic nature of this activity is striking. The business of dragging the dead whales to the ship, of removing the parts of the animal to be processed into the various products, and of rendering those parts into such products, was an activity that is directly parallel to the factories of the industrial centers of Europe and America. In the context of some of the primary mythic systems operating in the nineteenth century, as outlined in chapter 2, these processes and activities were at the core of the growing industrialization.

The emerging American economic system, the economic heart of America, afloat or ashore, was thriving. Much of this was thanks to exploitation of the native peoples, of the poorer immigrant communities that had been drawn to America's cities, and of the land and natural systems from which the resources needed for the manufacturing processes had been drawn. On the lower east side of Manhattan, there were factories staffed mainly by immigrants working on processes and in conditions very similar to those of the whaleship when rendering the body parts of whales. Staffed by immigrants and minorities and managed by white, Anglo-Saxon Protestants, they exploited the human system in much the same way, and with much the same effect on the environment, as the whaleship. The building of the railroads, dams, and canals to expand the capacities of the broader economic system used the same labor bases and had similar impacts on the environment as the whaling industry. The exploitation of the animal populations in the West (deer, elk, beaver, and buffalo) was pursued with much the same focus and waste. Whaling might have seemed more glorious, more epic in its stature, but it was all part of the same economic, societal system.

The *Pequod*, then, was, first and foremost, a business enterprise, owned and managed for profit, with limited liability to its owners and potentially disastrous risks, physical and economic, to its workers. It was spectacularly simple and most efficient in its design; it had only one focus: to produce certain products at a profit. Those products, however, had a limited, almost inconsequential value in and of themselves. They were simple everyday substances and materials, to wit: lamp oil, clean-burning candles, lubricants, and a host of small tools and products, much the same as the products of other commercial enterprises of the time. This vessel, commanded by Ahab as CEO and run by Starbuck, Stubb, and Flask as his VPs, was the archetype of the corporate enterprise of America, both of the nineteenth century and of today. We might as well label this enterprise The Pequod Incorporated.

The view of the *Pequod* as a commercial enterprise, though perhaps not in the same context as the corporate enterprises of today, was clearly in Melville's mind as he wrote *Moby-Dick*. It is clear that he meant to characterize it in that fashion from beginning to end, and that, in his construction of the final outcome of the voyage, he was alluding to some potentially ignominious end for the rush of industrialism of his time. A wonderfully illustrative quote to this effect occurs in the final moments of the *Pequod*, before Ahab is snatched from his whaleboat by Moby Dick for the final time. As Ahab watches the ship begin to founder from the whale's ramming, he cries, "The ship! The hearse! . . . its wood could only be American!" (426).

THE KEY PLAYERS

From the perspective of the mythic systems of the nineteenth-century American experience, the story of *Moby-Dick* is a story of three characters: Moby Dick, Ahab, and Ishmael. In this context, Melville's almost tiresome coverage of the whale as a species, and of the business of whaling, seems, as Howard Vincent points out, to have significant epic meaning. Melville's extensive description of the various aspects of the sperm whale, based on the knowledge of that animal that he developed from all the available sources of the time, creates a view of a glorious animal, a truly biblical Leviathan. It is also clear from more recent studies of the whale that the power, magnitude, and advanced state of evolution of the sperm whale are even more pronounced than the view communicated by Melville. In addition, with regard to the manner in which the story of Moby Dick unfolds, Ahab and Ishmael are the key protagonists.

Moby Dick, The Whale

Who or what was Moby Dick? What is the core or the significance of this entity as an element in Melville's story? Is it a primal existential force, a symbolic element of a larger presence or force? Alternatively, is it a character, an active player in the drama of Ahab, Ishmael, and the supporting characters of the *Pequod*? Or is it, in some different ways, both of these?

As outlined in chapter 2, Melville was familiar with the idea of a sperm whale ramming and sinking a ship from his having heard about and read the story of a rogue whale striking the whaleship *Essex* in 1820. Although the outcome of that story is similar to Melville's conclusion in *Moby-Dick*, there are also significant differences. We also know that Melville was aware of a particular rogue whale named Mocha Dick who was known to frequent waters in the vicinity of Mocha Island, off the coast of Southern Chile. According to Vincent, this is where the *Essex* was sunk. Mocha Dick and a few other rogue whales were known to attack whaleboats and ships with much less provocation than in the central story here.

While in the process of capturing other whales, the *Essex* was rammed by a large sperm whale that appeared out of nowhere and attacked the ship, seemingly without provocation, according to the account of its first mate, Owen Chase, in his book *Shipwreck of the Whaleship* Essex. In Melville's story, however, Moby Dick's destruction of the whaleboats was merely his retaliation to being attacked repeatedly, and ultimately being wounded. Moby Dick attacked the *Pequod*, only on the third day of assaults from Ahab and the *Pequod's* crew. Melville's various references to a certain maliciousness in Moby Dick are never separated in any meaningful way from the idea of the whale's destructive attacks being some form of immediate retaliation against assaults on him.

It also seems that, on the basis of his extensive treatment of the various species of whales and their characteristics, Melville has a view of the whale as a species, and of Moby Dick itself, a view that is quite reverential, despite the references to malign intents. The contrasting elements of Melville's treatment, his lengthy and inspired descriptions of the various species of whales, his various references to Moby Dick in terms that can only be characterized as exaltations, and then his describing the whale's cunning and ferocity as malicious, seem key elements in the underlying ethos of this story. This sense of malicious intent is a core of many conflicts in the story, particularly an emerging one between Ahab and Ishmael, as is seen later in this chapter.

In Melville's chapter 133, "The Chase—First Day," when Moby Dick is first spotted and the whaleboats pull alongside the serenely swimming whale, Ishmael is inspired by the majesty, the quiet power of the beast:

A gentle joyousness—a mighty mildness of repose in swiftness, invested the gliding whale. Not the white bull Jupiter swimming away with ravished Europa clinging to his graceful horns; his lovely, leering eyes sideways intent upon the maid; with smooth bewitching fleetness, rippling straight for the nuptial bower in Crete; not Jove, not that great majesty Supreme! did surpass the glorified White Whale as he so divinely swam. (409)

On the other hand, the descriptions of Moby Dick in which Melville uses the word *malicious* and its synonyms seem from a different perspective entirely. This perspective comes into play when he is describing the whale itself, its behavior, and its actions in fending off and retaliating against the attacks of whaleboats, ships, and men. To describe these tactics and actions of the whale, actions meant only to repulse attempts to inflict mortal wounds, as malicious, malignant, devilish, and evil, seems very much akin to the European, and, ultimately, the American settlers' attitudes toward the Native Americans. This can be seen from Professor Cave's study, reviewed earlier, wherein he describes the emerging views of the Native Americans after the Pequot war. In other words, the dichotomy of Melville's treatment of whales and his descriptions of Moby Dick's behavior as malicious seem to be another representation by Melville, albeit a bit subtle, of the perversity of some of the mythos of the time.

Studying the relationship of whale to man over the centuries prior to the advent of wide-scale commercial whaling in the seventeenth and eighteenth centuries, the various species of whale seem to have allowed themselves to be hunted, to resist but without fully using their incredible strength, such that the process of the hunt was generally a success for the native hunters. These facts seem to represent a functioning of the ecosystem much akin to the interaction of the buffalo and Native American tribes on the Great Plains of America before the mid-nineteenth century. But in the case of the whale, in the later stages of the history of commercial whaling in the nineteenth century, there were the experiences of rogue whales attacking whaling craft with incredible ferocity, specifically as related by Melville and others. It was almost as if this was a reaction to the expansion of whaling to levels that went well beyond the efficient and natural functioning of an ecosystem. Whales were now being hunted by the tens of thousands, merely for the harvest of only parts of their body, oil, and bone, much as the American buffalo were hunted by the white settlers largely for their hides. Consider Melville's description, in chapter 69, of the skinned and beheaded hulk of a whale floating away from the ship, after the commercially valuable parts have been harvested: "Beneath the unclouded and mild azure sky, upon the fair face of the pleasant sea, wafted by the joyous breezes, that great mass of death floats on and on, till lost in infinite perspectives" (247). The similarities of this scene and that of skinned buffalo hulks rotting on the plains are striking. Bringing it into more modern times, we may also draw parallels between these scenes and the scenes of mountains of discarded boxes, wrapping paper, and trash on our streets after major holidays.

Naturalist Gay Bradshaw has spent a significant part of her life among the elephants of Africa. In a number of articles, she reports the appearance of rogue elephants in Africa and India, elephants who have begun to terrorize villages and hunters without specific provocation. In an article in the October 6, 2006, edition of the *New York Times Magazine*, Charles Seibert, citing the work of Bradshaw and others, writes of "today's elephant populations . . . suffering from a form of chronic stress, a kind of species-wide trauma" seemingly in reaction to the exploitation of the species and the encroachment on their natural habitat. Are the rogue whales of which Melville and others report a manifestation of a similar sort of behavior, perhaps a collective resistance to the acceleration of commercial whaling? Might the malign intents and behavior ascribed to Moby Dick, however antithetical they may be to the glorious qualities Melville also describes, be a manifestation of such a trauma?

The realm of the whale, the deep, mysterious, unfathomable ocean which even today eludes our ability to understand fully, adds a significant level of mystery and complexity to the story. The whale

exists only in the sea, in a world so vast as to harbor the ultimate unknown. It is also a realm to which all living things, fish or fowl, beast
or man, seem to be eternally attracted, to seek connection and to find
refuge. The tale of *Moby-Dick* begins with Ishmael going to sea to cure
a seemingly deep malaise in his soul. In that same breath, Melville also
describes the people of lower Manhattan, who have very little history
or connection with the sea, other than as the medium over which they
came to America, congregating at the shoreline on holidays and staring out to sea for hours, perhaps to gain some respite from the anxieties of their daily lives in the mills of industrial New York. The sea, the
province of the whale, is the ultimate underworld, the realm in which
whale is both demon and vessel. The story of Jonah is instructive here;
it casts the sea and the whale as the ultimate alembic chamber in which
redemption and change can be wrought.

It seems that, in all his references and descriptions of the whale
and its environs, Melville is casting Moby Dick as some sort of god,
as a transcendent deific reality for which he, Melville, seems to have
spent most of his life in a desperate search. In mythic terms, the whale
could also be likened to Gaia, the mother goddess of the earth, or to
the *anima mundi*, the soul of the world. Through all the elaborate discussions of whales and whaling, of the sperm whale as the epitome of
the species, and of Moby Dick as the archetypal sperm whale, Melville
has molded a character of stunning numinosity, a mesmerizing entity
that is meant to hold significant power between two archetypal poles
of humanity, Ahab and Ishmael. It is in this context that Moby Dick,
as a character in the tale, holds so much attraction. It also becomes
clear why no animal other than the whale, and no species of whale
other than an albino sperm whale, could hold such a true sense of
epic power; and why no other being could carry the energy to effect
Melville's search for god and meaning.

Noted Jungian author Edward Edinger wrote a rather intense
depth psychological analysis of this story in his *Melville's "Moby-Dick":
An American Nekyia*. This book provides much groundwork for the

analysis here of the interrelationship of the whale, Ahab, and Ishmael. As an answer to the question, "What is the whale?" Edinger postulates that "the whale has too many meanings. Melville has gone to great trouble to provide an almost boundless network of associations to amplify the image of the whale. [It] becomes a Cretan labyrinth wherein one is almost sure to become lost" (75). Although the species of whale, virtually all species, had been hunted for centuries, there was something special about a white whale, according to Edinger, something that precluded its capture. Moby Dick was a white whale; it was also rumored to be seen in multiple places at the same time, a superstition to which Melville seems to acknowledge some foundation. Edinger labels Moby Dick "the collective whale soul, the essential, eternal whale [whose] sacred, special character . . . is indicated by his whiteness" (77–78). He likens it to the sacred white buffalo or white dog of certain Native American tribes or the white elephant of certain Eastern societies. Chapter 42 of the tale delves into the meaning of the whiteness of the whale in great depth; this will be discussed later in this chapter.

In the chapters encompassing the actual engagement with the White Whale, the incredible strength and cunning exhibited by Moby Dick lead to various references to it being holy and sacred, possessed of supernatural powers. Edinger also sees whales as the primitive, undifferentiated energies of nature, much as a raw undifferentiated natural life energy exists in all of us; he sees this also as a symbol of the objective self and "the transcendental reality behind the appearance of things" (79). In the references in *Moby-Dick* to Leviathan, especially in the references to Leviathan in the book of Job, Edinger portrays the White Whale as one of the manifestations of Yahweh, much as in the tale, Melville references Moby Dick as one of the incarnations of Vishnu (286).

Finally, Edinger asserts that the multitudinous references and implications of Moby Dick as sacred allow us to

> glimpse one of the fundamental meanings of Ahab's vengeful quest. It symbolizes the psychic dynamism which is

responsible for the radical secularization of the modern industrial world. The very notion of the sacred, the numinous, the superpersonal as a concept or category of experience is being extirpated from modern consciousness. (78)

From all of this we can conclude that the ultimate power of Moby Dick in this story is that of overarching numinous deity, a tangible expression of the majesty of both god and earth, and perhaps, some sort of collective goodness in the human soul. The references to Moby Dick as possessed of malign intents may be indicative of some of the shadows inherent in the American nation of the mid-nineteenth century, but they do not detract from Melville's clear sense of reverence. From the point of view of our focus here, this characterization, the idea of Moby Dick as deity, however defined, provides a spectacular counterpoint, a wondrous reference point to understanding the other two main characters of the novel, Ahab and Ishmael.

Ahab, the Captain

The significance of Ahab as archetypal whaling captain has already been mentioned. His name, as in other names in this tale, carries significant biblical meaning. Ahab was a king of Israel, ruling about a century after Solomon. He married Jezebel of Tyre, who convinced him to build a temple to the Tyrian god, Ba'al. Isaiah, the prophet, condemned him for this and predicted his death in a singularly ignominious fashion, along with the advent of serious decline and destruction in his kingdom. There is significant connection between the biblical Ahab and Elijah and the prognostications of the wretch named Elijah, whom Ishmael and Queequeg meet on the pier in the days before the initial sailing of the *Pequod*.

Melville describes Ahab's presence as a leader and whaling captain in both glorious as well as foreboding terms. He appears primarily as intelligent, alert, highly skilled and knowledgeable, and in absolute command at all times. In Ahab's first appearance on deck, the first time he is observed by Ishmael and the men of the *Pequod*, the energy the man projects, the sensation experienced by Ishmael, is both electric and terrifying. Ishmael says, "as I leveled my glance towards the taffrail, foreboding shivers ran over me. Reality outran apprehension; Captain Ahab stood upon his quarter-deck" (108).

The experience of Ahab as he revealed the real mission of this particular journey of the *Pequod* to the crew, in chapter 36, demonstrates the power of the man in commanding the crew's loyalty and commitment—even to a nefarious plan. Here, beyond the objective authority of command, Ahab exhibits a capacity to mesmerize, especially when he is challenged by Starbuck, correctly, on his intent to depart so wickedly from the normal goals of a whaling voyage. Ahab can command absolute obedience, even when enlisting men in a crime.

Chapter 41 describes the circumstances of Ahab's whaling career and the earlier encounter with Moby Dick, the episode in which he lost his leg. In perhaps one of the most powerful statements of a literary character being possessed, almost overcome with rage over a seeming injustice, Melville describes Ahab's temperament, his white hot rage at Moby Dick:

> The White Whale swam before him as the monomaniac incarnation of all those malicious agencies which some deep men feel eating in them, till they are left living on with half a heart and half a lung. That intangible malignity which has been from the beginning; to whose dominion even the modern Christians ascribe one-half of the worlds; which the ancient Ophites of the east reverenced in their statue devil;—Ahab did not fall down and worship it like them; but deliriously transferring its idea to the abhorred White Whale, he pitted himself, all mutilated, against it. All that most maddens and torments; all that stirs up the lees of things; all truth with malice in it; all that cracks the

sinews and cakes the brain; all the subtle demonisms of life and thought; all evil, to crazy Ahab, were visibly personified, and made practically assailable in Moby Dick. He piled upon the whale's white hump the sum of all the general rage and hate felt by his whole race from Adam down; and then, as if his chest had been a mortar, he burst his hot heart's shell upon it. (156)

The nature of the emotions and psychic orientation here is particularly fascinating from a Jungian point of view. Melville, writing twenty-five years before the birth of C. G. Jung, has described, as perfectly and as completely as seems possible, the Jungian phenomena of shadow and projection. This is the condition where a disturbing shadow element of an individual's or a collective's personality, one of which the subject is only partially or not at all conscious, is projected onto another, an object of only limited connection with the shadow element, and an obsession emerges that completely takes over the subject's view of the target. The White Whale is invested with "all the general rage" of an entire society, and Ahab becomes obsessed with its death. This is all despite the fact that such an outcome, having very little to do with the actual shadow (Ahab's false sense of dominion and his inadequacies in dealing with Moby Dick), will ultimately prove absolutely nothing.

In looking at the complexities of the literary character that Melville has created, Edinger provides some interesting additional observations. He portrays Ahab as having been "born from the deep mythological layers of the collective psyche, a modern self-revelation of the collective psyche" (53). He suggests that, for Melville, Ahab has been crafted as a manifestation of some of the trauma of Melville's experiences with his father, specifically, his father's business failures and untimely death during Melville's impressionable adolescence. In Melville's development of the strength of Ahab as leader, Edinger suggests that Melville may have been thinking of the very pronounced role that the two Peter Gansevoorts played in his early life. One was Herman's uncle, who helped his mother in the difficult years, and the other was his brother, who took on the role of family head and bread-winner after his father's death.

Last, Edinger envisions the name Ahab as conveying "the proto-type of the heretic" (54). He sees Melville in the same role, suggesting that much of Melville's work conveys his resistance to the teachings of his Protestant upbringing, "his opposition to the orthodox religions of the day" (54). The complexities of Ahab, the dark, sinister elements he seems to embody for Melville and the command he exercises over Ishmael, are critical elements in the view emerging here, that of a leader in a commercial enterprise who possesses many traits that enable him to be uniquely successful whether in the pursuit of economic gain or in malicious intents derived from deep in the soul, intents that serve only to demonize a deific being.

The strange birthmark, the "scar" that is reputed to run the length of Ahab's body, scarring for which the reader is given no explanation, is another element of the man, as created by Melville, that adds signifi-cant drama and mystery. It also creates another allusion in the story that Ahab is possessed of sinister and frightening origins and powers. Dennis Patrick Slattery, in *The Wounded Body*, addresses Ahab's scarring as be-ing "our emblem of the cosmic wound, the originary [original] wound that each of us carries inscribed on our own souls" (134). Slattery also talks of the relationship between Ahab's scarring and the multiple wounds, markings, and scarring on Moby Dick. If Ahab's markings are the "cosmic wound," might Moby Dick's woundings be the reflection thereof, the reflection of the scarring of nature caused by our Judeo-Christian belief in the fantasy of dominion, of our journey to conquer nature as the legacy of our having rejected the Garden in Genesis?

John Bryant, in his essay "*Moby-Dick* as Revolution," discerns an even more sinister side of Ahab, a righteous but pathological resolve to kill Moby Dick to confirm his own atheism (72). It is Ahab's core belief that there is only one god on the decks of the *Pequod* and that it is he. Might this be another manifestation of a similar belief in our modern psyche, our belief in our sense of dominion? Ernest Leisy, in "Fatalism in *Moby-Dick*," believes that the White Whale is "the cosmic will incarnate" and the fight against it is the central human struggle of the story (77).

The impact of Ahab's obsession, the deep pathological need plaguing him to exact revenge on Moby Dick, can be seen early in the story, in the incident of the pipe in chapter 30. In the previous chapter, Ahab has roundly chastised Stubb, the more hapless of the mates, for having the audacity to suggest the captain limit his walking on deck in off hours so that his ivory leg pounding on the deck would not disturb the men sleeping below. Ahab's lack of patience for Stubb, whom he frequently describes as a fool, and his intolerance for the idle chatter of fools, leads to Ahab's very harsh rebuke of the man. In the aftermath, Ahab sits on an ivory stool, at the bulwarks, smoking his pipe and staring into the sea. Melville draws the visage of the man Ahab "seated on that tripod of bones" as royalty. "For a Khan of the plank, and a king of the sea, and a great lord of Leviathans was Ahab" (113). After smoking for a while, Ahab withdraws the pipe and comments that "this smoking no longer soothes. . . . What business have I with this pipe? This thing that is meant for sereneness. . . . I'll smoke no more" (113). He then tosses the pipe into the sea. The heaviness of his journey, the burden of the vengeful quest leaves no room for simple pleasures. Melville adds that "the fire [from the pipe] hissed in the waves [and] with slouched hat, Ahab lurchingly paced the planks" (113).

And so, in the progress of the journey, Ahab's mood darkens as his intensity heightens. In this regard, there are some incidents mentioned previously that are worth expanding and there are others, not previously mentioned, that are worth introducing to gain a full sense of Ahab's encroaching madness and its effect on Ishmael and the crew.

In chapter 113, Ahab bids the blacksmith to make him a special harpoon to use in the battle with Moby Dick. He gives the blacksmith some "nail stubbs of the steel shoes of racing horses" which the blacksmith says are "the best and stubbornest stuff we blacksmiths ever work" (371). Ahab instructs the blacksmith, supervises him in the making of the harpoon, and gets the three harpooneers to give him some blood to temper the finished product. In a powerful moment, as he douses the hot steel in the blood, Ahab says, in Latin, "Ego non baptizo te in nomine patris, sed in nomine diaboli," which can be translated as "I baptize thee, not in the name of the Father, but in the name of the Devil" (371).

In chapter 119, the *Pequod* is engulfed in a terrific electrical storm, in which balls of lightning dance from the top of the masts. The crew is terrified, but Ahab defies the elements, refuses to allow Starbuck to lay the lightning rods over the side, and embraces the storm, saying,

"Oh! thou clear spirit of clear fire, whom on these seas I as Persian once did worship, till in the sacramental act so burned by thee, that to this hour I bear the scar; I now know thee, thou clear spirit, and I now know that thy right worship is defiance. To neither love nor reverence wilt thou be kind; and e'en for hate thou canst but kill; and all are killed. No fearless fool now fronts thee. I own thy speechless, placeless power; but to the last gasp of my earthquake life will dispute its unconditional, unintegral mastery in me. In the midst of the personified impersonal, a personality stands here. Though but a point at best; whencesoe'er I came; wheresoe'er I go; yet while I earthly live, the queenly personality lives in me, and feels her royal rights. But war is pain, and hate is woe. Come in thy lowest form of love, and I will kneel and kiss thee; but at thy highest, come as mere supernal power; and though thou launchest navies of full-freighted worlds, there's that in here that still remains indifferent. Oh, thou clear spirit, of thy fire thou madest me, and like a true child of fire, I breathe it back to thee." (382)

He then takes his new harpoon, has it catch the fire from the masts, and telling all the men that he is holding them to their oath to hunt and kill the White Whale, he says, "And that ye may know to what tune this heart beats; look ye here: thus I blow out the last fear" (383). Whereupon he blows out the flame.

Finally, as Ahab's incredible skill at tracking Moby Dick pays off and the White Whale is sighted for the first time, the hunt begins. In each of the three days, Ahab's boat is destroyed, as the White Whale's dominance over Ahab, the *Pequod*, and all of its crew is increasingly manifest. After each successive setback, Ahab and the men strive valiantly, with increasing effort and skill, to return to the fight and gain an advantage, but to no avail. Ahab resists Starbuck's last entreaties to desist. "Ahab is forever Ahab, man. The whole act's immutably decreed" (418). And as he hurls his harpoon a final time, in the final minutes of the last day's battle, he says, "from hell's heart, I stab at thee; for hate's sake I spit my last breath at thee," in his dying breath declaring his venom for the whale who deigned to wound him (426).

From his prose to his actions, Ahab is clearly one of the great characters in all of fiction. The force of his presence commands every scene. His singular, focused obsession with Moby Dick is legendary. As the archetypal whaling captain, superior in skill, intellect, and focused execution of the tasks of the commercial enterprise that is whaling, his obsession takes on mythic proportions. From the experience of his having been so seriously wounded by so noble a beast as Moby Dick, and of his having been denied what he perceived to be his right to capture this magnificent whale in the pursuit of his life's destiny to kill whales, there is evoked an incredible sense of man versus nature, of the misguided belief of man having dominion over the earth. And because Moby Dick is the archetypal whale, the grand ruler of all the beasts, the personification of the inherent deities that rule the earth, Ahab's obsession to hunt and kill it seems a projected need, a deep pathological need, to destroy the earth itself.

Ishmael, the Ordinary Seaman

In contrast to Ahab, Ishmael seems very subdued, more multidimensional and less significant in the unfolding of the story. Of the analyses of *Moby-Dick* published over the last eighty years, many have seemed to diminish Ishmael's importance, some either overlooking the character or the importance of his role. However, viewed from the perspective of Melville's times and experiences in world history, Ishmael emerges as equally significant as Ahab—perhaps even more significant. For the *Pequod*'s journey—the quest to conquer the archetypal whale, an expression of the soul of the earth—is very much the journey of Ishmael (and by extension, the journey of Melville) to find some meaning in the human experience within the ecosystem that is the community of humanity and the earth.

The story of Ishmael begins with his asking to be called the outcast, and by his telling that this is a journey he took some years in the past, "never mind how many" (18), to find some relief from a deep sense of disconnectedness, disenchantment, and melancholy. On the journey he presents himself as a man of no distinguishing characteristics or capabilities. He is open to meeting new people and to encountering new experiences. He is singularly tolerable of the new, different, and unusual. His befriending of Queequeg and the explorations into their contrasting views of the world is particularly instructive.

Queequeg opens himself up to Ishmael in an unusual and generous manner. He gives Ishmael half his money. He directs Ishmael to decide for both of them on which ship they should sign and sail; and he defers to Ishmael in many of the simple decisions of daily life. The bond that is established between them is unusual; Ishmael's acceptance of and reverence for Queequeg and his worldview seems to marry the two in an unusual way. Queequeg emerges as an alter ego of Ishmael's, an encapsulation of all that Ishmael reveres in humanity and of the man that he, Ishmael, would like to be.

Chapter 48, "The First Lowering," details Ishmael's first experience with an actual whale hunt. He is thoroughly shaken with how dangerous the work is and by how close they came to disaster, despite being in the boat with Starbuck and Queequeg. Starbuck's experience and skill are paramount, but Ishmael can't see any logic in their taking such risks. He sees it as a near-death experience. By contrast, Starbuck, Queequeg, and the other mates to whom Ishmael inquires of the experience, seem unfazed by it all.

As the journey unfolds, Ishmael emerges as a person with a singular lack of any particular talent or skill in whaling and with only limited enthusiasm for the tasks of the ordinary seaman. In fact, he seems a bit inept and wholly disinterested. In chapter 35, "The Mast Head," he characterizes himself as a terrible mast-head lookout, succumbing to the boredom and monotony of staring at the sea and empty horizon all day by dozing and dreaming:

> Let me make a clean breast of it here, and frankly admit that I kept but sorry guard. With the problem of the universe revolving in me, how could I—being left completely to myself at such a thought-engendering altitude,—how could I but lightly hold my obligations to observe all whale-ships' standing orders, "Keep your weather eye open, and sing out every time."
>
> And let me in this place movingly admonish you, ye ship-owners of Nantucket! Beware of enlisting in your vigilant fisheries any lad with lean brow and hollow eye; given to unseasonable meditativeness; and who offers to ship with the phaedon instead of Bowditch in his head. Beware of such an one, I say; your whales must be seen before they can be killed; and this sunken-eyed young Platonist will tow you

ten wakes round the world, and never make you one pint of sperm the richer. (135)

This paragraph is also instructive of a side of Ishmael that begins to emerge in the midst of the tale. Within his admissions about continual lapses and mistakes, he reveals a complete lack of enthusiasm for the work of whaling and, at the same time, a compulsion to study and analyze the ultimate meaning of such work. He confesses to a deep and abiding need for reflection on the meaning of the whole exercise of commercial activity.

Later on, in chapter 96, he falls asleep at the helm and wakes up to find himself staring at the stern of the ship, having nearly caused the *Pequod* to capsize. This episode occurs during the operation of the tryworks and he seems to be mesmerized by the fire, but the seriousness of his error frightens him. He admonishes himself, "Never dream with thy hand on the tiller" (328). But he is not admonishing himself for the tendency to dream, only for pretending to engage the work in the fashion required of the ordinary seaman.

Howard Vincent provides an interesting observation about the character of Ishmael, as Melville has crafted him and as he is seen in this analysis. He understands Ishmael as Everyman, from the morality plays of the High Middle Ages and Renaissance. "Ishmael is any man, anywhere, confronted with the flux of circumstance and with the chaos of his own being" (56). Vincent notes that without any concrete details about who and what he is, with nothing to create an image of the man, he becomes a vessel for the reflection of some of the key traits of other characters, traits to which he seems attracted. In addition, in the marginalization and disconnection of the name, Ishmael, the name he asks to be called, and in the grim soullessness he expresses at the threshold of the story, Vincent envisions him as "a profound symbol of the shelterless person in the face of almost absolute nothingness, when . . . the world has been revealed in its instability and unreliability" (58). In effect, Ishmael is the Everyman of the sinister economic society in which Melville finds himself and in which he feels lost, soulless, and abandoned.

Just after Ahab enlists the crew in his murderous quest and has them all swear a solemn vow, in chapter 41, "Moby Dick," Ishmael acknowledges his enthusiastic congruity with the rest of the crew in the oath so taken, but he confesses a "dread in my soul" (152). The remainder of this chapter is devoted to the known history of Moby Dick, as Ishmael is able to gather it from the crew, and to the experiences of Ahab in his earlier confrontation with Moby Dick, and his recovery from his wounding by the whale. In chapter 42, "The Whiteness of the Whale," Ishmael engages in his first expression of a view that begins to set him in the role of free agent in the tale. It starts with him describing his profound discomfort with the quality of whiteness. "It was the whiteness of the whale that above all things appalled me" (159).

In this discourse, Ishmael describes at some length the nature of the color white in things of beauty and virtue, the power of white as a symbol of regality and spiritual wholeness, on the one hand, and, on the other, the vision of white as symbolizing a desperate coldness, a void and a terror in the disparateness and abhorrence felt for the albino animal or man. "It is at once the most meaningful symbol of spiritual things, nay, the very veil of the Christian Deity; and yet . . . the intensifying agent in things the most appalling to mankind" (165). His conclusion is quite striking, and one that provides a critical insight into Melville, and a profound yearning in his soul:

> Is it that by its indefiniteness it shadows forth the heartless voids and immensities of the universe, and thus stabs us from behind with the thought of annihilation, when beholding the white depths of the milky way? Or is it, that as in essence whiteness is not so much a color as the visible absence of color, and at the same time the concrete of all colors; is it for these reasons that there is such a dumb

blankness, full of meaning, in a wide landscape of snows—a colorless, all-color of atheism from which we shrink? And when we consider that other theory of the natural philosophers, that all other earthly hues—every stately or lovely emblazoning—the sweet tinges of sunset skies and woods; yea, and the gilded velvets of butterflies, and the butterfly cheeks of young girls; all these are but subtle deceits, not actually inherent in substances, but only laid on from without; so that all deified Nature absolutely paints like the harlot, whose allurements cover nothing but the charnel-house within; and when we proceed further, and consider that the mystical cosmetic which produces every one of her hues, the great principle of light, for ever remains white or colorless in itself, and if operating without medium upon matter, would touch all objects, even tulips and roses, with its own blank tinge—pondering all this, the palsied universe lies before us a leper; and like wilful travellers in Lapland, who refuse to wear colored and coloring glasses upon their eyes, so the wretched infidel gazes himself blind at the monumental white shroud that wraps all the prospect around him. And of all these things the Albino Whale was the symbol. Wonder ye then at the fiery hunt? (165)

Edinger takes this a step further, seeing the whiteness as "pure undifferentiated archetype," "the original undifferentiated whole." To him, "whiteness is so devastating [to Ishmael] because it is infinite [and] Ahab's attack against the whiteness of Moby Dick represents the heroic effort of the ego . . . to refract and dismember the infinite" (82–85). It is in this context that Melville's dichotomy about the nature of evil and its presence in Moby Dick, measured against the numinosity of that being, is particularly striking. The whiteness as infinite puts the most terrifying meaning into Ahab's quest, and begins to make the catastrophic outcome seem a fait accompli.

Many authors tend to focus on the issue of Ishmael as outcast. In his essay, "The Image of Society in *Moby-Dick*," Henry Nash Smith contends "that Melville was intensely interested in at least one problem which involves 'society' as we understand it—the problem of alienation, of disturbance in the relation between the individual and the community" (63). He also says that the conflict of individualism and technology was of deep concern to Melville (62). His casting of Ishmael as the alien was to capture this sense.

Edinger sees Ishmael as "the prototype of the alienated man, the outsider who feels he has no place in the nature of things" (22). In using the name of Ishmael, Edinger sees Melville as speaking "from a position outside the orthodox and conventional . . . the antithesis of collective conscious values" (24). Edinger sees the use of the name Ishmael and the suggestion of a journey of redemption at the beginning of *Moby-Dick*, as the indication of a profound split within the Judeo-Christian system. The word *nekyia* of Edinger's title is meant to signify that *Moby-Dick* is as true a journey into the underworld of the American psyche as were the journeys of Dante and Faust in the societies of their times.

In all of this, the image of Ishmael is of the alienated self, the self-defined outcast from the society of his time, from all the mythic systems that define that society and which are fully inculcated in him, but in which he can find no refuge. His calling is, in the final analysis, to be the scribe and to record it all, not in the starkness of white, but in the vivid color of "deified nature" (165). The final outcome for Ishmael, as the only survivor, seems to confirm that the *Pequod*'s journey is Ishmael's journey. The journey is to confront the most powerful species on the earth, in the form of its absolute archetype, the albino sperm whale. The journey is to avenge, nefariously, a pure act of nature by an undifferentiated force of nature. The journey is to "prove," foolishly, man's mastery over the earth. Each of these is seen in the journey of Ishmael into the belly of the whale. And his return, his report of the knowledge gained from this journey, is that the concept of dominion is a fantasy . . . and that, in the community of man believing in dominion, Ishmael is just another orphan.

The Story, in Sum

For the purposes of this analysis, *Moby-Dick* the story, then, is about the interplay of three elements or characters whose energies are derived from the fundamental underlying ethos of the American, primarily economic, experience of the mid-nineteenth century: Moby Dick, Ahab, and Ishmael.

Moby Dick is the archetypal whale who also represents an existential force of nature. It is intelligent, cunning, and powerful beyond the normal experiences of whaling, and it cannot be subdued. Its actions seem to be a normal response to attempts to capture it, but they may stem from a collective will to repulse the massive exploitation of nature that American whaling, and the American economic experience, had become.

Ahab is the archetypal whaling captain, who has always been in command of his ship, his enterprise, and himself. He is the epitome of the commercial whaler of nineteenth-century America; he has developed a unique skill in finding and killing whales to fulfill a commercial need for a growing economy; and he is a celebrated captain among the whalers of Nantucket. Moby Dick has dared to challenge Ahab's right to capture the whale, providing Ahab with a nearly mortal wound; the whale's success in dismissing capture strikes at the heart of American whaling dominance; and its effrontery in such success is, to Ahab, outrageous. The White Whale must be killed; its continuing success brings the mythos of America under attack . . . and denigrates the Christian right to dominance over nature.

Ishmael is Everyman, a simple undifferentiated soul, who has found the world, the American world, a difficult place to be and who has sought an experience at sea to find answers to his anxieties. Along with the rest of the crew, a crew of men from all over the world, Ishmael is seduced by Ahab and enlisted in Ahab's diabolical quest. He retains some aloofness from the overall process, however, and is fearful from the start that Moby Dick, an albino sperm whale, cannot be conquered by man. In this belief, he makes the journey of the *Pequod*, for him, a journey to understanding and, as a result, he is spared to return to tell the tale. In the aftermath, however, he, Ishmael née Melville, remains the outcast, the orphan, for the rest of his life.

This story, this tale, is replete with many mythic strains, and, to echo Howard Vincent, Christopher Sten, and Edward Edinger, its symbolic content is almost limitless. Like many great literary achievements, it has a power that transcends its time. In focusing the analysis here on certain mythic themes present in the American economic society of the mid-nineteenth century, there are many, many elements of this story that have been, by necessity, ignored. However, it does, most assuredly, seem that the elements of this story that speak to the theme of the *Pequod* as an economic enterprise, central to the American economic experience of the nineteenth century, are a valid analogy for the economic society of today. It is the analogy of the exploitation of nature inherent in the enterprise of The Pequod Inc., that of destroying such a powerful and mythic element of the ecosystem as whales, as against the proliferation of similar, if not quite as dramatic, activities in our modern society. It is an analogy comparing two behavior systems, the ultimate outcome of which could be only catastrophic for both.

This is the central insight, then, for this society to gain at the beginning of the twenty-first century, from the rich interaction of the characters in *Moby-Dick*. The exploitive activities of our modern society, when carried out on the massive scale that they are today, more so than at any time in human history, will ultimately end in calamity for very large segments of our society. The task, the challenge that an intense analysis of *Moby-Dick* presents to us, is to understand how the players in our time, the larger societies of our century, might be operating from the same type of mythos as the men of the *Pequod* within the economic society of the mid-nineteenth century.

4 The Petroleum Age: A Titanic Story

The Great Heidelberg Tun

In 1851, when *Moby-Dick* was written, the energy fuels that powered the emerging economic societies of America and Europe were wood, coal, wind and water, animals, and animal fats and oils. Fireplaces and furnaces for providing heat and to run industrial processes burned wood and coal. Wind and rivers powered water wells and mills. Agriculture used various beasts of burden to clear and plow fields and harvest crops. Light for reading or working at night came from oil lamps and candles; whale oil was a primary lamp fuel, though oil and natural gas distilled from coal were also used. The railroads were powered by steam locomotives in which the steam was produced by burning wood or coal; the same process was used for river steamboats and sea-going steamships. Other than the railroads, the only nonpedestrian ground transportation was via bicycle, horse, or horse-drawn carriage.

In 1859, an individual by the name of Colonel Edwin L. Drake, using a drill and boring process driven by a steam engine, was the first to pursue the idea that oil, also called rock oil at the time, could be found in large quantities by drilling into the earth's crust. Rock oil had developed some minor uses as a lubricant and as an ingredient in some medical remedies. There was also a belief that parts of it could be used for illumination, but it had only been found on the surface in oil seeps and small pools, and its volume was just not enough to drive a commercial gathering and processing operation. Many such seeps existed in northwestern Pennsylvania, near Titusville, and an investor group had been formed in New Haven to explore the idea of drilling for larger accumulations beneath the earth's surface outside Titusville.

Drake, an individual of uncertain experience and skill, but unusually enthusiastic and tenacious, was chosen to execute the plan. His title of colonel was entirely fictitious, used to impress the citizens of Titusville; but his tenacity was real. Drake was an inspired nineteenth-century entrepreneurial soul who had an outrageous idea and, despite enormous obstacles, acted on it with a blind, obstinate perseverance. He spent the better part of almost two years assembling an operation, building a drilling rig, deciding on a location, and beginning the drilling process. There was a universal belief that oil did not exist in the earth in accumulations accessible by drilling and recoverable by pumping, as was the case for water, but this did little to deter Drake.

In fact, just outside Titusville, on August 27, 1859, Drake did indeed strike oil and commenced almost immediately to pump it out of the ground. Earlier that month, his investors had decided that, after the extensive delays, the project was not worth pursuing and wrote him to shut everything down. However, Drake did not receive the letter until after the twenty-seventh, so this unlikely beginning to the Petroleum Age was not derailed. What did ensue from that moment was the development of an industry, a society, and a way of life that continues, unabated, to this day.

The story of the petroleum industry, from that day in Titusville, is clearly paramount in the evolution of the economic society that has defined America through the twentieth century; petroleum has determined much of our economic development. Today, more than

90 percent of the products used and consumed in the daily life of all Americans are produced and delivered using petroleum in some fashion. Access to, and control of, supplies of oil have driven much of the political strategy of the major nations of the West since the 1930s. It is an industry that has so dominated our modern-day experiences that it is easy to call it titanic in both its influence and character. Its epic character also matches that of whaling. For it is clear that the countless individual efforts of the men and women who have built this industry find their mythological parallel in the journeys of the whalers so colorfully characterized in the stories that attended Ahab's famous quest.

ENERGY, THEN AND NOW

The word *petroleum*, whose etymology would suggest a meaning of rock oil, from the ancient Greek *petra* and the Medieval Latin *oleum*, encapsulates a myriad of products found in nature and grouped together as crude oil and natural gas. They were formed in the earth over geologic time from the decomposition of plant and animal life and are grouped together because their formation is of the same geologic system. They are all hydrocarbons, in that their chemical composition is a combination of hydrogen and carbon, the two elements that are the critical building blocks in the structure of all living things on this planet. Coal is a similar hydrocarbon, also formed from decomposed plant and animal matter, but as the result of a different geological process.

As a fuel source, petroleum had limited practical use before the mid-nineteenth century, whereas coal had been used in increasing quantities for centuries. The difference in their history as a fuel source is in their respective availability, their accessibility, and their ease of use. Over the history of humankind's use of energy, it can generally be said that energy sources will be accessed based on their ease and cost to acquire and consume, as well as their available supplies; the easiest and most plentiful to find, acquire, and burn are the first to be used. Coal existed in layers, relatively close to the surface, at least initially, and it could be mined easily. It could also be burned in its mined state with very little, if any, processing.

The most definitive treatment of the history of the Petroleum Age, which began in Titusville in 1859, is Daniel Yergin's Pulitzer Prize winning history, *The Prize*, first published in 1991. Yergin calls the Petroleum Age, the Hydrocarbon Age, and our current species of humanity, Hydrocarbon Man. Yergin's book is extremely intense and detailed; it is the definitive history of the Petroleum Age and is a basic reference used in this analysis. However, his use of the term *Hydrocarbon Age* to describe our petroleum history is not correct. Although the influence of petroleum on our society today is so deep and panoramic as to defy description, the true use of hydrocarbons as fuel and feedstock dates much further back than the nineteenth century. All fuels used by man prior to petroleum—wood, coal, and various plant and animal matter—could be considered hydrocarbons.

The earliest evidence of the use of hydrocarbons as a fuel is in the likelihood that an early predecessor of man learned how to control fire as early as five hundred thousand years ago (Ember, 119). These were fires involving wood, most likely, but there is evidence of the use of coal, tar, or bitumen, gathered or mined from the earth, and animal fats in many pre-history and early history cultures. The use of coal in large-scale quantities came into play in the early days of the Industrial Revolution, primarily in England and Europe. Coal was plentiful, at least initially, it could be mined easily from the surface with pick and shovel, and it could be burned to produce heat and power without needing any processing.

Petroleum, on the other hand, was not easily accessible; at least it was not believed to be prior to the drilling of the Drake well. It also could not be consumed without some sort of processing and, without the ready availability of commercial quantities, there was little incentive to develop efficient methods to extract consumable products from the heavy viscous substance that much of the crude oil of that day was.

Crude oil and natural gas, that is, petroleum, occur within the earth in the pores of sedimentary rocks. Over millions of years, plant and animal matter accumulated in drainage and river basins, and were intermingled with sediments from those basins. These sedimentary deposits were buried at greater and greater depths, as rock and other sediments were piled above them, and the greater depths resulted in higher temperatures and greater pressures. The effect of these more intense conditions, combined with a host of chemical reactions, re-sulted in the formation of petroleum within these sedimentary rocks. (Coal was formed by plant and animal matter aggregating in swamps and bogs in much denser quantities and then compressed into seams through similar processes of heat and pressure.) The nature of the specific conditions of each accumulation of petroleum, the depth and pressure of the reservoir rocks and the attendant temperature, de-termined the precise quality of the crude oil or natural gas in each location. The higher the temperatures and pressures and the longer the processes of change are at work, the lighter and better quality of crude. Because crude oil is a combination of a number of substances, its quality is generally determined by how light it is, by how much of its combined substances were of higher combustibility.

Natural gas, which is primarily methane, tends to be the lightest and most simple of petroleum substances, with the simplest of chemi-cal structures. Although some crudes contain natural gas in them, this substance is so light, with such a high level of combustibility, that it generally occurs in separate formations, attendant to, but separate from, crude oil. The quality of the particular petroleum deposits, then, is determined by its chemical composition, and the better-quality deposits were generally those produced in the most intense of sub-surface environments.

Over time, after being formed, the accumulations of petroleum tended to migrate through the pores in the sedimentary layers of rock in which they were formed. The movement through the layers of rock followed the natural laws of physics, driven generally upward by the pressures in the rock and by the ubiquitous presence of water. Because of the differences in density, petroleum will not mix with water but will generally float on top of it.

In these processes of migration, petroleum, in time, would meet the resistance of less permeable rocks; these would then form traps, eventually causing the petroleum to aggregate in significant quantities in sections called reservoirs. It is by drilling into these reservoirs, whose location is estimated by geologists and geophysicists evaluating surface and underground rock formations, that oil deposits are found. Once a reservoir is penetrated by the drilling operation, the oil can be propelled to the surface through the drillpipe by the natural pressure in the reservoir, or, if pressures are not significant, it can be pumped or forced to the surface by various mechanical means.

The process of formation of petroleum in the earth, its accumulation in specific quantities in various locations, the properties of the individual formations, and the problems involved in extracting the deposits, are quite complex and hardly uniform. The deposits are not in pools, but in porous rock, generally under pressure, and may or may not be extractable. Specific crudes can be quite different from one another, with radically different qualities and components. Petroleum is not one substance but a myriad of chemicals that can exist in individual formations of crude oil, in suspension in the oil, or in chemical combination with other substances. Today, the processes of finding and extracting petroleum, and of separating the various substances in refining processes to turn them into products for our use, has developed into a myriad of highly complex physical, mechanical and chemical systems.

In the world of northwestern Pennsylvania in 1859, however, the size of the sources of crude from the Drake well, and from the many wells that replicated his process in the ensuing months, resulted in the rapid development of simple processes to refine the oil into products that would serve the immediate market. The primary product derived from this activity was kerosene, a substance that would burn clean, without being too hot or dangerously flammable. It was produced by distilling the crude and could be sold profitably for an estimated $.25/gallon or less, versus $.75 to $2.00/gallon for whale oil at the time. Thanks, in part, to the difference in price, the Petroleum Age had begun.

To put this price discussion in context, in the period between 1861 and 1875 (and in prices of the time), sperm oil fluctuated between $1.31 and $2.55/gallon and whale oil sold for between $.45 and $1.45/gallon (Starbuck, 660). These were the wholesale prices paid for cargoes of oil in New Bedford and surrounding cities; the average of these prices at these sales points for this period were $1.72 and $.86, respectively. Data for the prices of kerosene are not available, but crude oil sold at the wellhead during that period was for prices in the range of $1.00 to $8.00/barrel (API Petroleum Facts, 71); the average for those fifteen years was $3.35. This price of $3.35/barrel converts to $.08/gallon, at the standard measure of 42 gallons to the barrel. From this we can surmise that, even accounting for the cost to refine the oil and for the waste associated with how much yield from an average barrel was not kerosene (greater than 25 percent), a sales price of $.25 or less is a reasonable estimate.

History of the Industry

The progression of this new industry in its early years was incredibly rapid. The success of the Drake well and the rapid development of the market for kerosene resulted in a drilling boom in western Pennsylvania which quickly spread to Ohio, western New York, West Virginia, Indiana, and Illinois. Over the ensuing decades, similar booms emerged in California, Oklahoma, Texas, and Louisiana, although these last two, the center of the oil business today, did not see the first discoveries of oil until 1901. Today there is production in thirty-one states, but these original ten states, plus Arkansas, Colorado, Wyoming, New Mexico, Utah, and Alaska, remain the focus of what is known in the industry as the oilpatch. The analysis here will not be an exhaustive review of the history of this business, or even a summary of all the stages and places of the business over the many decades. The attempt will be rather to touch on certain personages, events, developments, and organizations in the history of the business—from Rockefeller to the world wars to conflicts in the Middle East—that best convey the themes inherent in this focus.

The Phenomenon of Rockefeller and Standard Oil

The first and perhaps the most startling of these events is the appearance of John D. Rockefeller, a man who may have had the most lasting effect on this industry, if not on the entire history of American business, over the past 150 years. Rockefeller was twenty-six when he bought out his partner in a trading business in Cleveland and decided to focus on the business of refining oil in 1865. The price of crude oil had been very volatile, and Rockefeller believed that the more profitable opportunity lay in refining because of the higher cost to build and operate a refinery versus a drilling rig. In relatively short order, he began to build additional refineries and to discover ways to eliminate the volatility in the business by managing his geographical and competitive position in such a way as to create natural monopolies. His business practices gave him significant advantages over his competition, and economic power over his suppliers and customers, such that he could control both the price he paid for crude and the price he charged for kerosene.

Over the ensuing fifteen years, he developed a market position that was so dominant that by the late 1870s, he had a virtual monopoly in the emerging petroleum marketplace, controlling upwards of 85 percent of the market. He developed a uniquely focused method of doing business, maintaining rigorous records of his finances and constantly building a strong cash position so that he would never have to rely on investors or bankers. His discipline extended to every element of his personal and business life and included a highly secretive approach to every aspect of operations. He called his company, and the various interlocking entities through which he worked, Standard Oil, because it was his goal to create the standard by which the oil industry, and, perhaps, in his mind, any industry, should work. In many ways, his business approach and the speed with which he attained almost total control of the petroleum industry made him an archetypal businessman for the largely unregulated economic environment of the nineteenth century.

Rockefeller had an almost sociopathic approach to business, believing that by pursuing complete domination, he was instilling a discipline and a sense of order in the economy that did not exist otherwise. He believed that such conditions were so beneficial to the business environment as a whole that he was entirely justified in using whatever methods, however cruel and unethical, to accomplish his goals of crushing competition and gaining more economic power for Standard Oil.

One of his more nefarious tactics was his system of business relationships with the railroads. In its early years, oil moved mostly by rail. Rockefeller's position with the railroads became so strong, and the competition between the different railroad lines was so fierce, that he was able to negotiate secret rebates on many of his shipments, giving him a significant cost advantage vis-à-vis his competitors. He also developed an integrated approach to the business, taking positions in the businesses that supplied him, such as the sourcing of lumber and the attendant manufacturing operations for making barrels. Over the years, this concept of vertical integration became a standard for business operations, particularly in the international oil business.

In the states where he was dominant, in the early history of the business, he used his competitive advantages to routinely cut prices, sometimes drastically, to force out competitors. He called these tactics "a good sweating." Besides having the effect of restraining competition—no one would dare attempt to undercut Standard's prices without facing severe retribution—it also gave him many opportunities to buy out distressed competitors, competitors whose distress could have been largely Rockefeller's doing, at rock-bottom prices.

In early 1882, Rockefeller and his associates in Standard Oil formed the Standard Oil Trust, a mechanism they developed to avoid running afoul of state laws limiting interlocking business arrangements. The trust, as he organized it, allowed for the consolidation of the myriad of Standard Oil's operations, under a single management system without there being a perceived legal link between them. In the seventeen years since he started in 1865, then, Rockefeller had developed Standard Oil into the most powerful commercial enterprise in American history, to this day. Although he had generally avoided taking positions in actual wellhead operations (that is, in the business of owning the drilling operations and producing crude oil), he controlled 80 to 90 percent of the petroleum industry from the point of sale at the wellhead through the wholesale distribution to consumers. His business operations also began to stretch overseas as the oil business was developing in Europe and Asia, so that Standard Oil, as Rockefeller built it, was also a predecessor to the multinational company of the late twentieth century and to the concept of globalization as it is understood today.

His business practices had become so rapacious, however, that his reputation drew massive scrutiny from political, labor, and social organizations and from governments. In 1890, the Sherman Antitrust Act was passed to outlaw the existence of combinations of any sort that constituted "a restraint of trade." Standard Oil was clearly that type of combination, but it took another twenty years, a lot of investigative journalism, and the populist fervor of the Theodore Roosevelt administration, finally to break it up. That happened as a result of a Supreme Court decision in 1911 which directed the dissolution of Standard Oil into a number of separate entities. Amazingly, many of these entities became giants in the industry, controlling various aspects of the business down to this day. Some of these entities and their successor entities in today's market are shown in table 4.1.

The successor companies to these entities today (Exxon Mobil, ChevonTexaco, BP, and Conoco Philips) are four of the top five oil companies operating in the United States. The fifth is Shell, a company based in the Hague and started by an ancestor of Alfred Nobel in the oil fields of the Caspian region and southern Russia at the same time as the development of Standard Oil.

Table 4.1 Successor Entities of the Original Standard Oil

Original Entity	Business Operations and Successor
Standard Oil of New Jersey (Esso)	International operations of Standard Oil, now ExxonMobil.
Standard Oil of New York (Socony)	Standard Oil operations in New York and parts of Pennsylvania, became Mobil, now part of ExxonMobil.
Standard Oil of Ohio (Sohio)	Standard Oil operations in Ohio and parts of Pennsylvania. Bought by British Petroleum, now BP.
Standard Oil of Indiana (Amoco)	Standard Oil operations in Indiana and Illinois. Bought by BP.
Standard Oil of California (Chevron)	Standard Oil operations on the West Coast. Now part of Chevron Texaco.
Continental Oil (Conoco)	Standard Oil operations in the Rockies and midcontinent area. Now part of Conoco Philips.

Source: Author's compilation

In the intervening years from the breakup of the Standard Oil Trust in 1911 until the decade of the 1980s, when difficulties in the industry began a consolidation process that resulted in the companies listed in table 4.1, the worldwide oil business was controlled by seven companies, three of which were Standard companies. They became known as the Seven Sisters: Standard Oil of New Jersey (Esso), Standard Oil of New York (Mobil), Standard Oil of California (Chevron), Texaco, Gulf, Royal Dutch/Shell, and BP. Beginning in the 1980s, a wave of consolidation changed this configuration, reducing

131

the seven to five: Chevron purchased Gulf in 1984 and Texaco in 2001 to become ChevronTexaco; Conoco purchased Phillips, based in Oklahoma, in 2002, to propel them into the ranks of the majors. Of the original seven, Esso, or Standard Oil of New Jersey, emerged as the dominant organization coming from the 1911 dissolution, perhaps the de facto head of the group known as the Seven Sisters. Much more so than any of the other former Standard companies, or the other major oil companies, Esso, now ExxonMobil, retains the strong focus, disciplined practices, and rigorous management style of John D. Rockefeller to this day. Its continuing success as the world's top oil company over many decades is testimony to this fact.

In the intricate manner in which the worldwide oil operations of all these companies were connected, there continued to be various ways for them to collude on price and strategy after the dissolution of the Standard Oil Trust in 1911. Until the 1970s, they were a dominant force in the setting of international oil prices. They lost control when the host countries of many of their operations in the Middle East and elsewhere took charge of the indigenous operations within their own countries. It was this process that established the Organization of Petroleum Exporting Countries (OPEC). Today, OPEC is perhaps the world's most influential cartel, the most effective organization for influencing worldwide petroleum prices. OPEC is the subject of a separate section later in this chapter.

The Automobile and Motorized Transport

The second major event of interest to this review of the Petroleum Age is the introduction of the automobile. In the early days of the petroleum operations in Pennsylvania, Ohio, and elsewhere around the world, the primary product derived from oil refining was kerosene, used for lighting and heating. Whale oil had all but disappeared, although natural gas and a fuel oil refined from coal found some use for residential and commercial lighting and heating, and for street lighting. One of the by-products of the process of the refining of kerosene from crude oil was gasoline, which was lighter and more flammable than kerosene. It was too dangerous for use in the home, so it was generally discarded by refiners, dumped in rivers or flared. At the same time, during the 1880s, a number of different individuals in Germany and the United States, but primarily Karl Benz and Gottlieb Daimler in Germany, were working on designs for a motor-powered vehicle using various engine concepts.

The idea that emerged was that of an internal combustion, piston-driven motor. The plentiful and extremely cheap availability of gasoline, and its high combustibility, made this a natural fuel, so there was little reason for other designs or fuels to be pursued. Those that were developed were quickly made noncompetitive by the low cost and availability of gasoline. By the time of Henry Ford's development of the Model T in 1908, the gasoline-powered internal combustion automobile was the industry standard and, with that car's acceptance by the American public, the modern automobile industry was born.

The progression of the designs and growth of the automobile, from its original development in the 1880s to today, is further testimony to the power of the growing petroleum industry to define our lives. With gasoline so plentiful and cheap, it was a foregone conclusion that automobile design would favor the use of gasoline derived from crude oil. In the 1890s, an offshoot of the gasoline-powered engine was developed using diesel fuel; the design was a modification of the internal combustion engine. Diesel as a fuel was derived from crude oil, but it was a bit heavier than gasoline, more like kerosene. Early in the twentieth century, the development of electricity for lighting and of natural gas as a lighting and heating fuel resulted in much reduced demand for kerosene. This greatly facilitated the growth of diesel as a fuel because it could be produced from kerosene with only minor modifications to the refining process. The diesel engine proved more effective than gasoline-powered engines in meeting the need for large, more powerful requirements, so that it became the preferred engine for large trucks, train locomotives, and ships.

As the use of petroleum spread to these other areas, it transformed the entire transportation sector. The development of aircraft, which initially used gasoline-powered engines to drive the propellers before the development of jet engines, completed the sweep; petroleum became the only transportation fuel for the twentieth century. Jet engines did not change this, because jet fuel is another derivative of petroleum, also made from kerosene.

The development and introduction of electricity and electric lighting after the turn of the century was accomplished through electricity generation systems using large steam-driven turbines that employed coal, fuel oil (another product from crude oil), and eventually, natural gas, to make the steam. Therefore, beyond the transportation sector, the development of the power for large segments of the industrial societies of the twentieth century was also driven by petroleum.

As motorized transportation grew in importance, particularly with the growing use of the automobile, the structure of communities changed; the suburbs developed, relying on the automobile for transportation. Populations abandoned the cities for a less dense lifestyle in the suburbs and the development of the ground-based mass transit, mostly rail systems that linked the cities, internally and externally, virtually stopped.

The natural result of all this, from the perspective of the petroleum industry, was for the refining sector to focus its development on the maximization of transportation fuels, particularly gasoline, from each type of crude oil. It can be said, therefore, that the automobile industry, including most other forms of motorized transport, and all the elements of our society that emanated from the reliance on these forms of transportation, have had their primary genesis in the petroleum industry.

The World Wars

The third major event specific to this review of the Petroleum Age is the influence of petroleum on the wars of the twentieth century.

In World War I, the success of tank warfare and the fledgling use of aircraft signaled the value of a mechanized military. In the intervening years before World War II, the respective powers in Europe, the Far East, and America moved aggressively to mechanize their armies and to develop a petroleum-based fuel system. This is particularly striking for Great Britain, which was a major naval power that had used its vast supplies of indigenous coal to power its fleets. The much greater efficiency of the petroleum powered, internal combustion diesel engines versus coal-fired steamships, plus the ease of refueling with fuel oil rather than coal, made the transition a compelling, if not a natural, one for the British.

The use of petroleum, for all the nations central to the conflicts of the early twentieth century, raised one large question, however. Where was the crude oil and refined gasoline and fuel oil to fuel the military? This critical strategic question rapidly became a central focus for geopolitical policy, especially given that many of the European nations did not have an indigenous source. In World War II, the United States, with its still-growing supplies of crude and its rapidly growing refining capacity, did. Indeed, much of the development of the petroleum industry in the United States in the post–World War II era was driven by the infrastructure put in place to support the war effort in both Europe and the Pacific.

David Yergin in *The Prize* reviews the critical need for access to oil in the World War II strategies of both sides. He also finds compelling evidence that the defeat of both Germany and Japan was as much a function of their limited fuel supplies as it was to their actual defeat on the battlefield. The experience of both world wars, then, and of the buildup of the Cold War in the aftermath of World War II, left every nation on earth with an almost single-minded focus—to keep access to reserves of crude oil as a central tenet of its geopolitical strategies. The geographic focus of such strategies—the Middle East, Africa, and Southeast Asia—and the dangerous and deadly events that have marked recent history in those regions are poignant testimony to this fact.

The State of Texas

The fourth element of the history of the Petroleum Age of interest here is the fascinating role that the state of Texas has played. Oil was not discovered in Texas until 1901, when a well called the Lucas number 1, drilled on a hill called Spindletop, near Beaumont in the extreme southeastern corner of the state, "blew in." It spewed 75,000 barrels of oil per day (bpd) all over the surrounding area for ten days before the well could be capped. The explosive column of oil, driven by intense underground pressure causing it to leap into the air, was called a gusher, and, in its power and volume of oil, it was the first such experience in the American petroleum industry. The oil industry in Texas developed quite rapidly from that point, eventually touching every corner of the broad expanse of the state. In the early years of the twentieth century, the gusher experience was repeated a number of times and a number of famous companies and people were part of the scene. Most notable of the companies that began in those early years were The Texas Company, which became Texaco, and Gulf Oil, founded by the Mellon family of Pittsburgh. Each of these two became members of the Seven Sisters; they were the only two U.S. companies of the Sisters that didn't trace their roots back to Standard Oil.

In 1927, an oil promoter referred to as "Dad" Joiner put an investment group together to drill for oil in East Texas in a region that most thought was devoid of oil. After a number of setbacks, his Daisy Bradford number 3 well blew in. It was October 1930 and began what has been called the East Texas oil boom. Wells were drilled all over the area, each encountering similar oil finds, but it was not until mid-1931 that it was determined that all of this was part of the same field, the largest oilfield in the United States then and now. Called the East Texas oil field, it is still producing today. Covering one hundred forty thousand acres, it has had more than thirty thousand wells drilled in its environs and has produced more than five billion barrels of oil.

The most significant element about the discovery of the East Texas oil field is that it flooded the United States with oil and resulted in a major collapse in the oil price, from $1.30 to as low as $.15/barrel. Conditions in the various Texas oil fields became so desperate that, in late 1931, the Texas Railroad Commission (TRC), which was set up in 1891 to regulate the railroads in the state and had subsequently been given the responsibility to oversee the oil industry, decided to take action. The feverish activity in the field was also having the impact of damaging the oil reservoirs below ground, the result of so many producers trying to draw oil from the reservoir simultaneously. To correct this, the TRC assumed the authority of ordering oil producers in the state to limit the oil production from each of their wells to a percentage, called "the allowable," of their capacity.

The allowable was enforced by limiting the production of each well to a set number of days per month. However, though ostensibly set up to correct the damaging activity of too much production from the reservoir, which was the limit of the TRC's actual authority, the effect of this rationing system was also to limit oil supply. By limiting it to balance supply with demand, they also had the effect of controlling the oil price and introducing price stability in the market. Initially, the program was hotly opposed by the producers, and there were a number of battles in the courts. But the chaos in the field was so great that the plan was upheld and, to enforce the rationing system, the governor ordered the Texas Rangers into the East Texas field to police the cutbacks.

The TRC was largely successful and continued to operate as the mechanism to control supply in Texas for the next four decades. The oil business in the state, with Texas as the largest oil producer, was so significant that the TRC's ability to control supply kept the demand and supply balance in the entire United States, and to some limited extent, the world, stable until the 1960s. This is evident in figure 4.1, a chart of annual average wellhead crude oil prices over the history of the business up to 2006, before the most recent run-up in prices began.

By the late 1960s, however, the demand for oil in the United States was significantly outstripping U.S. supply as U.S. production began to peak, such that the rationing of Texas wells became moot. The shortfall in U.S. supply was made up by imports, largely from countries with significant oil available for export. These countries, mostly in the Middle East, gradually banded together to form OPEC. Since its formation, OPEC has operated under a charter to set production for its members based on the perceived needs of the market place, in a manner to attempt to control the price of oil. In effect, then, the model for how OPEC seeks to control the price of oil around the world was the Texas Railroad Commission.

Figure 4.1 U.S. Annual Crude Oil Price (dollars of that year)

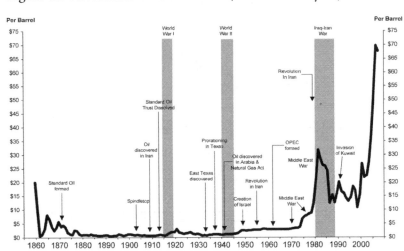

Source: Adapted and used with permission of Groppe, Long & Littell

From the TRC to OPEC

The last area of interest in this review of the history of the oil business is the nature and function of OPEC, particularly, its relationship to the primary consuming countries of North America, Europe, and the Far East. In the years following the breakup of the Standard Oil Trust, the seven oil companies that came to be called the Seven Sisters, three of which were remnants of the old Standard Oil (Esso, Mobil, and

Chevron), two of which arose out of the Texas oil bonanza following Spindletop (Texaco and Gulf) and the last two the giants of the European system (Shell and BP), consolidated their power and spread their activities to every corner of the world. Further discoveries in various parts of the oilpatch and, gradually, in a number of countries around the world, resulted in periods of excess worldwide supplies, even with the conflicts surrounding World War II. To deal with the excesses of supply, the seven companies began working together to attempt a system of allocation and rationing not unlike what the TRC had achieved in Texas, and in the United States, in the 1930s. Within the undeveloped world of the time, particularly the Middle East, where vast supplies of oil were being discovered, they began to allocate the activities of specific companies of the group to specific countries and, eventually, to ration their individual production amongst themselves to attempt to balance supplies with demand.

As the discovery of vast reserves and productive capacity in places like the Middle East and Venezuela focused the major oil companies on those countries, the arrangements they had with the host governments there became critical. Generally, these arrangements called for the oil companies to do the work of exploring for and producing the oil. The companies then took whatever production their internal systems needed, effectively limiting the overall production in those countries to those amounts. The oil produced, though taken into the oil companies' refining and marketing systems, was assumed to be sold at an agreed-upon price, and the profits from the assumed sale, after the costs to produce it, were split with the host governments in a variety of ways. In the early years, the host governments saw themselves as powerless to influence the oil companies, whose interdependent arrangements gave them almost unlimited power to allocate production and set prices. In many ways, these companies were so influential within the geographic regions of the oil-producing countries that they were de facto political organizations, effectively determining the policies toward those regions of the most influential of the Western governments.

There were two situations in the post–World War II era, however, that set the stage for the emergence of OPEC as a major independent force. The first was the developing conflict between the Arab world and the new nation of Israel. The support provided Israel in this conflict, particularly the tangible provisions of weapons and oil, by the Western consuming nations who were also the primary recipients of the growing oil production of the Arab states, increasingly infuriated the more bellicose of the Arab nations. The second situation was the economic power that the vast supplies discovered in these countries, primarily by the major oil companies, would ultimately give the host governments of OPEC.

In the years after World War II, the supply from these countries was becoming more than the developed world of Europe, America, and the Far East could absorb, despite growing demand in those areas. Although the major oil companies could control the supply flows, the growing excesses of productive capacities in those countries exerted a growing downward pressure on oil prices, which also limited the amount of money the major oil companies paid to the host governments. The experience of the continuing price reductions by the oil companies, at a time when the Western governments were supporting Israel to the detriment of the Arab world, led to increasing regional tension, particularly in the period between the two Arab-Israeli wars of 1967 and 1973.

OPEC was originally formed by Saudi Arabia, Venezuela, Iran, Iraq, and Kuwait in 1960. Its membership grew to thirteen by 1973, with the addition of various other countries primarily in the Middle East and Africa. With the conflicts surrounding Israel increasingly affecting the geopolitical tensions in the Arab world, the major oil companies, in the late 1960s and early 1970s, were finding it more and more difficult to negotiate with the host countries. The one country in OPEC that was in the center of all of this was Saudi Arabia, particularly because it was the largest oil producer of the OPEC countries, by far, and because it had the closest relationship with the United States.

Although its population was miniscule compared to many of the other OPEC members and its corresponding internal social and economic needs were quite a bit smaller, its aggregate production and its excess productive capacity dwarfed most of the rest of OPEC in 1973 and in 2006, as shown in table 4.2, and continues to do so today.

Table 4.2 Daily Production of Major OPEC Members (thousands bpd)

	1973	2006
Saudi Arabia	7,596.2	9,207.9
Iran	5,860.9	4,072.6
Kuwait	2,020.4	2,664.5
Venezuela	3,366.0	3,107.0
Libya	2,174.9	1,751.2
Nigeria	2,054.3	2,233.9
Iraq	2,018.1	2,020.1
United Arab Emirates	1,532.6	2,568.0
Total OPEC	**30,781.7**	**32,071.7**

Source: Author's compilation

The close relationship between Saudi Arabia and the United States had its beginning in February 1945, after the Yalta conference between Franklin Delano Roosevelt, Churchill, and Stalin. Roosevelt left Yalta and traveled on a U.S. warship to meet King Abdulaziz bin Abdulrah-man Al-Saud, also known as Ibn Saud, in the Great Bitter Lake in the middle of the Suez Canal. Major discoveries of oil in the late 1930s gave indication that Saudi Arabia could be a significant oil province and Chevron and Texaco were the only companies active in the country at the time, jointly owning a concession to explore for oil. This was an unlikely meeting between the two leaders, one of the country that was emerging as the leader of the developed world, the other of a loose ag-gregation of Bedouin tribes in the Arabian desert. The clear purpose of the discussion was oil. There does not appear to be any clear record of their talk, however, the meeting went exceedingly well, with Ibn Saud becoming enamored of Roosevelt, who showed the king an unusual deference. Two other U.S. companies, Esso and Mobil, were allowed to buy into the oil concession in 1948 and the four companies formed the partnership that became known as Aramco. No other country other than the United States, through the four Aramco partners, has been involved in the Saudi oil industry since that time.

The country has been ruled by Ibn Saud's descendants since his death in 1953 to the present day. The sons who succeeded him did much to maintain and develop the relationship with the United States, whose own production had peaked in 1971 as its consumption continued to grow. The close relationship over the years also included pledges by the United States to preserve Saudi sovereignty and the position of the Saud ruling family, presumably by force if necessary. But in the early 1970s, the overall conflicts between the Middle Eastern OPEC members and the West had deteriorated to a critical point. The Saudis had been a major restraining element in the Arab world because of their relationship with the United States, but in 1973 all of the conflicts came to a head.

In October 1973, Egypt and Syria attacked Israel, initiating the Yom Kippur War. When the United States provided substantial aid to Israel, the bellicose members of Arab OPEC prevailed on the Saudis to use oil as a weapon. The Saudi government then instructed Aramco to shut off all oil shipments to the United States and, specifically, to all U.S. military installations. This was particularly difficult for the managers and staff of Aramco, almost all of whom were American citizens stationed in the Aramco compound in Dhahran, Saudi Arabia, but they had to comply. At the same time, many of the OPEC members scrapped the process of price negotiations with the oil companies and put the sale of their oil out for competitive bid. With the world of the Middle East in turmoil, and shortages looming from the oil embargo instituted by the Arab countries, severe tensions infected the bidding process and oil was bid up to a posted price of $11.65/barrel. That price was set in December 1973; the previous July the posted price agreed on with the oil companies had been $2.90.

The relationship between the United States and Saudi Arabia remained relatively close and that continues to this day. Despite the eventual outcome of the Yom Kippur War, the success of the OPEC members in their economic confrontation with the West in 1973 and 1974 was complete. The fourfold increase in the price of oil held and, with their ability to control the flows of oil around the world, the balance of power in the economic world of oil was inexorably changed. As David Yergin writes, "The international order had been turned upside down" (633). The corporate descendants of John D. Rockefeller lost control of the markets they had dominated for so long and the mechanisms developed by the Texas Railroad Commission became the system that drives OPEC. Today, the members of OPEC, numbering thirteen, meet semiannually, or sooner as market conditions may dictate, to set production quotas, effectively prorating production among them.

In describing a 1975 scene in Algiers at one of the early OPEC meetings, after the success of 1973–74 had entrenched their solidarity, Andrew Sampson, in his acclaimed study of the major oil companies, *The Seven Sisters*, put the situation in picturesque terms:

> The Majesties sat next to the Brothers, the Africans congratulated the Arabs; and at the close of the conference President Boumedienne [of Algiers] suddenly presented himself as the peacemaker between two of the bitterest enemies in the Middle East who for years had been raiding across each other's frontiers. Saddam Hussien of Iraq walked across the hall to the Shah of Iran. The delegates all around the horseshoe stood up and clapped, and the two leaders kissed and embraced. (3)

Although the political regimes that rule most of the OPEC member countries do not always adhere to the quotas that they mutually set, and the absolute success of the cartel has been spotty, especially in periods of excess supply like the 1980s, it is one of history's most spectacular alliances. For a Western economic system that views access to oil supplies as a vital ingredient to economic societal health, the unlikely organization of countries that is OPEC may be the most dangerous one for the Western industrialized nations since the dissolution of the Warsaw Pact that had united all of Eastern Europe and Central Asia until the breakup of the Soviet Union.

What is most fascinating of all is that the control of this most valuable of all commodities, which in the industrialized societies of the West is the key foundation block for the bulk of economic activity, has moved from a few dominant economic institutions of the West into the hands of governments whose peoples had been the objects of centuries of Western economic colonialism. And, from another perspective, the Judeo-Christian West, which had been in conflict with the Islamic East across the entire border of those two worlds, from Gibraltar to Istanbul, for a thousand years, had now ceded a large part of the control of its future to this millennium-old adversary.

THE PETROLEUM AGE TODAY

At this writing, in 2010, the worldwide consumption of oil is approximately 85 million bpd. In the United States, it is approximately 21 million bpd, of which approximately 11 million bpd is imported. According to the Federal Highway Administration, there are approximately 245 million automobiles in the United States, including light trucks and SUVs, driving in excess of three trillion miles per year. Total U.S. gasoline consumption is running at approximately 9 million bpd, which translates into an average of 4,400 gallons per second, all day, every day. We access the supplies of this gasoline through a network of approximately one hundred thirty thousand gasoline stations and convenience stores in the United States. In excess of 90 percent of everything we consume uses some form of petroleum either as a feedstock in its manufacture, as an energy source in such manufacture, or in the transportation of the raw materials and finished products. The sources for much of the data of this section are the websites of various agencies of the U.S. government, specifically, the Energy Information Agency of the Department of Energy, the Federal Highway Administration and the National Highway Traffic Safety Administration of the Department of Transportation, and the National Surface Transportation Policy Study Commission.

Petroleum is an integral part of every aspect of our lives and the imbedded nature of this substance in our societies is hard to comprehend. The complexity of the substances, crude oil, measured in barrels, and natural gas, measured in thousand cubic feet (mcf), and how they fit into our national communities and our daily lives deserves some exploration. Earlier in this chapter we discussed the genesis of the sources of crude oil and natural gas, how they are the products of millions of years (geologic time) of physical and chemical processes in the earth, processes that break down plant and animal matter to produce petroleum. The precise nature of all these processes is not fully known and, given the time and conditions under which they occur, it is almost impossible to replicate them.

In contrast, the processes of taking these substances from the earth and producing materials that have uses today as fuel to produce heat or energy, or as feedstocks for the manufacture of everyday materials, were developed by humankind over the last 150 years using relatively simple physical and chemical processes.

The initial process of breaking down crude oil is to heat it to a vapor, which is then passed into a distillation column with various outlets arranged from top to bottom. The components in the crude condense along the column according to their boiling points, with the lightest components condensing and exiting the column at the top and the heaviest at the bottom. The various components of crude oil are quite numerous, but can be broken down into three groups according to their boiling points, and, generally, their combustibility.

At the high end are a large group of products that are generally referred to as *light ends*. These consist primarily of methane (natural gas), butane, propane, naphtha, and gasoline and multiple derivatives thereof. The next group are called *middle distillates* and consist mainly of fuels, particularly kerosene, jet fuel, diesel, and a light fuel oil which is used primarily for residential heating. The third group are a diverse mixture of heavy fuel oils and residuals, which consist of industrial and boiler fuels and coke, waxes, asphalt, and tar.

Crude oils vary considerably in their makeup; they are rated as to their quality according to an artificial method developed by the American Petroleum Institute (API). In general, this measures the weight and viscosity of a crude oil and then assigns it an API Gravity number, ranging from ten or less for the lowest quality, the heaviest and most viscous of crudes, to seventy or more for the highest quality, the lightest and least viscous. Generally speaking, the higher quality crudes have a higher proportion of the light ends and yield more of the products in this group and much less of the residuals; the lowest quality crudes yield the reverse.

The highest and most valuable product in the overall chain of components in crude oils is gasoline, because of its use in the highly voluminous automobile market. As a result of this, the focus of the refining element of the petroleum industry for most of the twentieth century has been to maximize the yield of gasoline from a barrel of crude oil. From the average barrel of crude oil, the atmospheric distillation process, as described above (distilling crude oil at atmospheric pressure) yields about 26 percent or about 11 gallons of gasoline per 42-gallon barrel of crude. To improve this yield, the other products from the atmospheric distillation process are subjected to a series of additional processes, many of which will yield additional gasoline as well as other products. These additional processes are numerous, but they can be grouped into three, as follows:

1. Processes to treat the middle distillates with heat and pressure, sometimes in the presence of a catalyst. This is meant to rearrange the molecules in the feedstock to yield more gasoline and

to yield other products in a form that have a ready market, for example, jet fuel and diesel.

2. Processes to treat the residuals under intense heat and in the presence of catalysts to extract more light ends.

3. Processes to treat certain of the light ends from all the other processes, to reform them, or some part of them, into a form that can be used as motor gasoline.

The end result of all of this, for the average barrel of crude oil today, is to improve the yield of gasoline to 48 percent or 20 gallons of gasoline per 42-gallon barrel. The remainder of the barrel today is primarily residential fuel oil and diesel, 20 percent or 8.4 gallons; jet fuel, 10 percent or 4.2 gallons; heavy or residual fuel oil, 7 percent or 3 gallons; lubricating oils, 7 percent or 3 gallons; and miscellaneous other products, 8 percent or 3.4 gallons.

The other primary form of petroleum, natural gas, is the lightest component in the petroleum chain; it generally exists in the earth in a gaseous state, so there is very little yield of this substance from the refining of crude oil. However, a number of other light petroleum substances may exist within the natural gas stream when produced from the earth, substances like ethane, propane, and butane, which may be suspended in the gas stream as it is produced. These are extracted from the natural gas stream after it is produced, in a variety of mechanical separation or cryogenic processes.

As we look at the processes to refine the petroleum stream into the components that fit our everyday use, a fascinating contrasting view to the physical and chemical processes that occur within the earth to form petroleum can be seen. Indeed, the entire circular process, from the origins of life on the planet in the synthesis of water, hydrocarbons in the earth, and solar energy into plant and animal life, to the decomposition of that plant and animal life within the earth in conditions of heat, pressure, and chemical change to form petroleum, to its recovery in the process of oil drilling and production, to its chemical

reconstitution and reformation in the process of refining, to its burning as an energy source that effectively releases the energy stored at the
beginning, and the return of the hydrocarbons to the atmosphere to
be absorbed again in the process of the generation of new life, seems
an elaborate, and very rich, alchemical cycle. The compound of petroleum, then, is a highly efficient form of stored energy, the energy of the
sun, which is the source of all energy in the solar system. Once it could
be mined and refined effectively, it is no wonder that its use prolifer-
ated in the way that it did over the past 150 years.

The processes of the formation of petroleum and of its mining
and use by humankind, the elaborate circular chain involved in all of
this, and the potential outcomes that humankind is facing today, do indeed have a mystical, alchemical quality. Can we look at them through
the imaginal lens of medieval alchemical theories and processes and
discern an outcome for our hydrocarbon society? From a more modern perspective, these processes almost seem like an endless stream of
chemical equations, in effect, material balance equations. The inherent
question that arises, though, is whither the balance?

In looking at the Petroleum Age as it has developed to today, it
is important to understand how big petroleum really is, both as an
aggregation of substances that are imbedded in virtually every aspect
of our lives and as an industry dominating our economic and sociological communities. Using the breakdown of petroleum products
listed earlier—light ends, middle distillates, and heavy oils—we can
summarize the extent of the petroleum society briefly.

Light ends include the lightest products, predominantly methane (natural gas), ethane, butane, propane, naphtha, and gasoline.
Besides the uses as fuels (natural gas, propane, and motor gasoline),
these chemicals are the feedstocks for a large number of processes
and product manufactures. All of this constitutes the general field of
petrochemicals. A sampling of the products in our daily lives made
with outputs of the petrochemical industry would include as wide a
range of products as plastic cups, bottles, and glasses; luggage and tote

bags; audio, video, and personal computing supplies and equipment; furniture, carpeting, and lighting fixtures; clothing and personal care products; surfboards, skis, and snowboards; motorcycle, snowmobile, and all-terrain vehicle components and helmets; building components for houses, stores, and factories; composite materials for planes, trains, and automobiles; and components for the heaviest of equipment used in all industrial processes. The range of synthetic products that have been developed out of these substances since the early twentieth century and the attendant science still evolving from this development is truly remarkable. What is even more striking is that the constant stream of new composite materials arising from the petrochemical industry today is also providing solutions for many problems associated with resource scarcities. A host of new composite materials to make cars, trucks, and airplanes lighter, more durable, and more energy efficient are notable examples.

Middle distillates include diesel fuel, jet fuel, lubricating oils, and light fuel oils. Most of the products in this range are fuels, but the variety and types of these fuels, developed for the different kinds of engines, are significant. For instance, beyond the use of motor gasoline in our automobiles and light trucks, our entire transportation and commercial delivery system, from the commercial trucking of goods to the transport of people and goods by air, rail, and ship, uses fuels that range in this class. More specifically, in the United States, these fuels power 7.9 million commercial trucks traveling 215 million miles per year, more than 10 million commercial airplane flights per year, and trains hauling 1.8 billion tons of goods traveling more than 1 billion miles per year.

Heavy fuel oils and residuals include heavy fuel oil, used for large industrial processes and for the generation of electricity by some local utilities, bunker fuel for ocean going ships, and tar and asphalt. Of significance here is the omnipresence of asphalt in our communities. It has been used as a major road surface in the 5.7 million miles of paved roads in the United States.

In terms of economic size, the petroleum business has also been one of the largest industries in the United States. In the days of the Seven Sisters, in the decades preceding the oil crisis of 1973, seven of the top twenty companies in the United States as ranked by *Fortune* magazine were oil companies. Three others were car companies (General Motors, Ford, and Chrysler) whose genesis, of course, was facilitated by the activities of the oil companies. Although the 1980s and 1990s were times of consolidation and restructuring for the petroleum industry, their dominance has not significantly deteriorated. Today, the aggregate equity market value of the publicly traded common shares of all the companies in the United States, the total for the major oil companies, the descendants of the Seven Sisters, is approximately $1.2 trillion. Although only three of the major oil companies are in the top twenty U.S. companies today, the total market capitalization for all the companies in all the sectors of the petroleum business is $4.2 trillion. This is 18.6 percent of the total market capitalization of all the publicly traded, nonfinancial companies, or $22.3 trillion (as of May 30, 2008).

Last, the petroleum industry, and the wealth created for its participants over the last hundred years, has also had a major impact in the philanthropic world. John D. Rockefeller founded the Rockefeller Foundation in 1910 to formalize a process for philanthropic giving that he started in 1889, when he became the major benefactor of the University of Chicago. Although the Rockefeller Foundation was not the first such entity, his structure became the model for philanthropic foundations of the twentieth century. Today, it is still ranked in the top fifteen, though it is dwarfed by the philanthropic activities of those, like Bill Gates, whose wealth grew out of the information technology phenomenon of the last twenty-five years. Two other foundations that grew out of the same wealth trend as Rockefeller, the Ford Foundation and the J. Paul Getty Trust, are numbers three and four in the ranking of U.S. foundations today. Rockefeller is number fifteen.

FROM WHALING TO PETROLEUM

In chapter 77 of *Moby-Dick*, Melville likens the head case of the sperm whale, where the reservoir of spermaceti is found, to the Great Heidelberg Tun. This is an enormous barrel that rests in the cellars of Heidelberg Castle in Germany. Simply a tourist attraction today, it was once much more. The Great Heidelberg Tun is reported to have held in excess of 50,000 gallons. Melville contrasts the Tun with its elaborate engravings and its use as a repository for the best of wines with the sperm whale's case:

> And as that famous great tierce is mystically carved in front, so the whale's vast plaited forehead forms innumerable strange devices for the emblematical adornment of his wondrous tun. Moreover, as that of Heidelburgh was always replenished with the most excellent of the wines of the Rhenish valleys, so the tun of the whale contains by far the most precious of all his oily vintages; namely, the highly-prized spermaceti, in its absolutely pure, limpid, and odoriferous state. (269)

The spermaceti organ was a dominant feature of the sperm whale, setting it apart from its cetacean brethren. Melville's celebrating it in this way is poignant and his analogy to the Heidelberg Tun is one we might extend to close our analysis of the Petroleum Age. As we look at the Petroleum Age today, the petroleum economic society in which we live could be likened to that Tun. We have filled it, the Tun of our society, with the most extraordinary amalgamation of substances and processes, some of vital importance to our daily lives, some suited only for frivolous use. Although some of the legacy of the Petroleum Age is quite regrettable, a wealth of knowledge has been gained about the nature of the universe and our very existence. We have filled this Tun of ours with a most amazing body of knowledge about the earth in all its wonders, much of which has given us a wide range of capacities to alter outcomes for ourselves and our planet. In the proliferation of ideas and knowledge gained, we have effectively adorned the outer casing of this Tun, the external profile we present to the universe, with equally rich and meaningful symbolic renderings. In its sheer size, breadth, range, and complexity, the nature of our Tun, its contents and the meanings we ascribe to it, is amazing. We should look at what has been so created, from the imaginations of all of the societies that have participated in it, with a certain sense of reverence. For, in many ways, it is glorious. However, at this point in the cycle of life for ourselves and our planet, as we look at what has been done and where we stand today, the fundamental question is this: How shall we use it?

5 Challenges of the Petroleum Age

A Bower in the Arsacides

Behind the wonder and accomplishments of the scientific and technological breakthroughs spawned by the Age of Petroleum, some very dangerous conditions have also arisen from the single-minded focus on petroleum. As we look at what oil has wrought, we see some fundamental questions that we, the human species, must face. These can be summarized as follows:

- *Peak oil.* Are we reaching that point in the life cycle of petroleum where the available daily supplies, at a cost that our societal systems can bear, have peaked, such that, not only can we no longer grow our consumption of petroleum, but our supplies will soon begin to inexorably decline?
- *Peak pollution.* Is our hydrocarbon society reaching a point of size and complexity that its daily operation is altering the ecosystem of the earth in such a way that, in time, it will destroy the mechanisms that support human life?
- *Peak population.* Is the total size of the population of the species, at the rate it is growing today and functioning with regard to the earth as it does today, rapidly becoming too large for the underlying ecosystem?

These concerns—peak oil, peak pollution, and peak population—are at the center of significant debate in the worldwide culture today, debate about the nature, size, and severity of today's conditions. Very little of this debate, however, challenges the facts of these conditions, only their severity and potential outcomes. It is not the intention here to engage such debate in any way, or to assume the validity of specific positions. Such engagement would entail a level of exploration into fact and theory beyond the focus of this analysis. The effort here will be only to describe, in limited detail, the known data of these conditions, which are the result of the last 150 years of the petroleum society, and to do so as a means to address the potential effects of our long-term exploitation of the petroleum resource base of the earth.

PEAK OIL

The use of energy by humankind to this point in our history, particularly energy for heat, light, and transportation, has been a process of moving from the fuel that is the most accessible and available to gather and use, to that which is more difficult. This is a process known as "progressive economic exploitation." In the history of humankind, we have gone from wood, to animal fats and oils, to coal, and finally to petroleum. All of these are hydrocarbons, made from the elements of life on earth, in the synthesis of light (solar energy), chemicals from the earth, and water. The earliest fuels were forms of life that had relatively short histories, that is, wood, plants, and animal products. The later ones, coal and petroleum, were forms that had been manufactured and assembled into energy stores in the earth over geologic time. Because of the long-term chemical and physical processes of formation of these later fuels, they are also much more condensed and potent; in effect, they had been made into very efficient, enhanced forms of stored solar energy. (Nuclear energy, which is also ultimately sourced in the energy of the sun, follows the same dynamic. However, although nuclear energy stores are many times more concentrated and more extensive than any other energy source, they are beyond the scope of this analysis.)

Given their higher degree of potency, their higher energy content, these later hydrocarbon fuels—coal and petroleum—also enabled humankind to rapidly increase the amount of work a group of individuals or a society could perform. The result was that they greatly enhanced the process of commercial and industrial development. Coal was an efficient fuel for the initial stages of Industrial Revolution in Britain and Europe; it is one of the reasons that Britain and northern Europe were the centers of industrial development in the eighteenth and early nineteenth centuries. Oil was even more condensed and, once refined, much easier to use. As refining processes developed that enhanced its energy content and made it easier and more efficient, its effect on industrial development accelerated. The vast supplies of petroleum in North America were one of the main reasons the United States was able to propel itself into the position of dominance in the industrial world by the last half of the twentieth century.

Progressive economic exploitation, the process of moving from the simplest and most accessible forms of energy to the more complex and more difficult to aggregate in usable forms, also applies to the evolutionary process of the use of each type of fuel. In the Middle Ages, the wood that was gathered for heat was first harvested from the edge of the forest adjacent to the village. As consumption depleted the stores nearby, the villagers had to forage farther and farther into the forest, and eventually to use carts and wagons to gather wood from the forest's depths. So it is with oil. The supplies of oil that Colonel Drake and his emulators, and, ultimately, John D. Rockefeller and Standard Oil, began to exploit were readily easy to find, produce, refine, and deliver.

Today, oil exploration is conducted in remote and difficult locations, under harsh conditions, at costs that are orders of magnitude higher than those of only a few decades ago. Much of today's new supplies of oil also require the development of extensive infrastructure to aggregate the resource and deliver it to markets. Exploration efforts today range all over the earth, from the Arctic Circle to the depths of the ocean. Drilling in the Gulf of Mexico is being done at water depths of up to eight thousand feet and into the earth's crust to a distance of twenty-five to thirty thousand feet. By comparison, the initial Drake well was in the midst of the emerging industrial heartland and it struck oil at sixty-nine feet. The Lucas well on Spindletop outside Beaumont in 1901 blew in when the rig was down to eleven hundred feet and the Daisy Bradford number 3 well in 1931 was at thirty-six hundred feet when it spewed oil into the East Texas sky.

Besides the phenomenon of progressive economic exploitation, the other major principle related to humankind's use of modern energy fuels is that coal and petroleum are not renewable. The time required for these resources to be formed in the earth is so great that no new supplies have been, or will be, manufactured in the lifespan of the human species. This was not considered a problem with regard to coal or petroleum in the past because the amounts of the ultimately recoverable resources in the earth were so large as to mitigate any serious concern about depletion. Although coal resources remain enormous today, evidence indicates that the recoverable resources of petroleum, particularly oil, may be reaching a critical phase.

In 1956, a well-known geologist by the name of M. King Hubbert, working for Shell Oil in Houston, presented a thesis about the future of the petroleum business to a meeting of the American Petroleum Institute in San Antonio. Hubbert had researched the performance of individual oilfields and general oil provinces, and, in such analyses, he noticed that they all tended to follow the same pattern. From a slow start, as knowledge about the field developed, production would begin to increase rapidly until it reached a peak. At that point, although new technology might prolong the peak for a time, the production from all those fields would begin to decline and, eventually, to decline dramatically. There were no exceptions to the inevitability of declines.

When looking at oil-producing regions, so-called oil provinces like the Texas-Louisiana Gulf Coast, he noticed that they generally tended to follow the same pattern. As more was learned about the province and new discoveries were made, production from the aggregate of all fields in the province tended to increase rapidly until it reached a peak. The peak usually followed a number of years after the number and size of new oil discoveries began to decline. All these estimates, of increasing production, peaking and inevitable declines of individual oilfields and oil provinces, could be plotted as simple bell curves.

Hubbert's presentation in 1956 showed that oil production in the United States as a whole was rapidly reaching its peak as an oil province. He estimated that total production would peak in the early 1970s. Figure 5.1 was taken from Hubbert's actual presentation and shows his prediction of oil production in the United States.

Figure 5.1 Hubbert's Peak: U.S. Crude Oil Production

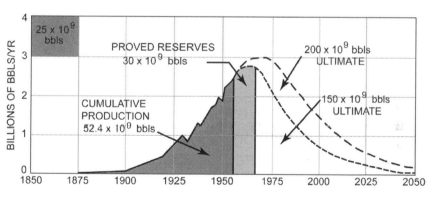

Source: Adapted and used with permission of American Petroleum Institute

The shaded areas under the bell curve show the amount of cumulative production to the date of the presentation and the projected production from existing reserves that petroleum engineering estimates show to be "proved reserves." The two downward sloping curves show the estimates based on two different assumptions of ultimately recoverable crude oil in the United States, estimates that Hubbert determined based on his analysis of all the major oil producing provinces.

The validity of his analysis was substantially proven when oil produc-tion in the United States peaked in the early 1970s at approximately 9.6 million bpd. It has been declining ever since and today stands at approximately 5.1 million bpd.

In his presentation, Hubbert performed the same analysis for the world as a whole. Although he was not in a position to perform this analysis with the same amount of detail and with the same level of rigor as he did for the United States, he produced the chart shown in figure 5.2, in the same format as the one for the United States.

Figure 5.2 Hubbert's Peak: World Crude Oil Production

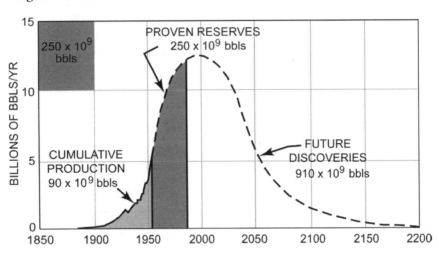

Source: Adapted and used with permission of American Petroleum Institute

This chart shows a peak for world oil production in the year 2000. That this did not turn out to be true does not change the validity of the analysis. The limited available data for an analysis of worldwide production at the time, and the fact that the United States as an oil province was much more mature in 1956 than many areas of the rest of the world were, made Hubbert's estimates for the world much more prone to errors in timing than those for the United States. The size and complexity of all the oil provinces of the world, the limited experience with some of the more remote and difficult areas that have been explored since 1956, and the development of many more uses for petroleum have had an enormous impact on the value proposition of oil as a core element in the economic societies of the West. Additionally, the enormous price spikes in petroleum and petroleum products in the late 1970s and again over the last five years have changed the dynamics of the business considerably. Sustained prices in the $15 to $35/barrel range between 1975 and 1983, and in the $40 to $140 range from 2004 to date have provided the type of economic stimuli that provokes more drilling and exploration and that raises total estimated volumes of the overall reserve base.

However, the effect of these forces and of changes in technology that provide for more opportunity to find oil, is only to extend the top of the curve, to delay or plateau the peak, and to forestall the inevitable decline . . . because the certainty of an ultimate decline, in the production of recoverable oil for the human species from the planet Earth, is an inexorable fact. Moreover, this fact is intuitively derived from the very nature of petroleum as a nonrenewable resource of the earth that has been exploited by humankind for 150 years.

The idea of peak oil does not mean that, when a peak is reached, all future supplies cease to be available. It means that production cannot grow from the peak levels and that any additional resources found will serve only to slow the decline, to replace only a portion of the production from the existing oil fields that are depleting. However, because the easiest reserves have been discovered, produced, and consumed first, the effort and cost to find additional production can only rise, most likely significantly. The effect of less total oil production and a higher cost to find new production only serves to push oil prices higher. According to the economic laws of supply and demand, one of the effects of rapidly rising prices would assuredly be a reduction in demand; in the face of higher prices, consumers ultimately decide to buy fewer petroleum products. However, the effect of the declining supplies of petroleum, and continuingly higher costs to find new supplies, would tend to keep the demand/supply equilibrium in a position of supporting continuing high prices. Of course, this assumes that we are not faced with severe economic contraction that could serve to seriously reduce oil demand and price. There is much debate about the issue of peak oil, specifically its timing, but little about its inevitability. The critical consideration in this debate is that the ultimate reserves of oil is not the issue; rather it is how much can be produced in the required time frames and at reasonable costs. The best evidence of the principles of peak oil is seen in the following graph of the total production from the United States over the past sixty years (figure 5.3).

Figure 5.3 Annual Crude Oil Production

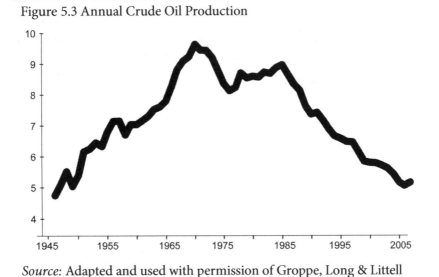

Source: Adapted and used with permission of Groppe, Long & Littell

The United States is an aggregation of a number of very large oil provinces. As a nation, it is the oldest in terms of its oil history and the largest in terms of aggregate oil production. The United States is also the largest consuming market for petroleum and its derivatives; exploitation of petroleum resources in the United States will always have priority over development in more remote regions of the earth. With the petroleum industry's lengthy history and experience of operating in all environments in the United States and the wealth of knowledge about petroleum geology and engineering gained from more than 150 years of operation, it is reasonable to conclude, categorically, that the experience of U.S. petroleum production is as absolute a model of the geology and mechanics of worldwide petroleum recovery as can be developed.

Recent years have seen a growing belief within the oil industry and in broader scientific, economic, and political communities that we are in the early stages of the experience of worldwide peak oil today. The very high level of oil prices, and the fact that, despite high prices, oil production has not grown very significantly in recent years, would seem to provide evidence of that. A contrary view indicates that it could be another fifteen to twenty years before worldwide production begins to peak. Those who hold this view believe that increasingly improving technology in finding and producing new oil supplies and the incentives in place from the experience of high oil prices today will result in incremental new supplies from existing fields and from entirely new oil discoveries. Such proponents point out that there tend to be significant lags between the development of new technology and resulting increases in oil exploration and actual oil production. It is also believed that the experience of the peak in oil production, whenever it comes, will be more like a plateau, of a number of years' duration, followed by the inevitable decline.

It is not the intention here to engage in a discussion about the nature and experiences taking place in our petroleum economy that might suggest the timing for peak oil; it is also not to take a specific position with regard to the extent and timing of the peak. To do so in enough detail for it to be useful is well beyond the scope of this analysis. However, the nature of petroleum as a nonrenewable resource of the earth and the intuitive facts about what happens to a nonrenewable resource when it becomes valuable, as borne out by the experience of the petroleum economy over the last 150 years, can only lead to the conclusion that it doesn't matter when peak oil will actually occur, for it most assuredly will happen. The evidence that the peak is approaching is compelling enough. Its very occurrence is a monumentally serious outcome for the economic societies of the West, if not for the planet, and the consequences of not addressing its inevitability are severe.

Considering the imbedded nature of petroleum as the foremost strategic commodity in the world economies and as an ingredient in virtually every aspect of our lives, an approaching peak and eventual decline in available productive resources must be seriously evaluated. These will change the economic bases of the developed and developing societies in ways that are difficult to imagine. Equally significant is that the principles behind the concept of peak oil apply to every nonrenewable resource in the earth. In ways similar to oil, the same phenomena may be happening to other valuable minerals and substances of the earth, such that the maintenance of our society, as we have constructed it to this day, on a basis that is sustainable without serious disruption, may be almost impossible to achieve beyond the next few decades.

PEAK POLLUTION

The experience of the Petroleum Age has also been occasioned by the generation of a myriad of useless and at times harmful by-products: refuse, effluent, gaseous materials, and trash. The accumulations of these materials continue to grow. All the elements of our existence, the air we breathe, the water we drink, and the earth that sustains us in so many ways, are increasingly infused with substances resulting from the consumption of petroleum, substances that cannot be recycled by the ecosystem or absorbed in a sustainable manner.

The purpose here is to put this phenomenon into some context to understand the impact that this characteristic of the Petroleum Age is having on the human society and its earth. Three elements of the earth—air, water, and land—are recipients of this legacy of refuse and trash, which can be grouped as gases, liquids, and solids. The website of the U.S. Environmental Protection Agency (EPA) lists a number of categories of pollutants and wastes generated by our municipal, industrial, commercial, and residential systems. The individual substances number in the hundreds; only some are sourced from petroleum and its derivatives. In addition, only limited data is available on the accumulations of many of these substances. However, for the petroleum sector, all such substances come from the following four processes within the flow of oil from its source in the earth to its consumption by humanity: discovery and production, transportation and refining, petrochemical manufacture, and marketing and consumption. The substances that present the greatest threat to planetary ecosystems number only a few of the dozens listed by the EPA. The intention here will be to deal only with those where the impact is the most severe and which originate from the most imbedded elements of our use of petroleum.

The petroleum industry, the aggregation of economic enterprises that are involved in all the processes delivering petroleum products to consumers, has been the object of significant regulation over the years. In general, the regulatory processes that have focused on petroleum have sought to improve the nature of the business operations sufficiently to reduce air, water, and land contamination and provide for a sustainable approach to the planet. Although there are some examples of industries and individual companies modifying business practices in advance of regulation, most changes to more sustainable practices have come in response to regulatory requirements.

In this context, however, the history of this business is rife with examples of environmental catastrophes. While the effect of regulation over the years has been to significantly limit the effect on the environment of the production, transportation, refining, and marketing activities of the industry, the experiences of the more visible disasters have tended to stay within the collective consciousness. Witness the crude oil spilled in the multitudinous early experiences like Spindletop and East Texas; the numerous pipeline and refinery explosions over the years; the incidents of effluent leaching into ground water from oil terminals and gasoline station tankage. In ocean environments,

163

accidents like the tanker spills off the Brittany Coast in the English Channel (1978) or in Prince William Sound of Alaska (1989), and the major production leakages in the Santa Barbara Channel (1969), the Bay of Campeche in Mexico (1979), or the most recent event in the Gulf of Mexico create startling images of ecological trauma in the collective consciousness.

Notwithstanding the April 20, 2010 BP Horizon blowout in the Gulf of Mexico and its repercussions in the region, the overall experiences of the last few decades have been such that the incident rate of such mishaps has been trending lower, especially in proportion to the aggregate size of the overall industry measured against the historical experiences. This has not been the case with consumption, however.

In the process of consuming petroleum products, the legacy effect of emissions and accumulations of trash is increasingly serious. The key elements here are the emission of greenhouse gases (GHGs), specifically carbon dioxide, methane, nitrous oxide, and a number of fluorinated gases, and the discard of plastic products—including cups, glasses, utensils, plates, bottles, and personal care product containers—many of which are used for fleeting instants and then idly trashed.

The EPA, in its 2006 reports, "Inventory of U.S. Greenhouse Gas Emissions" and "Municipal Solid Waste Generation" provides the most detailed indication of the extent of these contaminants. Carbon dioxide is the dominant GHG (85 percent of all GHGs) and, in 2006, according to the EPA, over 95 percent of all carbon dioxide was generated from the burning of fossil fuels. In that year, the United States generated 6,595.2 million tons of carbon dioxide, or 18.1 million tons per day, from the consumption of petroleum and coal.

Municipal solid wastes (MSWs) include all of the nonindustrial, nonconstruction, and nonhazardous solid wastes generated by all of our communities. The EPA lists nine separate categories of MSWs, as follows: auto batteries, steel cans, yard trimmings, paper and paper board, aluminum cans, tires, plastic milk and water bottles, plastic soft drink bottles, and glass containers. According to the EPA, all of these totaled 251.3 million tons of MSWs in 2006; this translates into 687 thousand tons per day or 4.6 pounds per person per day. The EPA does not categorize these wastes by original origin, so it is difficult to determine how much is derived from petroleum. However, the EPA does say that plastics comprise approximately 12 percent of the totals. Additionally, much of our rubber products today are synthetic, made from petrochemicals, so that some part of the 7.3 percent of MSW that the EPA says is from rubber, leather, and textiles would also have a petrochemical origin. If it is assumed, then, that approximately 15 percent of total MSWs is from petrochemicals, then plastic and synthetic materials waste in the United States totals approximately thirty-eight million tons per year. It is estimated that, within this annual pile of trash, there are more than twenty-four billion water bottles, fifty million per day. Only 30 percent of all this plastic is recycled.

GHGs have the effect of trapping heat in the atmosphere of the earth. Carbon dioxide is also produced naturally and is absorbed in the earth through numerous natural processes. However, although the larger ecosystems of the earth are in the constant process of recycling carbon dioxide and other GHGs, the magnitude of the emissions released into the atmosphere as a result of human industrial and commercial activity over the last century appears to be at a level significantly beyond what can be absorbed. Because carbon dioxide that is not absorbed remains in the atmosphere for an extended period and exacerbates the greenhouse effect by trapping heat in the atmosphere, there is reasonable probability that the GHGs emitted from our industrial and commercial societies are creating a dangerous condition within the global climate systems. The effect of such conditions— changing climates and more severe weather patterns and diminishing ice caps and higher sea levels—would appear to present the possibility of dire consequences for the ecosystems supporting human life.

Plastic wastes find their way into MSW landfills and miscellaneous trash heaps; however, the material does not decompose in any reasonable time frame. As a result, the accumulated trash continues to build and remains as an inert, nonbiodegradable amalgamation of material; it presents the possibility of future toxicity from its ultimate accumulated size and impact on a myriad of natural systems. A large area of the Pacific Ocean between Hawaii and Alaska has become infested with enormous amounts of plastic trash. Over many years, discarded material, mostly plastic, has found its way into rivers around the West Coast of North America and the northern Pacific Rim. This waste meanders and drifts in the river systems, eventually flowing into the ocean and, carried by tides and currents, it becomes trapped in an area of the northern Pacific by the natural circular flows of currents in this part of the ocean. The accumulation has become increasingly concentrated by the circular currents, and it continues growing, becoming more dense as more debris finds its way into the ocean. *The San Francisco Chronicle*, in an article dated October 19, 2007, reports that this "Great Pacific Garbage Patch" has been growing for decades. At the time of that report, it was estimated to be the size of Texas and to contain as much as one hundred million tons of plastic (Berton, W-8).

The fact of these accumulations in the air, on land, and at sea, and the nature of the human processes that are adding to them in enormous amounts every year, are such that any debate about how serious they are is irrelevant. They are growing and, in time, will be so large that the consequences of ignoring the problem will become moot. The human species will be at risk at such a level that it will require much more massive adjustments to daily life than are contemplated now.

PEAK POPULATION

In 1750, at the dawn of the Industrial Revolution, the population of the world was an estimated 700 million. By 1850, when the United States was in the grip of the new industrialism, the world population was an estimated 1.2 billion, and by 1950 it had more than doubled to an estimated 2.5 billion. As we approach the end of the first decade of the twenty-first century, it is an estimated 6.5 billion and is projected to grow to in excess of 9 billion by 2050.

We have added almost six billion people since industrialism began and, in the Petroleum Age, we have added almost five billion. Industrialization over the past 250 years contributed in large part to this growth because the mechanization associated with the new economic systems allowed for a massive reconstruction of society and more efficient and sustainable living systems. Cities drew people from the countryside, as industrialism began to dwarf the traditional agrarian systems. However, the farms also grew in productivity since the work could be performed with machines taking the place of men and animals. Farms could be larger with much more production per man hours worked. Food could be produced at greater distances from cities and transported in larger mechanized vehicles. Industrialization brought improvements in health and social services, and, though large segments of the population could not easily access such improvements, birth rates and life expectancy increased.

The near tripling of the world's population in the last sixty years is radically straining the resources of the earth. Lester Brown of the Earth Policy Institute in Washington, DC, provides one of the best reviews of the extent of planetary distress caused by the exploding population of the human species and the continuing proclivity of the species to exploit its resources. Beyond the issue of the depletion of nonrenewable resources, he posits that

> we are consuming renewable resources faster than they can regenerate. Forests are shrinking, grasslands are deteriorating, water tables are falling, fisheries are collapsing, and soils are eroding. . . . in addition, we must deal with . . . expanding deserts, deteriorating rangelands, dying coral reefs, melting glaciers, more frequent crop withering heat waves, rising seas and more powerful storms. (3–5)

The interconnectedness of all the ecosystems of the earth make all these conditions, though serious in their individuality, critical to the sustainability of the overall ecological structures. The systems of the earth are rapidly reaching a point at which the resource base, all resources, will not be able to support even the existing levels of population, let alone the increases that growth rates suggest.

Looking again at the situation with nonrenewable resources, the implications of continuing to operate societal systems in a business-as-usual fashion can be seen in the current trends in the consumption of oil. Table 5.1 presents data on oil consumption per capita broken down by region. In terms of petroleum use today, the concentration of per capita usage is much higher among traditionally developed societies.

Table 5.1 World Population and Oil Consumption in 2006

	Population (millions)	Consumption (million bpd)	Per Capita (bpd)
United States/Canada	340	22.7	.067
Industrialized Europe (including Russia)	535	16.3	.030
Industrialized Asia (excluding China and India)	225	10.3	.046
Middle East	185	5.9	.032
Latin America	585	7.1	.012
China/India	2,400	10.6	.004
Rest of the world	**2,230**	**11.3**	**.005**

Source: Author's compilation based on UN Population Division 2007; *BP Statistical Review 2007*

The energy use in terms of oil, by the industrialized world, which comprises only 17 percent of the world's population, is approximately 60 percent of total world supplies. The United States alone, at only 5 percent of the world's population, uses almost 25 percent of the oil. As the rest of the world, particularly China and India, continues to develop and to adopt commercial systems and consumption habits that mimic the industrialized world, the demands they will put on oil supplies will be enormous. For instance, if both China's and India's per capita oil consumption approximated that of the industrialized world, the additional amount of world supplies needed to meet the incremental demand would approximate 96 million bpd, bringing the requirement for total worldwide supplies to 180 million bpd. Obviously, with the prospects for peak oil being imminent, such supplies will, in all likelihood, not be available.

Similar trends are being experienced with other nonrenewable resources, and world systems of common renewable resources, such as potable water and basic foods, are similarly becoming seriously strained. With regard to potable water, as natural reservoirs and river systems are depleted beyond the capacity of earth systems to replenish them, water for growing human population centers must be sourced from more remote and less accessible systems. Making such water available to population centers will require the consumption of significant amounts of energy, exacerbating the problem with energy supplies.

Consider California, as an example. Because the population concentrations in Southern California are many miles from any water sources, the state currently uses approximately 20 percent of its electricity and 30 percent of its natural gas supplies just moving and treating water to make it available to its citizens. This condition, with depleting stores of water in all the natural systems hydrating California, is deteriorating. If rising GHG levels are warming the planet and reducing snow and glacial caps, then hydroelectric power will also be in shorter supply, for the West Coast of the United States and other areas around the world.

Decreasing snow and glacial caps are presenting a potentially critical situation for the water supply of many billions of the world's population, particularly in Asia. The measurable depletion in the Himalayan snow and ice cap is especially worrisome because the Himalayas are the source for a number of key rivers in Asia, notably the Indus, Ganges, Yangtze, Yellow, and Mekong. These rivers hydrate the populations of India, China, and Southeast Asia, where approximately of 25 percent of the world's total population reside.

HYDROCARBON SOCIETY AND THE EARTH

These conditions, born of the Petroleum Age and inexorably intertwined in the web of life of the earth, put the human species in a precarious position with regard to the planet from which we draw life and meaning. Resources depleting, natural ecosystems deteriorating, and costs of living rising increasingly stress our economic, social, and political systems, with precious few signs of progress in relieving the underlying pressure. Peak oil will occur and the energy resources to power the economic engines of all societies will be increasingly more expensive, if available at all. Growing gaseous, liquid, and solid waste accumulations in the ecosystems, together with population concentrations exacerbating the looming resource shortages, are assuredly darkening the prospects for human life at the pinnacle of the Petroleum Age.

In 1850, as Herman Melville was writing *Moby-Dick* and as the United States was in the grip of the early industrialism that so alarmed him and his American Renaissance contemporaries, the country was still a predominantly agrarian society. Eighty-five percent of the population lived outside the major cities. For such people, many of the items of everyday life were found relatively close to the homestead, from sources with which the residents had some contact. Even the residents of the major cities had some sense of the processes of production that were involved in the products of their daily consumption.

Thoreau's retreat to Walden Pond and his elaborate chronicles of experiences with the most minute elements of nature were an attempt to gain a deeper insight into the processes of nature of which he, and his contemporaries, already had some sense. Seventy-five years prior, Thomas Jefferson, as he was writing the Declaration of Independence, provided a most compelling evidentiary point about the connection of the people of colonial America to the land they had so richly populated. He wrote,

> When, in the Course of human Events, it becomes necessary for one People to dissolve the Political Bands which have connected them with another, and to assume *among the Powers of the Earth*, the separate and equal Station to which *the Laws of Nature and of Nature's God* entitle them. . . . (Commager, 100, emphasis added)

Today, at this pinnacle of the Petroleum Age, we seem to have declared a different form of independence, absolving ourselves not from allegiance to man, but from allegiance and responsibility to nature. The goods and services we use are sourced from locations wholly unknown to us, in some cases many thousands of miles away. The surfaces upon which we live, at home, in the office, even at play, are heavily synthetic, predominantly manufactured from some derivative of petroleum or in whose production petroleum was the primary energy source utilized. Even much of the air we breathe and the water we drink have been conditioned in some fashion. Precious little of our daily lives puts us in direct sensory contact with the primary elements of the earth. What might all this mean?

In chapter 102 of *Moby-Dick*, "A Bower in the Arsacides," Ishmael endeavors to probe the depths of the whale, to go "into the subterranean parts" in an attempt to extend his descriptions of various aspects of whales. At first he admits to some hubris associated with his doing this, he being just a simple seaman. But he explains himself by talking about an experience he had many years hence when he had occasion to visit his "royal friend Tanquo, King of Tanque, one of the Arsacides," an island chain in the Solomons, in the western Pacific Ocean. This king had amassed a collection of a wide range of artifacts from different places, for he was "gifted with a devout love for all matters of barbaric ventu," a term meaning "strange and rare objects of art" (344).

The community there had also salvaged the skeleton of a dead sperm whale that had washed up on the beach in a storm. They moved it to the interior of the island and used it as the center hall of a temple-like structure, adorning it with much of Tanquo's collection. The skeleton was surrounded by trees and vines, all of which had intermingled with the bones in an incredible weave. In his effort to delineate the internal size of the whale, Ishmael describes how he moved through the maze-like structure in an elaborate process of measuring the whale's dimensions. He articulates his vision of the live trees and vines woven through the dead whalebones in quite unusual, even mystical terms:

> It was a wondrous sight. The wood was green as mosses of the Icy Glen; the trees stood high and haughty, feeling their living sap; the industrious earth beneath was as a weaver's loom, with a gorgeous carpet on it, whereof the ground-vine tendrils formed the warp and woof, and the living flowers the figures. All the trees, with all their laden branches; all the shrubs, and ferns, and grasses; the message-carrying air; all these unceasingly were active. Through the lacings of the leaves, the great sun seemed a flying shuttle weaving the unwearied verdure. Oh, busy weaver! unseen weaver!—pause!—one word!—whither flows the fabric? what palace may it deck? wherefore all these ceaseless toilings? Speak, weaver!—stay thy hand!—but one single word with thee! Nay—the shuttle flies—the figures float from forth the loom; the freshet-rushing carpet for ever slides away. The weaver-god, he weaves; and by that weaving is he deafened, that he hears no mortal voice; and by that humming, we, too, who look on the loom are deafened; and only when we escape it shall we hear the thousand voices that speak through it. For even so it is in all material factories. The

spoken words that are inaudible among the flying spindles; those same words are plainly heard without the walls, bursting from the opened casements. Thereby have villanies been detected. Ah, mortal! then, be heedful; for so, in all this din of the great world's loom, thy subtlest thinkings may be overheard afar.

Now, amid the green, life-restless loom of that Arsacidean wood, the great, white, worshipped skeleton lay lounging—a gigantic idler! Yet, as the ever-woven verdant warp and woof intermixed and hummed around him, the mighty idler seemed the cunning weaver; himself all woven over with the vines; every month assuming greener, fresher verdure; but himself a skeleton. Life folded Death; Death trellised Life; the grim god wived with youthful Life, and begat him curly-headed glories. (345)

The beauty of these images bespeak a massive interconnectedness of life, an ultimate interconnectedness of industrialized life and of nature embracing death in such a world in the vision of how the vibrant green vines surround the stark white of whalebone. Christopher Sten sees this episode, in the juxtaposition of its telling in *Moby-Dick* and the actual event later in Ishmael's life, as an indication in the story of Ishmael being on the threshold of the successful completion of his hero's journey. According to Sten, some years later in life, in the Arsacides, Ishmael is able to move in and out of the belly of the whale, and to achieve a difficult task with some measure of ease and confidence. He had survived the journey of the *Pequod*, facing the whale and certain death, to grasp the vision of the power of nature. As a result, he can now visit the interconnectedness of Life and Death in the industrialized world with some element of impunity, for he is the scribe of this larger story as well.

There is much for us to envision here, in this image of a bowerlike chamber whose frame is of an old world, adorned with all manner of artifacts of such world, but whose strength, beauty, and dynamism are derived from the intricate weaving of a natural system. We stand today at the threshold of a doorway between two worlds, the old an increasingly grim skeleton of a once glorious society of our own creation, the new a vibrant recreation of a verdant paradise where nature and man, the earth and humankind, in blissful harmony, build structures of limitless complexity, with an ease and speed that are seamless. It is within our grasp. We have the knowledge and power to do it, lacking only the wisdom to see its infinite potential. What must we do to pass this threshold?

6 Industrialism and the Economic Society: Origins of the Mythos

All the General Rage. . . .

Earlier in this book, in the beginning of chapter 3, the concept of myth is explored in some depth. The societal themes that permeated the world of the United States in the first half of the nineteenth century, as outlined in chapter 2, are used to explain the ethos that seemed to drive the main characters and the unfolding of plot in *Moby-Dick*. Myth as a pattern of beliefs was found to inform, at times symbolically, the prevalent attitudes that drive societal behavior. Today, in this American economic society at the pinnacle of the Petroleum Age, many of the mythemes of Melville's time continue to operate, albeit in different forms and at differing levels of intensity. Other mythic structures have also emerged to propel the collective ethos to the heights of commercial and industrial activity that have been achieved. How might we describe the mythos of the American economic society of today? What themes emerge as we seek to explain the behavior of this modern culture, especially as it continues to exploit the consumptive patterns wrought by petroleum?

In this analysis of *Moby-Dick*, the focus has been that of Ahab and the economic organization that was the *Pequod* pursuing the business of whaling, of hunting and killing whales to derive a fuel for

175

lighting as well as miscellaneous other products for the emerging commercial and industrial landscape. The root elements of the process of killing and rendering whales at the wide-scale commercial level of the time is seen as part of the fundamental mythos of the Industrial Age. The conflict between Ahab, archetypal whaling captain believing in his own whaling invincibility, and Moby Dick, a legendary albino whale of unusual strength and cunning in repelling the attacks of whalers, is developed to carry the mythos of an exploding Industrial Age. It was an age in which humankind, especially in the Judeo-Christian West, increasingly exulted in its ability to bend nature, the physical earth, to its will. Although Ahab's belief in his own invincibility and that of his ship and crew proved to be false, he nevertheless struck out at Moby Dick with his dying breath, taking this core belief with him to his watery grave. By extension, we could say that the collective ethos of the entire industry of whaling and perhaps of the Western industrial society of the time carried the same sense of invincibility.

In this Petroleum Age, the processes of pursuing commercial development by exploiting plant, animal, and mineral resources of the earth have been expanded in many ways; so much so that resource supply constraints, systemic weakness in the underlying ecosystems, and explosive population growth are converging to create the real possibility of societal catastrophes within the foreseeable future. Although the ethos that drives this activity could be seen as a continuation or extension of the ethos of Melville's time, the extent to which we have taken the concept of development seems much deeper. John D. Rockefeller could be seen as a corporate leader of the nineteenth century much in the archetypal dimensions of Ahab in whaling; but he also represents archetypal elements of much more staggering proportions for our modern society. What corporate leader of today does not strive to achieve some semblance of the market dominance of Rockefeller, even though Rockefeller's quest for complete dominance over the marketplace ultimately proved as elusive as Ahab's quest for dominance over Moby Dick?

Modern society has developed levels of technological break-through and opportunity that are beginning to strain the imagination. Much of this is quite striking and miraculous, opening up opportunities to use the natural systems of the world in very promising ways. But much of it is also frightening, depleting vast stores of nonrenewable resources and consuming renewable resources so rapidly that the process of renewal is largely outstripped . . . and, at the same time, so much is pursued only for temporary or frivolous purposes.

There seems to be something deeper and more fundamental at work here than the process that drove the Industrial Revolution of the eighteenth and nineteenth centuries. There would appear to be three conditions in the core of the Western psyche today, all of which derive their mythos from its Judeo-Christian, Greco-Roman roots. These conditions, to be analyzed in depth in this discussion, can be initially summarized as follows:

- *The fantasy of dominion.* The belief that the human species has an innate, fundamental mandate to dominate the natural world, even though that mandate has no firm basis in reality.
- *The hero in the underworld.* The sense that the journey of a modern day hero, to unite the species and the earth in the collective consciousness, lacks a fundamental vision; in effect, the symbolic hero delineated in the hero myth of Western culture seems to be lost in the underworld.
- *The tyranny of moneyed wealth.* The single-minded focus of the Western, particularly American, psyche on the accumulation of financial, moneyed wealth as a primary motivator of individual and collective human behavior.

These conditions, these fundamental belief systems that form the mythological backdrop to our modern economic society, are significantly interconnected and interwoven, so much so that it is difficult to discern their independent characteristics. Nevertheless, it is important to attempt a clear articulation of each if we are to gain some grasp of the alternatives for our collective future.

THE FANTASY OF DOMINION

The first and second chapters of Genesis, the first book of the Bible, perhaps the most mythic text in the collective Judeo-Christian psyche, contain the primary accounts of the creation of the world by the God of the Judaic tradition. With regard to humankind, Genesis 1:27–28 says this:

> So God created humankind in his image, in the image of God he created them; male and female he created them. God blessed them, and God said to them, "Be fruitful and multiply, and fill the earth and subdue it; and have domin-ion over the fish of the sea and over the birds of the air and over every living thing that moves upon the earth."

According to a number of biblical scholars, the ancient Hebraic words used in the context of *subdue* and of *dominion*, as translat-ed in this edition, generally carry the meaning and energy of those words as we currently use them. Theodore Hiebert of the McCormick Theological Seminary in Chicago writes that this language "grants hu-mans the right and responsibility to rule, to govern the rest of creation. It establishes a hierarchy of power and authority in which the human race is positioned above the rest of the world" (19). Some scholars, while acknowledging the authority to rule, temper the language by suggesting that such dominion carries a sense of obligation. Walter Bruggeman of the Eden Theological Seminary in Missouri sees an I-Thou relationship between man and nature, in which the charge from God is "a command to order, maintain, protect and care for, i.e., to exercise control in the best interest of the subject, in our case, nature" (1166).

The entire rendition of the creation of humankind in Genesis 1, however, still places humankind in a significantly superior position. Man and woman are created by God separate from the earth; they are created "in the image of God." That phrase, the image of God, is emphasized and repeated. Man and woman are powerful, co-creative beings independent of the earth. Much of the rest of the world flows out of a process of creation from within, the waters and the earth bringing forth "swarms of living creatures" (1:20–24), but man and woman are created directly by God, in his image.

Interestingly, a second, largely different, rendition of the creation of man is presented in Genesis 2. Here the overall creation story is much more involved, with the waters and the earth interacting in a fascinating pattern. Here, "the Lord God formed man from the dust of the ground and breathed into his nostrils the breath of life; and man became a living being" (2:7). God also creates Eden and places man therein "to till it and keep it" (2:15). God creates the animals and birds out of the ground, to provide a sense of community for man; he has man provide names for them all. Recognizing man's loneliness, a sense of loneliness that the animals cannot fill, he then creates woman from a rib of man's side and man and woman "become one flesh" (2:24). The process here is much more one of man being with the earth and of man and woman forming a communal, nourishing bond with each other and with the earth, rather than their being co-rulers in a charge to "fill and subdue."

Much analysis and scholarly study of these two accounts has been done in recent years. Hiebert refers to the study of the two versions as the Theology of Dominion and the Theology of Stewardship, respectively. In the context of our analysis here, there is significance in the two accounts and in the amount of study of their meaning. Joseph Soloveitchik, a rabbinical scholar of some renown teaching at Yeshiva University, wrote a fascinating account, *The Lonely Man of Faith*, of what he calls the two Adams. He understands Adam the first as majestic and practical, with a firm desire to understand the cosmos, and a compulsion to master its secrets. Adam the second, on the other hand, is communal and connected, with a deep sense of the need for community, of man and earth and God, without a strong compulsion to order or to dominate.

Soloveitchik sees the man of faith in today's world as lonely, perhaps even in exile, because the experience of humanity over the recent centuries has been increasingly that of Adam the first, to whom faith is a difficult virtue. Although he recognizes that the two creation stories, the two Adams, emanate from two separate biblical traditions in the history of the Judaic system, Soloveitchik believes that the existence of the two creation stories is important in its own right and that a crucial element for humanity is the ultimate need to attempt an integration of the two. However, the experience of modern man and the predominance of Adam the first makes that difficult and any attempt at integration today leaves one with a deep sense of isolation. Soloveitchik suggests that "the whole theory of the social contract, brought to perfection by the philosophers of the Age of Reason, reflects the thinking of Adam the first, identifying man with his intellectual nature and creative technological will" (29).

The progression of humanity, particularly in the West, in recent centuries has been to study, plan, organize, and work to gain dominance over nature, over the physical world; as his cognitive and adaptive skills have flourished and accomplishments have built on accomplishments, the spirit of Adam the first has grown to dominate the human psyche to an inordinate extent. Nowhere has this been more apparent than in the progression of the Petroleum Age.

Consider what Adam the first has achieved over the past 150 years. He has learned to exploit all the resources of the central energy source of the universe, the Sun, from its stores in the earth in the form of coal, natural gas, and oil, to its central core in the nucleus of the atom itself. Using this energy, he has developed the ability to travel anywhere on the earth in a single day, a feat that took months only two centuries ago. He can rearrange the molecules of a host of basic earth substances to create new materials of incredible strength and durability. He has conquered infectious diseases and doubled his lifespan. He has soared into the stratosphere of the earth, and he has walked upon the surface of the moon.

The depth of this elemental spirit in humankind of the Petroleum Age is at the core of our mythological makeup. We feel it at the deepest part of our being. On January 28, 1986, Ronald Reagan spoke to the world in the aftermath of the space shuttle *Challenger* disaster, saying, "We will never forget them this morning as they prepared for their journey and waved goodbye and slipped the surly bonds of earth to touch the face of God." This last part was from a poem called "High Flier" by nineteen-year-old Royal Canadian Air Force pilot John Magee, who died in December 1941 over England. Reagan's use of these words was brilliant because it spoke to the heart of the psyche of Adam the first, the spirit that ruled the activities of all the peopleof the world who participated or witnessed the conquest of the skies and the regions of space. They struck at the fabric of all of us who lived through this time, for it was our overriding quest to "slip the surly bonds of earth," to unite with and fulfill the will of God, as commanded in Genesis 1.

Adam the second is still within us, as is made clear from the myriad of ways that a reverence for the earth sneaks into our psyches, however we might continue our consumptive and exploitive lifestyles. However, a stronger sense of Adam the second will continue to elude us while the power of Adam the first still rules. How fascinating it is how much the mythos of Herman Melville's *Moby-Dick* contains the epitome of the psyche of Adam the first.

Consider the business of whaling and the journey of Ahab, the archetypal whaling captain, and his crew of the archetypal whaleship *Pequod*. The sperm whale was the great leviathan of the earth, capable of destroying most all the whaling craft it encountered. The business of whaling was a commercial enterprise designed to produce substances from the bodies of whales that the societies of the earth could use for a myriad of purposes, both significant and trivial. The journeys to capture, kill, and render sufficient whales to make for a successful commercial voyage were long, harrowing, exhausting, and extremely dangerous, and the business of whaling was the first in which the United States was the dominant producing country. The journeys of whaling ships like the *Pequod* were mythic in their power within the American psyche and epic in their scope and activity.

At the core of the spirit that drove the men of the *Pequod*, and Ahab, in particular, was their belief that they ruled the seas and that they were supreme in the right and talents to hunt, kill, and render whales. In chapter 36, "The Quarter-Deck," Ahab says to Starbuck, "I'd strike the sun if it offended me" (140). Considering the psyche of a man who would say that, reflecting on how this spirit has grown since the time that Melville penned his tome, and realizing how much has been accomplished in commerce and technology since that time, is it not compelling to see *Moby-Dick* as a valid augur of the Petroleum Age?

THE HERO IN THE UNDERWORLD

The myth of the hero is known as a monomyth because it finds a parallel in many different cultures. Joseph Campbell's 1949 book, *The Hero with a Thousand Faces*, provides a complete and comprehensive analysis of the mythic systems surrounding this concept, the journey of the hero through a series of adventures resulting in an achievement that provides some type of breakthrough, an element of enlightenment or a sustainable experience of salvation, for a particular community of humankind. The myth of the hero also seems to be a particularly powerful one for the Western, particularly American psyche, of the last three hundred to four hundred years.

In the Campbellian context, the myth of the hero encompasses a journey in multiple stages, a journey of discovery, of trial and renewal and, finally, of initiation or redemption. It starts with a call. An individual, group, or community is in crisis and one or more chosen members are impelled to take a journey, to pursue a course of action to resolve the crisis. The chosen accept the call or reject it. Those who accept it begin the journey with some sort of separation, a physical, social, or philosophical separation from the original group or ethos. The journeyers go through a difficult struggle or series of trials, a mythical underworld, perhaps aided by a physical or spiritual guide; and eventually achieve a deep and profound understanding of the nature of the crisis and of prescriptions for a remedy. The journeyers then return with the newfound knowledge, which Campbell labels as the "boon" (36–37), and then work to integrate the solution into their lives. If from a group or community, the journeyers are most often reintegrated into the group or community and achieve a sense of redemption from the crisis for the collective.

Varieties of this myth operate at all levels and in all versions of the human experience. Many of the myths have either an initiatory or a redemptive core. This monomyth's appeal to the Western psyche, and particularly to the American psyche, stems largely from its resonance in the experience of the Christ, and many of the religious and social leaders that emulated his life over the intervening years; all were archetypal Campbellian heroes in the Judeo-Christian experience. This resonance is particularly strong in America, due to the nature of our history as a people. From the original settlement experiences of the early colonists, through the struggles of the fight for independence from Britain and of the founding of the new nation anchored strongly in revolutionary humanistic principles, to the immigrant experiences of the nineteenth century, and to the settlement of the West—they all bespeak a variety of heroic journeys of Promethean proportions. There are a profusion of individual and collective examples, in both historical and literary accomplishments, in the entire American experience.

John Shelton Lawrence and Robert Jewett, in *The Myth of the American Superhero*, focus on the elements of the hero myth in late twentieth-century American pop culture, particularly in film. They define the "archetypal plot formula ... seen in thousands of popular-culture artifacts" as follows:

> A community in harmonious paradise is threatened by evil;
> normal institutions fail to contend with this threat; a selfless
> superhero emerges to renounce temptations and carry out
> the redemptive task; aided by fate, . . . the superhero then
> recedes into obscurity. (6)

It is primarily a redemptive ethos. Lawrence and Jewett see the "supersaviors in pop culture . . . as replacements for the Christ figure . . . their superhuman abilities reflect[ing] a hope for divine, redemptive powers that science has never eradicated from the popular mind" (7). This theme has been repeated in scores of movies and stories, and is most powerful in the cult movie series, *The Matrix*. The storyline is of a modern society unconsciously trapped, under the control of an artificial machine intelligence that enslaves the whole of society and creates an alternate reality, the Matrix, that takes over their consciousness. A simple, average citizen, Neo, is chosen to lead a band of rebels in a seemingly impossible struggle to dismantle the artificial system. He performs superhuman feats in his hero's journey and, finally, after learning the secrets of the machines and how to destroy them, ascends to a place above the earth and independent of the machines. However, there is no change in the underlying condition of the Matrix or the enslavement of the overall society.

This is a significant twist in the mythos of the hero's journey, a twist found in many similar stories in modern media, a twist that is at the core of the distinction being explored here. Despite having achieved some understanding of the crisis, there is no fundamental redemption of society's underlying malaise. The hero, as representative of the collective society, is lost in the underworld, still seeking a redemptive mythos. With regard to the theme of this analysis, our modern society is caught in the cycle of exploiting the earth, struggling for a solution.

The nature of the story line of *The Matrix* and its high techno-scientific modern orientation are significant in that there have been many movies, before and after, that carry the same plotline. Analyzing the ethos underlying our economic society over the 150 years of the Petroleum Age, the rush to exploit and consume the resources of the earth seems emanating from some sort of haphazard search for a sense of connection and redemption. A society that derives its psychical history so profoundly from a Judeo-Christian grounding has achieved a level of technological and economic development that is truly profound. The process to do so seems fully imbedded, but the achievements do not seem to provide any lasting sense of deep satisfaction and personal accomplishment. It is as if we are lost in a maze of furious activity, ever pursuing higher and higher levels of technological achievement and consumption but attaining no breakthrough of spirit. We are enslaved to our own matrix, our own complex, technologically interwoven societal system, finding no redemption despite the intensity of our achievement and consumption.

The mythic systems imbedded in the concept of the hero's journey work on many levels; they can easily involve large segments of a society in the personage of the hero, and may involve a significant timespan. It is also true, as Lawrence and Jewett point out, that the myth of the hero has a powerful resonance in the American psyche. In this context, it seems clear that the nature of the ethos of our modern consumptive society could be interpreted in two ways. The first is as a society in the midst of a crisis, desperately looking for a redemptive process to be initiated by a hero presence, as portrayed by the popular iconic stories of film, video, and print media outlined by Lawrence and Jewett . . . but no such hero, individual, group, or collective is prepared to heed the call. Or it is a system in crisis where a Campbellian hero— again, an individual, group, or collective— has heeded the call, but is trapped in the underworld. In this case, the hero is slaving through a series of trials and conflicts either with no clear sense of resolution, or no clear avenue to a redemptive breakthrough that would constitute a return and an integration into society. The latter may be a more accurate interpretation of the focus of this analysis but, in either case, the implications are the same; that is, the progression of the Campbellian journey is thwarted.

Moby-Dick, as the story of Ishmael, can also be interpreted in the context of the myth of the hero; as such, it provides parallel patterns here. Ishmael receives a call to go to sea to relieve some sense of anxiety or troublesomeness of spirit. We are not told what such anxiety entails, but it could be inferred that it relates to the same sort of personal anxieties that took Melville to sea in 1839 and 1841, when he was struggling with the world of commerce in which he and his family had found themselves. In Ishmael's journey, he encounters obstacles in New Bedford and Nantucket but he is befriended by Queequeg, who guides him through his deliberations about whaling. Together they ship out on the *Pequod*. The journey takes Ishmael and his shipmates into a series of more and more difficult encounters until they finally confront the White Whale. In the process of getting to this point, Ishmael gains a sense of the futility of the quest and begins to distance himself from the mythos of whaling as an industry. In the final confrontation, Ishmael alone survives. It can be said that, at this point, his salvation is a function of his having achieved an understanding of the true nature of the journey to kill the White Whale and of the nature of the business of whaling as an economic enterprise. It is this understanding that seems to represent some core element of the boon. The discovery and delivery of the boon, Ishmael's story, while providing some sense of resolution for Ishmael, still does not have the requisite resolution for the underlying society.

Christopher Sten speaks in *The Weaver God, He Weaves* of Ishmael's journey to confront the whale. He describes Ishmael's final confrontation: "He has seen beyond his own death and is now prepared to do something worthy with the life that is left to him." He goes on, "Like every epic hero once he has come to his journey's end, Ishmael possesses the power to save others, to guide the chosen few along the path of trials to the same life-transforming spot" (200). The severe personal trials of Melville's early life around the failures of his father's and his brother's commercial activities were a large part of Melville's view of commerce and industry and the experience of the economic society that was, and is, the United States. Ishmael's survival to tell the tale, to be the scribe in the chronicle of the confrontation of Ahab and Moby Dick, seems very much to be the boon, the gift of the "power to save others" as Sten describes it, even though this boon never achieves its attendant "power." The parallel for the modern society of today— the reason we are all a collective hero lost in the underworld—is that, unlike Ishmael, we have not found the requisite understanding of the malaise and the redemptive power or boon.

C. G. Jung provides an analysis of the nature of modern man that is also instructive here. In a 1928 essay, "The Spiritual Problem of Modern Man," Jung describes modern man as someone who has attained a relatively high level of consciousness of the human experience, but who is not necessarily representative of the full spectrum of society. He calls him "the man who stands upon a peak, or at the very edge of the world, the abyss of the future before him, above him the heavens, and below him the whole of mankind with a history that disappears in the primeval mists" (*Collected Works* 10:152–55).

Having lived through both world wars, the economic Armageddon of the interlude between them, and the threatened atomic Apocalypse of the aftermath, Jung was especially concerned about the future of humankind and oriented to a sense of a collective unconscious. He wrote his essay early in the progress of those fateful years of the first half of the twentieth century, but it spoke presciently about the struggle that the Petroleum Age has brought so poignantly to the fore. Jung's modern man had a sense of the objective psyche that saw promise in the technological and intellectual developments of the twentieth century but was distressed by the inability of collective humanity to avoid conflict and catastrophe. Jung spoke of humanity being "at the threshold of a new spiritual epoch" (*Collected Works* 10:149) but stuck in the web of old belief systems with no apparent avenue to enter its new epoch. This view seems to mirror the idea of a hero mired in underworld conflicts, unable to find the break-through leading to redemption.

The Campbellian hero, Ishmael, *The Matrix's* Neo, and Jung's modern man have experienced the turmoil of the Petroleum Age, have gained a sense of the reparation and change that must come, but, with society so mired in the cultural mythos of the time, they are lost and unable to integrate back into society and initiate a process of salvation. Each is, like Ishmael on the deck of the *Rachel*, just another orphan.

THE TYRANNY OF MONEYED WEALTH

The pursuit of wealth as a primary aim of life seems firmly imbedded in the American, if not the Western, psyche; furthermore, considering the events of the worldwide credit markets in 2007 and 2008, the complexity of our monetary and financial systems defies ordinary comprehension.

Of course, in this American economic society, societal stratification dictates the nature of wealth. At the top are families of significant ancestral wealth, individuals and their families at the top levels of corporate organizations, financial brokers and traders, principals of investment groups, popular sports and entertainment figures, and the advisors and counselors who tend to each of these groups. For these, the accumulation of wealth tends to be delineated primarily in financial terms, well beyond their interest in or their ability to acquire nonfinancial assets or services. Next are the people of some means, professional types, midlevel business types, and those at the top strata of the governmental, academic, and nonbusiness organizations. For these the accumulation of wealth tends to track their lifestyles, where their goal is to provide an entirely comfortable life for their families and to provide for a comfortable, if not lavish, retirement.

Next would be those who struggle to meet the needs of a socially acceptable lifestyle for their families, a nice home, schooling, acceptable medical care, and the occasional vacation, but where the effort to do so requires substantial family adjustment, particularly by adopting multiple income streams. Last are those at the bottom, the homeless, unemployed, or working poor, who struggle to make the necessary means to live a simple life on either side of the poverty line.

The common denominator of all these is the pursuit of, or the struggle to make, money. The people at the bottom may beg, work odd jobs, or try to maintain a job at the bottom of the employment food chain, all to buy food, housing, clothes, and bare necessities for self and family. As we move up the chain, the focus increases to better housing, clothes, personal and medical care, schooling for children, and maybe some luxuries like toys for the family (all ages), and access to entertainment and vacations. At some point up the chain, as income and wealth accumulate, the interest in or ability to accumulate significantly more nonfinancial assets ("stuff") diminishes and the pursuit becomes that of financial wealth alone. The focus in such pursuits is to provide for a comfortable retirement and, eventually, to build a substantial estate for descendants. Beyond this, the last piece may be to build a philanthropic legacy, although, in recent decades, the growth of philanthropy, though significant, has lagged behind the growth of overall financial wealth.

Most striking is the focus on money as the goal within a system that is incredibly complex and intertwined in our lives. Of course, at the lowest strata, money is merely the means to provide for the barest necessities of life. But as we move up the chain, as money provides an increasing level of comforts, the pursuit does not diminish in intensity. Indeed, it may be seen to intensify such that, at the top most levels, it is all-consuming. Witness the profusion of financial iniquities at the top levels of the business world in the United States and elsewhere today, where the rampant and wholly mischievous exploitation of complex financial structures has caused the most significant dislocation in the capital markets since 1933. For, what has transpired in the period leading up to this day, to the severe financial disruptions of 2007 and 2008, is the expansion and intensification of an incredibly nefarious process of creating highly complex derivative securities from other financial assets, ostensibly to provide opportunities for high yielding investment or for risk mitigation strategies for a myriad of investors in the worldwide financial marketplace. However, because many of these structures were based on questionable underlying financial assets, notably subprime and notably high risk mortgages, and because the volume of these was so staggering, they became a house of cards that overwhelmed the core of the financial markets. The result is becoming, today, a type of financial meltdown, a risk of financial Armageddon that harkens back to the disruptions that plagued the commercial world of Allan, Gansevoort, and Herman Melville.

The focus of those who engineered these activities, the single-minded efforts of the primary executives, brokers, and traders up and down the organizational structures central to these affairs, has been near-term financial reward, their own financial gain to the exclusion of most all other motivations. The personal financial wealth built amongst these groups has been enormous. What is most distressing is that so much of it seems to have happened with very little thought as to consequence or to enduring societal value.

Of course, in the process of these pursuits, on Wall Street and on Main Street, among the wealthiest as well as the poorest of families, there is also an inordinate rush to consume, even if the wealthiest choose not to spend it all. In this process, the exploitation and consumption of the resources of the earth begin to take on the appearance of havoc and, at the level that has been achieved in the modern day, this havoc seems largely mindless. Benjamin Barber in his 2007 best seller, *Consumed*, provides some wonderful detail on the almost infantile nature our consumptive lifestyle, particularly in the way that products and services are marketed to us and in our responses to such marketing. Barber posits that "business mandates profligate spending on faux wants while ignoring real human needs" (77). Barber elaborates in great detail how the economic system in America is focused on the consumer, on "addressing those whose essential needs have already been satisfied but who have the means to assuage 'new' and invented needs" (9). The system is focused on turning all of us into ravenous, lifetime consumers, from children at the TV or computer bombarded with high image advertising, to college and university students granted multiple credit cards as part of their registration process, to adults whose appetites are constantly being heightened and intensified to crave products and services they do not need and which have limited redeeming human value.

In the southeastern corner of California, in an area known as the Imperial Valley, there is a large expanse of sand dunes, much of which lies in a national recreation area. This location is many miles from any major metropolitan area, two hundred miles from San Diego, more than two hundred miles from Phoenix or Tucson, three hundred miles from Los Angeles. Yet on President's Day weekend every year, upwards of one hundred fifty thousand people descend on this area, with the sole purpose of traversing the extent of these dunes in every type of off-road, motorized vehicle known to man. The scene is striking, the noise is deafening, and the participants seem enthralled by the experience and rush of speed and risk as they cruise over the dunes. The distances traveled to get there, by car, house trailer, motor home, or RV, are large, and the costs, particularly for the total of fuel consumed, are not minimal; yet one hundred fifty thousand people consider this a good way to spend a long winter weekend. To what end might we ascribe such an activity?

From the outside, it is hard to imagine what the attendant value in such activities and consumptive patterns might be and whether they can ever warrant the expense of resources consumed. Behind all the examinations of why, behind all the curious explanation of motive, however, there is a much larger truth: the ultimate realization that, intrinsically, money has no value. As coins or currency in our pockets, the substantive value of the metal or paper is negligible. As numbers on a bank statement or an investment ledger, it has even less value. Some psychical energy may be associated with these representations or symbols of money, given how circuitously they travel to us, but, intrinsically, they have value only in how they are ultimately used.

The use of money began in the late stages of human development, approximately three thousand years ago, primarily as a medium of exchange, to facilitate the exchange of goods in what was primarily a barter system. When the species began aggregating in larger groups and villages and needed a means to trade and distribute food, clothing, tools and the implements of life, money became a primary means of exchange. In most of its history, however, from ancient societies into the twentieth century, money always derived its value from some sort of link to a natural or physical asset. Its value was based on some index denominated in a physical asset—animals, produce, or precious stones or metals.

In some form, this persisted well into the latter half of the twentieth century. Until 1973, for instance, the U.S. dollar was pegged to gold at the rate of $35 an ounce and the thesis that the U.S. Treasury would redeem its currency for gold at that rate of exchange was generally accepted. After World War II, with the dollar so pegged, all other currencies were valued based on the dollar. In 1973, however, the United States severed this tie and any connection between the dollar and the value of gold, or any other physical asset of the earth, ceased. This shift is significant because, though the U.S. dollar was seen to be the most solid in value vis-à-vis all other currencies and was used by other countries as a reserve currency, its disconnection from gold meant that any index of money with the natural world, any effort to ascribe its value to something tangible in the earth, had come to an end.

Separately, over the centuries following the Protestant Reformation in Europe, another fundamental shift occurred with regard to money and wealth. For most of history before that time, accumulated wealth carried an obligation with it, a broad obligation to use it to build a sense of community. Beginning with the advent of the Calvinist and Wesley traditions in northern Europe, however, it slowly became a worthy pursuit to accumulate money solely for its own sake. The most accomplished study of this is by Max Weber, the early sociologist. Weber's book *The Protestant Ethic and the "Spirit" of Capitalism* was based on a vast amount of sociological research in which he observed significant differences between the traditional Catholic attitudes toward work and that of the Protestants within the communities of the growing Industrial Revolution. He saw that the Catholics tended to stay in single enterprise labor and work only as hard or as long as was necessary to maintain their standard of living. Protestants, on the other hand, pursued factory work, specifically, positions requiring a high level of skills, positions that also led to management opportunities. As Weber delved into the nature of these orientations, he found that the Calvinist and Wesley traditions, which dominated much of the area of Europe that he was studying, had developed a strong sense of the obligation of humankind to pursue a calling to work, which included an obligation to accumulate the fruits of one's labors and to invest it to build wealth. In a religious system that struggled with the conflict of free will and predestination, where much of humankind was doomed to eternal damnation even if they spent a lifetime seeking the grace of redemption, an individual's or a family's success in an industrious life came to be seen as a sense of having attained that grace, of having been favored in the eyes of God.

Initially, this Protestant work ethic focused on saving and eschewed an ostentatious show of wealth. Toward the end of the nineteenth and into the twentieth century, however, it began to change and "conspicuous consumption" to achieve some level of recognition in society became the norm. The idea of conspicuous consumption was first developed in 1899 by educator Thorstein Veblen in *The Theory of the Leisure Class*. Veblen focused on the history of the most affluent in various societies, observing that "persons whose occupation is vicarious leisure come to undertake a new subsidiary range of duties—the vicarious consumption of goods [where] the most obvious form in which this consumption occurs is seen in the wearing of liveries and the occupation of spacious quarters" (43).

In the aftermath of World War II, as Western societies worked to rebuild their economies and the United States assumed the role of pre-eminent world economic power, the sense of conspicuous consumption became the standard by which many U.S. families lived their lives. The exploding availability of credit in the closing decades of the twentieth century, and homeowners' ability to extract every last measure of value in their homes to generate more money to spend, brought us to the point we find ourselves today, where the proclivity to work, to earn, and to spend seems limitless. The extent to which we have taken these proclivities is quite striking, especially given that, with one of the highest per capita incomes of the major industrialized countries of the world, the savings rate in the United States, the percentage of its income that the average family saves, is the lowest. In the third quarter of 2005, it was actually below zero. Thus, for that period, the average U.S. family spent all of its income and saved nothing—nothing for medical needs, for children's schooling, or for retirement.

The fact of money and moneyed wealth in our lives seems so entrenched in our psychical makeup that it is even difficult to engage in any reasonable dialogue about it. No one seems willing or even capable of talking about an alternative to pursuing money as a primary lifetime activity. Even if we believe our lifetime pursuits are not about money at all, even if we are loathe to think of ourselves in the same mental framework of a New York investment banker or money trader, we must still spend a large part of our lives thinking and worrying about money, about where we will find the resources to live out our lives. For many of us today, it seems that "enough money" is always somewhat more than we have. And as our moneyed society pursues these goals of access, even to the point of excess, our disconnection from the earth and our proclivity to exploit its resources is blindly enabled.

In its deeply mythical orientation, *Moby-Dick* provides us with a sense of these shadow elements of this economic society of ours. As has been mentioned, the *Pequod* was a business enterprise, an archetypal whaling ship carrying out a preeminent U.S. business activity.

This was during the early years of the American Industrial Revolution when business cycles were acute and quite severe for the unprepared. In the early years of Melville's own life, his father's business failed, forcing the family to flee from New York to Albany, with eleven-year-old Herman accompanying his father in a midnight boat ride up the Hudson River. His father's untimely death in the aftermath of this failure, followed by his brother's business failure a few years later, and then Herman's own lack of success in the business world seems to have left the author with a strong sense of the imbedded nature of commerce and its potential for catastrophe in the American system. Additionally, given that the predominant religious system of the colonial and early national system of America was Protestantism and Melville's family was steeped in the Dutch Reformed system of the Calvinist traditions, as exposed by Max Weber, the inability to achieve long-term success in commerce must have been a severe family burden.

Reading with this background in mind brings us to the conclusion that transmitting a profound sense of the shadow element of an economic society was part of Melville's literary intent. The shadow exists in the progression of the journey of the *Pequod*, and in Ishmael's journey through the mythical belly of the whale. Ishmael is the only survivor left to tell the tale, and he is left with a sense of the futility of the hunt for Moby Dick. We, as modern-day readers, might then see the mythos of our moneyed pursuits as an enhancement, an escalation of significant proportions beyond the developing societal themes on which Melville chose to dwell.

Chapter 41 of *Moby-Dick* was discussed earlier, in chapter 3 of this text. We return to Ishmael's recounting of Ahab's obsession with Moby Dick. This extract, with its vivid, Jungian terms warrants repetition because of its import to our focus:

> The White Whale swam before him as the monomaniac incarnation of all those malicious agencies which some deep men feel eating in them, till they are left living on with half

a heart and half a lung. That intangible malignity which has been from the beginning; to whose dominion even the modern Christians ascribe one-half of the worlds; which the ancient Ophites of the east reverenced in their statue devil;—Ahab did not fall down and worship it like them; but deliriously transferring its idea to the abhorred White Whale, he pitted himself, all mutilated, against it. All that most maddens and torments; all that stirs up the lees of things; all truth with malice in it; all that cracks the sinews and cakes the brain; all the subtle demonisms of life and thought; all evil, to crazy Ahab, were visibly personified, and made practically assailable in Moby Dick. He piled upon the whale's white hump the sum of *all the* general rage and hate felt by his whole race from Adam down; and then, as if his chest had been a mortar, he burst his hot heart's shell upon it. (156, emphasis added)

In the modern economic society, the manner in which we deal with the earth, in our sense of dominion, in our having lost a sense of purpose to our journey as a species, and in our obsession with money and wealth as the primary end of life, our behavior can seem as obsessive as Ahab's. In the futility of our pursuits, the obsession to continue to acquire, exploit, spend, and consume, our behavior can be likened to Ahab's projection of "all the general rage" onto the White Whale, only in our case the projection is on the earth itself, the ultimate source of the resources we crave. Our futility, that inability to achieve any sense of peace and contentment in our pursuits, is much like Ahab's inability to achieve dominion over Moby Dick.

From Dominion to Stewardship

A scene in the 1997 movie *Titanic* reveals Thomas Andrews, architect of the vessel, explaining the extent and seriousness of the damage to the ship from the collision with the iceberg. He concludes with an expression of the inevitability of the outcome. Bruce Ismay, chairman of the board of White Star Line, the ship's owner, says, "But this is the *Titanic*. This ship can't sink!" Andrews retorts, "It is made of iron, sir. I assure you it can, and will, sink."

Many of the successes and achievements from the early years of the Petroleum Age were particularly awe inspiring in their time. Certainly the magnificence of the vessel *Titanic* in its size, power, and luxurious features was mesmerizing. And yet the beliefs that arose with such advancements slid all too easily into ideas that defy simple natural laws . . . and for intelligent men to believe that forty-six thousand tons of iron and steel, by itself in the middle of the Atlantic Ocean, could not sink defies logic.

As we ponder the circumstances in which humankind finds itself today, at the pinnacle of the Petroleum Age, it is easy to become despondent and to see catastrophes as the only possible outcomes. As the supplies of our energy and physical resources become critically short, as the impact that our consumptive behavior patterns have on the hierarchies of ecosystems begins to alter the balance of life on the planet, as the growth of populations exacerbate these problems, the threat of catastrophic events becomes more present in individual and collective consciousness. Potential catastrophes could take many forms: resource shortages will create severe economic and physical hardship that could lead to armed international conflict; climate change will introduce new, life-threatening weather patterns that could result in eco-catastrophes in regions of intense population; and the continuing high birth rates will severely aggravate starvation and population dislocations in critical world regions. Each of these catastrophic scenarios falls in a high range of probability within the coming decades.

We are all agents of these conditions; we are all agents of the Petroleum Age. It may seem easy to find culprits in an "other," in people and institutions that appear to be independent progenitors of the more regrettable of conditions. Assuredly, some individuals and institutions are, and have been, much more involved in the development and progress of the activities that promoted these conditions. However, we must acknowledge that all of this happened with our collective concurrence, our collective acquiescence, in some fashion. And the process of scientific and commercial exploration within the petroleum sphere over the past 150 years has also given us a body of knowledge about the earth that will be critical in developing a sustainable future.

So, in truth, there really are no ultimate villains in the progress of humanity to this point. Similarly, there really are no heroes in the process of change. Yet. The evolution of the Western psyche to this point involved a progression of events and trends that made the emergence of industrialism and of an economic society a natural process from the time of Plato. Though some of us may believe we have lived a world apart from these systems, in truth, today we all live within a world society that depends on, and is seemingly inextricably tied to, hydrocarbons. Many of us may see ourselves as agents of change or would like to. Undoubtedly, we all should work toward change; but precious few of us can be in this world, in any capacity, and live hydrocarbon-free, carbon-neutral lives. Today's conditions are a problem for all of us and all of us must engage, together, in a process of change.

What is most encouraging is that, in the past decade, extensive dialogue and exploration have emerged on the nature of the planetary circumstances created or exacerbated by the activities of humankind.

What is developing is the belief that the means to a set of energy and resource systems that are infinitely sustainable and in harmony with the ecosystems of the earth are real and available to us. To achieve these, however, the vigorous and aggressive exploration of a host of energy and resource systems, both old and new, will be required. The possibility does exist that sometime later in this century, when petroleum has gone the way of whale oil, the systems that will have replaced petroleum will be ones that may not even be visible to us today.

The progression of energy systems in the past has been from more and more concentrated sources of stored solar energy, from plants and animal matter, wind and water, to coal, petroleum and, eventually, nuclear energy. Because the sun is the source of all energy in the solar system, the future will take us further into this dynamic, developing the existing sources into carbon-neutral and eco-balanced systems and finding new, as yet undeveloped, derivatives of the sun (for example, hydrogen or fusion).

Additionally, a major set of initiatives around the much more efficient use of hydrocarbons is developing that will have the effect of significantly reducing the impact of our current fuels and manufacturing feedstock systems. Amory Lovins of the Rocky Mountain Institute is a highly credentialed scholar who has worked at various levels of government, academe, and business in the study of energy consumption for more than thirty-five years. His 2004 book, *Winning the Oil Endgame*, details a number of processes, from ultralight vehicle and aircraft design using existing technologies, to much more efficient building and home construction, to continued development of more productive technological systems, to vastly different business and lifestyle models, all of which can radically change how we use energy. Lovins accurately points out that we have halved the amount of energy used per dollar of GDP since 1975 and he predicts that, using more efficient methods and standards, we can do that again by 2025. More efficient use of hydrocarbon energy does not solve the problem of peak oil and peak pollution, but, given the massive size of our energy society today, it does provide the mechanism for an orderly transition to different systems, eventually free of fossil fuels.

It is my belief that the conceptual mechanisms needed to get to the optimum portfolio mix of sustainable energy sources exist in the current social, fiscal, and governmental systems of the world economic societies today. If markets are allowed to allocate supply and demand through a free-flowing price mechanism, if fiscal and governmental policies are set to burden the consumption of each energy source with its full economic and societal costs (for example, some sort of carbon tax system for hydrocarbon fuels), and if revenue neutral schemes are developed to allocate tax revenue to appropriate programs, then the incentives will be in place to develop alternative sources. Government support systems should be used as incentives to new technological development, as long as such support systems do not inadvertently favor a particular solution that may be counterproductive (for example, corn ethanol); and social payment schemes may be needed to relieve a disproportionate burden on certain societal groups. A set of systems can be developed to allow the private markets to find the best long-term solutions. The most promising experiences of the developments of the Petroleum Age, the experiences that gave us the extensive knowledge of the earth we have today, arose primarily from the free operation of such systems . . . and it will be the knowledge gained from those developments that will lead us to the wisdom we need to imagine and develop a new future.

The fundamental issue in all of this is the underlying mythos: how do we move the collective consciousness away from the felt-sense of dominion and a pursuit of moneyed wealth as an underlying core of the psyche and begin to embrace a sense of planetary stewardship? Joseph Solovietchik provides a wonderful view here. He posits that

> Adam the first is trying to carry out the mandate entrusted to him by his Maker who . . . summoned him "to fill the earth and subdue it." It is God who decreed that the story

of Adam the first be the great saga of freedom of man-slave who gradually transforms himself into man-master . . . transcend[ing] the limits of the reasonable and probable and venture[ing] into the open spaces of a boundless universe. . . .

Adam the second is also intrigued by the cosmos. Intellectual curiosity drives them both to confront courageously the *mysterium magnum* of Being. However, . . . Adam the second responds to the call of the cosmos by engaging in a different kind of gesture. . . . He asks "What is the purpose of all of this? What is embedded in organic and inorganic matter, and what does the great challenge reaching me from beyond the fringes of the universe as well as from the depths of my tormented soul mean?" (19–22)

To Solovetchik, there seems to be a natural progression from Adam the first to Adam the second, from Adam as master of the universe to Adam as minister or shepherd, seeking a deeper understanding of the nature of the universe and of God's mandate to all of us to serve. In the much closer connection of Adam the second to the earth as the garden and to Eve as the extended community of humanity, Soloveitchik sees a natural progression of humankind to a closer union with the earth and God than could have been achieved solely through Adam the first.

In a similar vein, Joseph Campbell provides a sense of his view of a possible future. In conversation with Bill Moyers, included in *The Power of Myth*, Campbell recalled his having seen the first views of the earth from the surface of the moon, this spectacular blue-green orb shrouded in white clouds, vividly reflecting the light of the sun against a backdrop of darkness, with no national boundaries nor any sense of any divisions of humanity in its visage. After all his decades of work, analyzing the hundreds of mythic systems spanning the entire known history of the human species, Campbell came to believe that there was only one focus for the future mythic systems of the species:

> And the only myth that is going to be worth thinking about
> in the immediate future is one that is talking about the plan-
> et, not the city, not these people, but the planet, and every-
> body on it. That's my main thought for what the future myth
> is going to be. (32)

To Campbell, then, this journey of humankind is the hero's journey, to re-discover the resource power of the entire planet and to integrate with it in some form of sustainable partnership of spirit. In doing
so, perhaps, the mantra of our everyday lives in a new economic society can go from today's "our resources are boundless, like the ocean" to
"we must live in harmony with the ocean and its creatures."

Finally, the portion of Ishmael's journey that, for my purposes
here, is the core of *Moby-Dick*, is also highly instructive as we look at
the future beyond the Petroleum Age. The idea of the *Pequod* as a commercial enterprise, and its voyage in the tale as the story of the journey of Ishmael, has been discussed at length. It has also been explored
that Melville's life bore a number of economic hardships that severely
influenced him, hardships that were spawned by the economic activities of the emerging commercialism and industrialism of the time.
It can also be inferred that a parallel exists between the elements of
Melville's experience with economic hardship and Ishmael's deciding to go to sea. His choice of whaling and the position of whaling
within the American economy of the time both add much power to
the theme. With this in mind, there is some value in our looking at
this journey of Ishmael one more time, as we close our analysis here.

Ishmael goes to sea in a most respected profession, that of whaling. At the time, whaling was indeed a respected profession, but also
one that had been advancing in an exploitative fashion, beyond the
level that could be supported by the ecosystems of the sea. Melville
casts the voyage as a mythic, epic voyage to kill the most powerful
Leviathan of the earth, the White Whale, full of mythic symbolism
for the natural systems of the earth. Ishmael grows to respect the

majesty of this creature and to recognize the futility and tragedy of Ahab's hunt. At the same time the voyage is primarily an economic enterprise, designed to meet a need for the energy of light among the world's populations. Ishmael gradually begins to see the connection of the two as the voyage, and the journey, venture deeper and deeper into the ocean and deeper and deeper into darkness and impending doom.

Ishmael completes his journey through the underground, through the mythic belly of the whale, in all its Campbellian and biblical connotations, and returns with a boon. The boon is the obligation to tell the story, the story of Moby Dick and of the devastation of rampant, excessive slaughter of whales. However, something is operating at a much deeper level here. The boon really is to convey something to the emerging economic society of the time, and, by extension, to the world of the Petroleum Age and today. It is to convey the futility of a pursuit of hydrocarbon energy beyond a level that is sustainable and balanced within the ecosystems of the earth.

In closing, then, it is useful to reflect on Solovietchik's belief in the coming ascendancy of Adam the second and in the power that such a spirit can have promoting our collective psyche toward change. In considering this belief, we can recall the condemnation and inherent challenge to that psyche, expressed by an aging Melville in *Clarel,* that we not become "the graceless Anglo-Saxons who, in the name of Trade, deflower the world's last sylvan glade."

Bibliography

Abrams, Kathleen C., ed. *The Story of the American Oil Industry*. The Woodlands, TX: Pioneer Publications, 1981.

Allums, Larry, ed. *The Epic Cosmos*. Dallas, TX: Dallas Institute, 1992.

Arvin, Newton. *Herman Melville*. New York: William Sloane, 1950.

Barber, Benjamin R. *Consumed. How Markets Corrupt Children, Infantilize Adults, and Swallow Citizens Whole*. New York: W. W. Norton, 2007.

Beale, Thomas. *The Natural History of the Sperm Whale*. 1839. Reprint, Worthing, West Sussex, UK: Littlehampton Book Services, 1973.

Beard, Charles A., and Mary R. Beard. *A Basic History of the United States*. New York: Doubleday Doran, 1944.

Beinhocker, Eric D. *The Origin of Wealth: Evolution, Complexity, and the Radical Remaking of Economics*. Boston, MA: Harvard Business School Press, 2006.

Berger, Bill, and Kenneth Anderson. *Modern Petroleum: A Basic Primer of the Industry*. Tulsa, OK: Pennwell Books, 1992.

Berton, Justin. "Continent-Size Toxic Stew of Plastic Fouling Pacific Ocean." *San Francisco Chronicle*, October 19, 2007, W-8.

BP Statistical Review of World Energy, June 2007. London: BP, 2007.

Braswell, William. *Melville's Religious Thought*. New York: Pageant, 1943.

Brodhead, Richard. *Hawthorne, Melville, and the Novel*. Chicago: University of Chicago Press, 1976.

Brown, Lester. *Plan B 2.0: Rescuing a Planet under Stress and a Civilization in Trouble.* New York: W. W. Norton, 2006.

Bruggeman, Walter. "King in the Kingdom of Things." *The Christian Century* 86 (September 10, 1969): 1165–66.

Bryant, John. "*Moby-Dick* as Revolution." In *The Cambridge Companion to Herman Melville*, edited by Robert Levine, 65–90. New York: Cambridge University Press, 1999.

Bryant, John, Mary K. Bercaw Edwards, and Timothy Marr, eds. *"Ungraspable Phantom": Essays on Moby Dick.* Kent, OH: Kent State University Press, 2006.

Campbell, Joseph. *The Hero with a Thousand Faces.* Princeton, NJ: Princeton University Press, 1949.

———. *The Masks of God: Primitive Mythology.* New York: Penguin, 1959.

———. *The Masks of God: Oriental Mythology.* New York: Penguin, 1962.

———. *The Masks of God: Occidental Mythology.* New York: Penguin, 1964.

———. *The Masks of God: Creative Mythology.* New York: Penguin, 1968.

Campbell, Joseph, with Bill Moyers. *The Power of Myth.* New York: Doubleday, 1988.

Cave, Alfred A. *The Pequot War.* Amherst: University of Massachusetts Press, 1996.

Chase, Owen. *Shipwreck of the Whaleship* Essex. New York: Corinth, 1963.

Cheever, Susan. *American Bloomsbury: Louisa May Alcott, Ralph Waldo Emerson, Margaret Fuller, Nathaniel Hawthorne, and Henry David Thoreau: Their Lives, Their Loves, Their Work.* New York: Simon & Schuster, 2006.

Coghlan, Andy. "Whales Boast the Brain Cells that 'Make Us Human.'" *New Scientist* 2580 (December 2, 2006): 6–7. www.newscientist.com/article/dn10661-whales-boast-the-brain-cells-that-make-us-human.html (accessed July 9, 2010).

Commager, Henry Steele, ed. *Documents in American History*. New York: Appleton-Century-Crofts, 1958.

Cowan, Bainard. *Exiled Waters: Moby-Dick and the Crisis of Allegory*. Baton Rouge: Louisiana State University Press, 1982.

Deffeyes, Kenneth. *Hubbert's Peak: The Impending World Oil Shortage*. Princeton, NJ: Princeton University Press, 2001.

Delbanco, Andrew. *Melville: His World and Work*. New York: Alfred A. Knopf, 2005.

Dryden, Edgar. *Melville's Thematics of Form*. Baltimore, MD: The Johns Hopkins University Press, 1968.

Edinger, Edward F. *Melville's "Moby-Dick": An American Nekyia*. Toronto: Inner City Books, 1995.

Ellis, Joseph L. *Founding Brothers. The Revolutionary Generation*. New York: Vintage, 2000.

Ellis, Richard. *Book of Whales*. New York: Alfred A. Knopf, 1985.

———. *Men and Whales*. New York: Lyons, 1999.

Ember, Carol, Melvin Ember, and Peter Peregrine. *Anthropology*. 10th ed. Upper Saddle River, NJ: Prentice Hall, 2002.

Emerson, Ralph Waldo. *The Essays of Ralph Waldo Emerson*. Garden City, NY: Famous Classics Library, 1941.

Gore, Al. *An Inconvenient Truth: The Planetary Emergency of Global Warming and What We Can Do About It*. New York: Rodale, 2006.

Grimal, Pierre. *The Dictionary of Classical Mythology*. Oxford: Blackwell, 2000.

Hayford, Harrison, and Hershel Parker, eds. "Before *Moby-Dick*: International Controversy over Melville." In *Moby-Dick*, by Herman Melville, 465–70. New York: W. W. Norton, 2002.

Hiebert, Theodore. "Rethinking Dominion Theology." *Direction: A Mennonite Brethren Forum* 25 (Fall 1996): 16–25.

Homer. *The Homeric Hymns*. Translated by Charles Boer. Woodstock, CT: Spring Publications, 1996.

Hubbert, M. King. "Nuclear Energy and the Fossil Fuel." In *Drilling and Production Practice*, 7–25. Washington, DC: American Petroleum Institute, 1956.

International Energy Agency. "Statistics." www.iea.org/textbase/stats (accessed July 11, 2010).

Johnston, Louis D., and Samuel H. Williamson. "What Was the U.S. GDP Then?" MeasuringWorth, 2008. www.measuringworth.org/usgdp (accessed July 11, 2010).

Jung, Carl Gustav. "Psychology and Literature." In *The Collected Works of C. G. Jung*. Vol. 15, *The Spirit in Man, Art and Literature*, translated by R. F. C. Hull, 84–105. Princeton, NJ: Princeton University Press, 1978.

———. "The Shadow." In *The Collected Works of C. G. Jung*. Vol. 9, *Aion: Researches into the Phenomenology of the Self*, translated by R. F. C. Hull, 13–19. Princeton, NJ: Princeton University Press, 1978.

———. "The Spiritual Problem of Modern Man." In *The Collected Works of C. G. Jung*. Vol. 10, *Civilization in Transition*, translated by R. F. C. Hull, 74–94. Princeton, NJ: Princeton University Press, 1978.

Lawrence, D. H. *Studies in Classic American Literature.* New York: Penguin, 1977.

Lawrence, John Shelton, and Robert Jewett. *The Myth of the American Superhero.* Grand Rapids, MI: Wm. B. Eerdmans, 2002.

Leisy, Ernest E. "Fatalism in *Moby-Dick.*" In *Moby-Dick Centennial Essays,* edited by Tyrus Hillway and Luther Mansfield, 76–88. Dallas, TX: Southern Methodist University Press, 1953.

Leyda, Jay. *The Melville Log: A Documentary Life of Herman Melville 1819–1891.* 2 vols. New York: Harcourt Brace, 1951.

Lovelock, James. *The Revenge of Gaia: Earth's Climate Crisis and the Fate of Humanity.* New York: Perseus, 2006.

Lovins, Amory, et al. *Winning the Oil Endgame.* Snowmass, CO: Rocky Mountain Institute, 2004.

Magee, John. "High Flier." *Quote...Unquote* 2 (April 1992). www.qunl. com/rees0008.html (accessed July 11, 2010).

Matthiessen, F. O. *American Renaissance: Art and Expression in the Age of Emerson and Whitman.* New York: Oxford University Press, 1941.

McNally, Robert. *So Remorseless a Havoc: Of Dolphins, Whales and Men.* Boston, MA: Little, Brown, 1981.

Melville, Herman. *Clarel: A Poem and Pilgrimage in the Holy Land.* Evanston, IL: Northwestern University Press, 1991.

———. "Hawthorne and His Mosses." *Moby-Dick,* 517–32. New York: W. W. Norton, 2002.

———. *Moby-Dick.* Edited by Hershel Parker and Harrison Hayford, 2nd ed. New York: W. W. Norton, 2002.

————. *Typee: A Peep at Polynesian Life; Omoo: A Narrative of Adventures in the South Sea; Mardi and a Voyage Thither; Redburn: His First Voyage; White-Jacket or The World in a Man-of-War; Moby-Dick or, The Whale; Pierre or, The Ambiguities; Israel Potter: His Fifty Years of Exile; The Piazza Tales; The Confidence-Man: His Masquerade; Uncollected Prose; Billy Budd, Sailor*. 3 vols. New York: Library of America, 1982, 1983, 1984.

Metcalf, Eleanor Melville. *Herman Melville*. Cambridge, MA: Harvard University Press, 1953.

Miller, Edwin H. *Melville: A Biography*. New York: George Braziller, 1975.

Murphy, Jim. *Gone A-Whaling: The Lure of the Sea and the Hunt for the Great Whale*. New York: Clarion, 1998.

National Surface Transportation Policy Study Commission. *Transportation for Tomorrow*. Washington, DC: U.S. Department of Transportation, December 2007. www.transportationfortomorrow.org/final_report/pdf/final_report.pdf (accessed July 10, 2010).

Needleman, Jacob. *Money and the Meaning of Life*. New York: Doubleday, 1991.

New Oxford Annotated Bible. 3rd ed. New York: Oxford University Press, 2001.

Parker, Hershel. *Herman Melville: A Biography*. 2 vols. Baltimore, MD: The Johns Hopkins University Press, 1996 and 2002.

Pater, Walter. *Essays on Literature and Art*. Edited by Jennifer Uglow. London: J. M. Dent & Sons, 1990.

Pease, Donald. "*Moby-Dick* and the Cold War." In *The American Renaissance Reconsidered*, edited by Walter Benn Michaels and Donald Pease. Baltimore, MD: The Johns Hopkins University Press, 1985.

Philbrick, Nathaniel. *Revenge of the Whale: The True Story of the Whale-ship* Essex. New York: Penguin, 2002.

Reynolds, David. *Beneath the American Renaissance: The Subversive Imagination in the Age of Emerson and Melville.* Cambridge, MA: Harvard University Press, 1989.

Russell, Dick. *Eye of the Whale: Epic Passage from Baja to Siberia.* New York: Island Press/Simon & Schuster, 2001.

Sampson, Andrew. *The Seven Sisters.* New York: Viking, 1975.

Scammon, Charles. *The Marine Mammals of the Northwestern Coast of North America.* New York: Dover, 1968.

Scoresby, William. *An Account of the Arctic Regions and the Northern Whale Fishery.* New York: Augustus M. Kelley, 1969.

Sealts, Merton. *Melville's Reading: A Check-List of Books Owned and Borrowed.* Cambridge, MA: Harvard University Press, 1950.

Seibert, Charles. "An Elephant Crackup." *New York Times Magazine,* October 8, 2006.

Simmonds, Mark. "Into the Brains of Whales." *Journal of Applied Animal Behaviour Science* 100 (October 2006): 1–2.

Simmons, Matthew R. *Twilight in the Desert: The Coming Saudi Oil Shock and the World Economy.* Hoboken, NJ: John Wiley & Sons, 2005.

Slattery, Dennis Patrick. *The Wounded Body: Remembering the Markings of Flesh.* Albany: State University of New York Press, 2000.

Slijper, E. J. *Whales.* Translated by A. J. Pomerans. Ithaca, NY: Cornell University Press, 1958.

———. *Whales and Dolphins.* Translation of Riesen des Meeres. Ann Arbor: University of Michigan Press, 1976.

Smith, Henry Nash. "The Image of Society in *Moby-Dick*." In *"Moby-Dick": Centennial Essays*, edited by Tyrus Hillway and Luther S. Mansfield, 59–75. Dallas: Southern Methodist University Press, 1953.

Soloveitchik, Joseph B. *The Lonely Man of Faith*. New York: Doubleday, 1965.

Starbuck, Alexander. *History of the American Whale Fishery*. Secaucus, NJ: Castle, 1991.

Sten, Christopher. *The Weaver-God, He Weaves: Melville and the Poetics of the Novel*. Kent, OH: Kent State University Press, 1996.

Stowe, Harriett Beecher. *Uncle Tom's Cabin*. New York: Penguin, 1981.

Tarnas, Richard. *The Passion of the Western Mind*. New York: Ballantine Books, 1996.

Taylor, Charles. *Sources of the Self: The Making of Modern Identity*. Cambridge, MA: Harvard University Press, 1989.

Thompson, Lawrence. *Melville's Quarrel with God*. Princeton, NJ: Princeton University Press, 1952.

Thoreau, Henry David. *Civil Disobedience and Other Essays*. New York: Dover, 1993.

———. *Walden. A Fully Annotated Edition*. Edited by Jeffrey S. Cramer. New Haven, CT: Yale University Press, 2004.

UN Population Division."World Population Prospects: 2006." New York: United Nations, Department of Economic and Social Affairs, 2007. www.un.org/esa/population/publications/wpp2006/wpp2006.htm (accessed July 10, 2010).

U.S. Census Bureau. "History." www.census.gov/history (accessed January 26, 2009).

———. "Census of Population and Housing." www.census.gov/prod/ www/abs/decennial (accessed June 2, 2010).

U.S. Department of Commerce. Bureau of Economic Analysis. "National Economic Accounts Data." www.bea.gov (accessed January 26, 2009).

U.S. Department of Energy. Energy Information Administration. "Country Energy Profiles." www.eia.doe.gov/country (accessed January 26, 2009).

U.S. Department of the Interior, Bureau of Land Management. *Profile of the 2006 Visitor to the Imperial Sand Dunes Recreation Area.* El Centro, CA: U.S. Department of the Interior, May 2008.

U.S. Department of Transportation. Federal Highway Administration. "Publications and Statistics." www.fhwa.dot.gov/pubstats (accessed January 26, 2009).

———. National Highway Traffic Safety Administration. www.nhtsa.dot. gov (accessed January 26, 2009).

U.S. Environmental Protection Agency. "Inventory of U. S. Greenhouse Gas Emissions 1990-2006." www.epa.gov/climatechange/emissions/ downloads/2008InventoryPublicReviewComments.pdf (accessed July 10, 2010).

———. "Municipal Solid Wastes (MSW) in the United States: 2007 Facts and Figures." www.epa.gov/osw/nonhaz/municipal/msw99.htm (accessed July 12, 2010).

Van Dyke, Kate. *Fundamentals of Petroleum.* 4th ed. Austin: University of Texas Press, 1997.

Veblen, Thorstein. *The Theory of the Leisure Class.* New York: Dover, 1994.

Vincent, Howard. *The Trying-Out of* Moby-Dick. Carbondale: Southern Illinois University Press, 1965.

Voltaire (Francois-Marie Arouet). *Micromegas*. New York: Hippocrene, 1999.

Weber, Max. *The Protestant Ethic and the "Spirit" of Capitalism*. Edited by Peter Baehr and Gordon Wells. Introduction by Peter Baehr and Gordon Wells. New York: Penguin, 2002.

Whale Rider. DVD. Dir. Niki Caro. Perf. Keisha Castle-Hughes, Rawiri Paratene, Vicki Haughton. Screenplay by Niki Caro and Witi Ihimaera based on novel by Witi Ihimaera. 1987; ApolloMedia, 2002.

Whitehead, Hal. *Sperm Whales: Social Evolution in the Ocean*. Chicago: University of Chicago Press, 2003.

Yergin, Daniel. *The Prize: The Epic Quest for Oil, Money and Power*. New York: Free Press, 2003.

ABOUT THE AUTHOR

A banker for more than forty years, Robert D. ("Bob") Wagner, Jr. has worked for four major institutions in New York, Los Angeles, and Houston. Since moving to Houston in early 1974, Wagner has focused on advising and financing the oil and gas industries in Texas. He continues these endeavors today in an independent, nonaffiliated advisory role.

Wagner came to Texas in the immediate aftermath of the Yom Kippur War of October 1973, when the oil industry—if not the whole world of energy—went from a decades-long period of relative stability to the volatile world of wide swings in supply and price still being experienced today. Throughout these years, he was an active participant in the companies and banks trying to deal with this volatility. One particularly difficult time was the period of the early 1980s, when the Texas banks were struggling with the effects of the massive collapse in oil prices and the resulting reverberations throughout the Texas economy. For most of this period, Wagner ran the energy department of the largest financial firm in Houston, a firm with a heavy commitment to energy loans and investments. The investments made in the boom years of the late 1970s proved exceedingly difficult for all involved. Ultimately, all nine of the major Texas bank holding companies collapsed or were sold, and none remain among the major banks operating in Texas today.

As a long-term member of the Independent Petroleum Association of America and a former president and director of the Petroleum Club of Houston, Wagner's experience in the field runs deep. His activities in the distressed environment in Texas oil finance led to many speaking engagements and to the publication of multiple newspaper and magazine articles on his experiences. His speeches and articles have focused on the nature and potential outcomes of the volatility experienced by the energy and banking industries over the past thirty years.

Wagner had a classic, liberal arts Jesuit education in the 1950s and early 1960s, graduating from College of the Holy Cross in 1963. Three years as an officer in the U.S. Marine Corps, with service in Vietnam, preceded the beginning of his career in finance in late 1966 and his earning an MBA at night from New York University's Stern School of Business in 1971.

His grounding in liberal arts gave Wagner a strong interest in history and in the philosophical, social, psychological, and economic events and trends that we, as humans, have experienced throughout known history. This orientation eventually led him to Pacifica Graduate Institute in Santa Barbara, California, where he earned a PhD in mythological studies in 2008.

While Wagner continues his activities in the financial side of energy, he is also pursuing a process to analyze, dissect, and explain the events and trends of our economic and petroleum worlds from the point of view of myth and depth psychology. This book, *"Moby-Dick" and the Mythology of Oil,* is one of his first attempts at such endeavors.

5750049R0

Made in the USA
Charleston, SC
29 July 2010